LOOKING FOR
BETTY MacDONALD

LOOKING FOR

Betty
MacDonald

THE EGG, THE PLAGUE,

MRS. PIGGLE-WIGGLE, AND I

Paula Becker

UNIVERSITY OF WASHINGTON PRESS
Seattle and London

Printed and bound in the USA
Design by Thomas Eykemans
Composed in Electra, typeface designed by William Addison Dwiggins in 1935
Display type set in Futura, designed by Paul Renner in 1927
20 19 18 17 16   5 4 3 2 1

UNIVERSITY OF WASHINGTON PRESS
www.washington.edu/uwpress

LIBRARY OF CONGRESS CATALOGING-IN-PUBLICATION DATA
Names: Becker, Paula, author.
Title: Looking for Betty MacDonald : the egg, the plague, Mrs. Piggle-Wiggle, and I /
    Paula Becker.
Description: Seattle : University of Washington Press, 2016. |
    Includes bibliographical references and index.
Identifiers: LCCN 2016007016 | ISBN 9780295999364 (hardcover : alk. paper)
Subjects: LCSH: MacDonald, Betty Bard. | Authors, American—20th century—
    Biography. | Children's literature—Authorship.
Classification: LCC PS3525. A1946 Z434 2016 | DDC 813/.54 [B] —dc23
LC record available at https://lccn.loc.gov/2016007016

The paper used in this publication is acid-free and meets the minimum requirements of American National Standard for Information Sciences—Permanence of Paper for Printed Library Materials, ANSI Z39.48–1984. ∞

For

Betty and Mary, and for

Blanche Hamilton Hutchings Caffiere
(1906–2006),

with whom we all were friends

CONTENTS

Plates follow pages 66 and 126

NOTE TO READERS

Portions of the material in this book appear on HistoryLink.org, the free online encyclopedia of Washington State history. All letters not cited to an archive were in a private collection at the time I was granted access to them. Quotations from such letters are cited by writer, recipient, and date only. I have opted to cite recipient family members and close friends exactly as Betty MacDonald addressed them in the letters in addition to identifying them by their full names, in the hope that if these materials become part of a public collection, future researchers will be better able to locate specific letters despite my current inability to give archival citations. All quotations from Betty MacDonald's books are taken from the original J. B. Lippincott editions.

Regarding the published and unpublished recollections of Bard family friends Blanche Hamilton and Margaret Bundy, this book refers to them as Blanche Hamilton and Margaret Bundy Callahan throughout. Both women changed their names on marriage during their long friendships with the Bards. Blanche Hamilton became Blanche Hutchings and then Blanche Caffiere. Under the name Caffiere, she published a book about the Bards, *Much Laughter, a Few Tears*. Margaret Bundy married the painter Kenneth Callahan in 1930.

The House and I

W AS it the house I fell for first? Or was it Betty Bard Mac-
Donald, who wrote *The Egg and I* and *Mrs. Piggle-Wiggle*,
and who described the house with such affection?

> According to real estate standards, Mother's eight-room
> brown-shingled house in the University district was just a modest
> dwelling in a respectable neighborhood, near good schools and
> adequate for an ordinary family. To me that night, and always,
> that shabby house with its broad welcoming porch, dark wood-
> work, cluttered dining-room plate rail, large fragrant kitchen,
> easy book-filled firelit living room, four elastic bedrooms—one of
> them always ice-cold—roomy old-fashioned bathrooms and huge
> cluttered basement, represents the ultimate in charm, warmth,
> and luxury.[1]

The house that Betty wrote about was in Seattle, but it could
have been anywhere. For her millions of readers, it *was* anywhere, or
rather it was our own place, a memory we had—or wished we'd had. It
evoked that place of shelter and acceptance we spend our lives trying
to find our way back to, a home both actual and iconic.

I knew about the house because I'd recently stumbled on Betty
MacDonald again after a whirlwind acquaintance with her books in
childhood. I was beginning to learn about Betty's world, to slip into her
books, thinking and daydreaming about her life, about her family, and
especially about her houses. Betty MacDonald's books describe almost

all of her homes and what those places meant to her. This house, in Seattle's Roosevelt neighborhood, sheltered her family during the 1930s, the period described in her books *The Plague and I* and *Anybody Can Do Anything*. More than any of Betty's houses, I'd tried to picture this one. Perusing old Seattle city directories—those dusty volumes languishing in libraries and historical archives that record who lived where, year by year—I came upon the listing for "Bard" with a jolt: 6317 15th Avenue Northeast, Seattle. I knew that house. It was six blocks from my own address, on a busy arterial street I drove down many times each day. Betty MacDonald was almost a stranger to me that day in the library—not yet a nearly constant focus, not yet a calling.

It was a hunch, but I thought this house might have been Betty's inspiration for the upside-down cottage where her beloved character Mrs. Piggle-Wiggle lived. I could imagine it from Betty's description: "The most remarkable thing about Mrs. Piggle-Wiggle is her house, which is upside down. It is a little brown house, and sitting there in its tangly garden it looks like a small brown puppy lying on its back with its feet in the air."[2]

The house on 15th Avenue Northeast was right side up. But it was comfortably slouchy, faded and worn in a favorite-sweater kind of way. It looked like someone had once cared for it, and maybe still did. Children who clattered across the broad wooden front porch would not be damaging anything. The house just felt Piggle-Wiggly. So did the neighborhood, full of old Craftsman-style houses set far enough back from the sidewalks to showcase those tangly gardens, full of tall hollyhocks, overgrown and deeply scented rose bushes, snapdragons like the ones my cousins and I played with in my grandma's backyard, pinching and releasing the blossoms' bases to make them "talk" to one another.

It was in El Paso, Texas, in 1971, that I first encountered Betty Bard MacDonald, on the dust jacket of a Piggle-Wiggle book. I was eight years old. The book was from my classroom's tiny library, and I had carried it in my turquoise-flowered suitcase to Grandma's house.

I had been trying and failing to learn to ride my big new red bicycle, finally giving up for the day. I opened the book in Grandma's shady guest room. The book was cheering. Mrs. Piggle-Wiggle seemed to understand that children had complicated feelings, that doing new things well sometimes took time. She was so wise and kind that even the parents in the book sought her advice. I felt almost as if I knew her—as if we would be friends if I could visit her. I read all four of the Piggle-Wiggle books as quickly as I could find them and longed for more.

Mrs. Piggle-Wiggle's last page told me that its author, Betty MacDonald, had been born in Boulder, Colorado, and had grown up in Butte, Montana, and Seattle, Washington. It was the first I'd heard of any of those places, but the names stayed with me. Washington was the state that put stickers on my sack-lunch apples: "Grown in Washington." When I moved to Seattle twenty-two years later, I thought about those stickers, and I remembered that long-ago author description. Betty MacDonald lived here, I thought idly sometimes. I wondered where she might have lived, and what became of her.

People in Seattle knew Betty's name, but many of them knew her best for writing a different book—a best seller whose catchy title I recognized, although I'd never read it: *The Egg and I.* I found the book easily and started reading.

"Critics are cackling over *The Egg and I,*" proclaimed a blurb on the cover. "She has a hilarious sense of the ridiculous. If you've forgotten how to laugh, this book is what the doctor ordered!"

The Egg and I was published on October 3, 1945, and American readers—parched for laughter after enduring World War II—instantly embraced its tart, self-deprecatory humor. The publisher, J. B. Lippincott, took note of the book's early popularity and ramped up its publicity, dedicating much of their precious war-rationed paper to feeding the presses that churned out *Egg,* impression after impression, barely keeping up with the rising tide of national and then international demand. Before a year was up, *The Egg and I* had sold more than a million copies and was topping nonfiction best-seller lists, showing no sign at all of slowing down.

The book was Betty's story, or a version of her story: a childhood in a warm, rowdily eccentric family and her marriage in the 1920s to an insurance salesman turned chicken rancher named Bob, who whisked her off into the boondocks of Washington's Olympic Peninsula. There she endured the ceaseless rain and learned "to hate even baby chickens."[3] She was forced to rely on the dubious assistance of her nearest neighbors, a slapdash couple with a brood of a dozen-plus children. Betty dubbed the pair Ma and Pa Kettle. Hundreds of chickens, one burst water tower, a baby, and several years later, Betty and Bob decamped to a more modern farm, one with electric power rather than kerosene lanterns, closer to Seattle. Or so the story went in *The Egg and I*.

I found *The Egg and I* hilarious and bracing, but kind of mean. I learned there was another book, *The Plague and I*, about Betty's yearlong battle with tuberculosis nearly a decade after leaving the egg farm. *The Plague and I* intrigued me, both with the story Betty told and with the way she told it. What kind of person wrote about tuberculosis with such twist, such quirkiness, that the fear of death was beaten down with laughter? By the time I read Betty's next book, *Anybody Can Do Anything*, I was hers. Betty MacDonald not only made me laugh, she transported me. I didn't know it yet, but those dual qualities were Betty's special magic, part of the reason so many readers treasured her books and frequently reread them.

Anybody vividly describes a 1930s Seattle. It recounts Betty's hardscrabble years as a single mother during the Great Depression, frequently desperate but buoyed by the support and companionship of her mother and siblings and by her own dark sense of humor. Betty's descriptions of her terrors and frustrations, and the way her idiosyncratic family's sense of humor and hyperbole shaped every situation—in short, their ways of being Bard—hung in the air as if Betty had just left the room.

Betty's final autobiographical book, *Onions in the Stew*, tells of her second marriage and of the pratfalls and pitfalls she encountered while raising teenagers on Vashon Island, a mostly rural outpost a short ferry ride from Seattle. This book was different from its predecessors: slicker, more restrained and constricted, as if molded by one of those 1950s girdles. The voice was clearly still Betty's, but it was less spontaneous, as if she'd sensed a laugh track and tailored her story to sync with it. For me, though, that was a minor point. Through Betty's words, I was starting to see the past—her life, lived decades ago in many of the places where I was living my present. I was beginning to catch glimpses of Betty's 1930s, '40s, '50s—shimmering through my 1990s and 2000s. It was literary time travel, seductive, satisfying.

Betty's quick wit and acid humor laced through her four works of autobiography. She produced these books in rapid succession, interspersed with four sparkling Piggle-Wiggle books for children and the fairytale-like *Nancy and Plum*. Betty—her fresh, smiling face made globally famous by its presence on all but the very earliest editions of *Egg's* front cover—was a celebrity. When Universal-International Pictures released the film version of *Egg* in 1947, Betty's character was played by the glamorous movie star Claudette Colbert, who swanned pluckily through her scenes on the tidy chicken-ranch set costumed with great chic by the designer Adrian.

Betty's books transformed her and those around her into characters, skewering friends, neighbors, and adversaries alike. Her books all magnify the Bard motto "Don't be a saddo." Life is hard. All we can control is our response to it, and laughing beats crying. This sentiment cheered and encouraged readers worldwide. Her books—*Egg* overwhelmingly—were all best sellers in their time. Her Piggle-Wiggle books are children's classics. Betty's Ma and Pa Kettle characters quickly became iconic.

During the thirteen years following *Egg's* publication, Betty churned out books, conducted hundreds of print interviews, made scores of radio appearances, waded through mountains of fan mail, battled two libel lawsuits brought by former neighbors who saw themselves in Betty's characters, hobnobbed with movie stars, cashed royalty checks, endured family crises, and moved from an idyllic rustic home on Vashon Island near Seattle to an equally idyllic property in Carmel Valley, California.

Four decades after Betty MacDonald moved to California, in my Seattle, I read her books and was entranced by her rendering of our shared metropolis. I read the books again and again, as if hoping that reaching back into Betty's stories would let me somehow graze fingertips with her. I wanted more and more to really know, in whatever way it might be possible, the woman behind the books.

There must be a biography of Betty MacDonald, I thought. People still read her books. But I couldn't find one. How could it be that *The Egg and I* has never been out of print, and yet there was no biography of its author? I imagined adults whose mothers had introduced them to that book wondering whatever happened to Betty MacDonald. I pictured all the children who'd ever read a Piggle-Wiggle book standing in line, with me at the head, asking their third-grade teachers for more details about the woman who'd invented that delightful character.

To satisfy my own curiosity, I started looking for Betty MacDonald, beginning with the houses that her books described. It was a treasure hunt through Betty's past, and through Seattle's.

I wanted to understand more about the physical place we shared and how Betty's world compared to mine. Old city directories led me to most of the addresses where Betty lived and to the homes of her older sister, Mary Bard Jensen, who also wrote autobiographical books and a children's series (*Best Friends*). With my three children in their booster seats behind me, I drove my red Volvo station wagon from house to house, gazing at the doors to which the Bard sisters once held keys, imagining the lives they might have led.

My kids took these field trips in stride. As I discovered more about Betty's world, I shared the details with them. "Is that a Betty house?" they'd ask me sometimes as we drove through quiet Seattle neighborhoods. They were on first-name terms with the Bards, as if they were family friends, albeit friends who never actually came to visit: "My mom is really into Betty and Mary," four-year-old Sawyer told his friend Sam.

I often sat in traffic in front of the house on 15th Avenue Northeast (which my kids and I started calling the *Anybody* house), wondering about Betty's family. I felt I knew them from reading her books.

Thinking about that, though, as I waited for the light to change, I realized it wasn't true. Like Betty's other readers, I knew only a clutch of tantalizing details.

Betty's books painted her family broadly as eccentric but added finely detailed touches about each individual. Her paternal grandmother, Gammy, wore her corsets upside down and baked her grandchildren frugal cookies that combined every ingredient lurking in the corners of the icebox. These inedible rocks were slipped to unsuspecting neighbors when Gammy's head was turned. Betty's mother, Elsie Bard, was known to everyone—even her children—as Sydney. In Betty's books, Sydney is silent, implacable, a cipher, like the ghost light left burning overnight at every theater to keep stagehands and others from the peril of total darkness. And what of Darsie Bard, Betty's father, a professional mining engineer to whose premature death she allocated but a single line, as if to further probe the story might precipitate hemorrhage?

Above all the other family members glistened Betty's older sister. Mary was the sun around which other family members revolved, whether they wanted to or not. She was feisty, bossy, opinionated, never without a plan. Betty had three younger siblings as well: Cleve, the only boy; Dede, the only small, dark-haired one among tall, ginger-tressed sisters, droll and quick-witted; and Alison, the youngest, brought up helter-skelter by the rest. In the corners, darting through the stories, squabbling like the children in need of Mrs. Piggle-Wiggle's cures, were Betty's own daughters, Anne and Joan. And telling the tale was Betty, the bard, a Bard, her words carrying me into the past.

I felt haunted by Betty's world and how she saw it—by her books, her face, her story. When I read what was happening behind the doors of those houses, I wondered what she hadn't said. Her world was still alive for me. I wanted to go there, to know her better than I knew her from the books I had read. I wanted, maybe, to haunt her back.

I became tenaciously attached to knowing her better. I thought of myself as a sort of skip tracer, trying to locate Betty and her associates like a bill collector trying to find a missing debtor. I was skip tracing the dead.

Did I have any right to do so? I can only say that in the way she haunted me, there was a kind of urging on. As the years passed, that urgency grew stronger. Betty and Mary, I sometimes joked, were hungry ghosts. Whenever I thought of them at all, they grabbed my mental steering wheel. I felt they wanted me to go off road, to find and tell the other parts of their story.

I began dipping into history books and photography archives, trying to see Betty's world when the *Anybody* house was hers. I wrote an article about the *Anybody* house, "Time-Traveling the Roosevelt District with Betty MacDonald," for the weekly *Seattle Press*.[4] I wondered frequently what that house looked like from the inside.

Driving past the house, I sometimes lurked in the car, the engine idling. One summer morning in 2005, as I was parked in the alley behind the house, trying to picture the kitchen, a woman pulled her car up beside mine and looked at me quizzically. "Do you live here?" I asked. "I'm interested in an author named Betty MacDonald, who lived here in the 1930s."

"Oh, I know about her," the woman said, "I have a newspaper article." Her name was Tanya, and she invited me in.

The house was very nearly as Betty had described it in her books: the ample living room with a fireplace, where the Bards played Chinese checkers and piano and listened to football and dance marathons on the radio; the main-floor back bedroom that was always cold. Tanya, like Betty's mother, Sydney, was a painter, and she used that room as a studio. The house felt worn but tended to, with a carelessly eccentric air that I think the Bards would have appreciated.

As Tanya walked me through, I looked for details that might have been there in Betty's time — doorknobs, windows, the bathroom mirror. Tanya led me up the tight front stairs to a small hallway with three bedrooms. Tanya slept in the front bedroom, which Betty had said was Sydney's room. When I saw the issue of the *Seattle Press* containing my article next to the bed, time bent for me. For just a moment, I felt I was reaching through the temporal boundaries separating me from the Bards and their life in that house. I felt their echo, and it thrilled me. The next day I left copies of *The Plague and I* and *Anybody Can*

Do Anything in Tanya's mailbox, thinking, as I dropped them off, that this was where the Bards got their mail.

After that day, I felt the *Anybody* house had somehow given itself to me, bestowed the gift of retrospective clairvoyance, its cheerful, shabby rooms revealing the past. Going inside the house fully ignited my quest to find Betty. I started traveling beyond Seattle. I wanted to go everywhere Betty had lived, to the places she'd written about extensively and places she'd skimmed over with a line or two. I wanted to find all the houses and see inside them if I could. I wanted to glean all the details I could from historical records about the way those places had been when Betty lived there. I called these research trips, but they were pilgrimages.

I traced Betty to the solitary old house in Boulder, Colorado, where her life began. I followed her to a modest house set high above a quiet street in Butte, Montana, and to a large brick school nearby. I found an empty road in Placerville, Idaho, where a small cabin once endured the bitter winters. I found homes in Seattle: a grand place overlooking Lake Washington that said, "We have arrived"; a sprawling, comfortable country house that told the world, "We're staying, and we welcome you"; and the much more modest *Anybody* house on its busy street, which sighed, "Things didn't quite turn out as we'd planned."

There was an empty field along a winding road in Chimacum, Washington, where a small farmhouse once nestled. Betty never loved that house, but people around the globe read what she wrote about it and traveled long distances to see it, to walk around and through it, tell friends they'd been there.

There was an island home clinging to Vashon's steep slope, smelling of wood smoke and salt air and echoing with ferryboat whistles. There was a town house bought and lavishly decorated with unanticipated windfalls. And finally, there was a sprawling ranch in Carmel Valley, California, with slopes of sagebrush that rolled on and on beneath a powder-blue sky, as if the land was telling its own story.

At the beginning of this treasure hunt, I wanted to find Betty. By journey's end, I wanted others to find her, this young woman whose face was as familiar during the 1940s and 1950s as any movie star's, whose voice was the first—male or female—to entrance readers around the planet with a story deeply rooted in the great Pacific Northwest. I wanted none of her story lost. And I wanted modern readers—who knew her for the Piggle-Wiggles, if they knew her at all—to understand how richly Betty MacDonald deserved to be found.

LOOKING FOR
BETTY MacDONALD

CHAPTER ONE

The Richest Hill on Earth

B ETTY MACDONALD never saw herself as destined for greatness. Anyone taking odds on which Bard family member might achieve fame would have backed young Betsy's father, Darsie, who worked so diligently, or else her older sister Mary, who had the boundlessly resilient ego for it. Betsy grew up in their shadows. She was shy but shared her family's instinct to reframe life's haphazard details into story. Bard family exploits were the ingredients for these tales. Bold adventure became bolder in the telling, and what was funny became hilarious. This was the way all of the Bard siblings, even quiet Betsy, claimed membership in the family tribe.

As a young woman typing away on the manuscript of her first book, *The Egg and I*, during the dark days of the Second World War, Betty MacDonald did not know that this prodigious storytelling muscle would be her literal—literary—gold mine. Picking her way through the tale of her first marriage, Betty began with family stories: her childhood traipsing the mineral-rich Western United States, her rambunctious siblings, and her parents, Darsie and Sydney Bard.

Betty's parents began their married life in Butte, Montana. For the four Bard children who lived there when they were young, Butte was an outrageous place to form their first conceptions of normalcy, and it was rich with the material for story. In March 1903, when the newly married Sydney Bard stepped off the Northern Pacific train that had carried her from Boston to Butte, nearly ten thousand men labored in the mines beneath her feet.[1] It was a raw place for an Eastern bride.

Sydney had fallen in love with the serious but dashing Darsie Bard, a tall young Harvard student with jet-black hair, steady gray eyes, and whiskers that were copper-hued when he let them grow. Could she have imagined, when the couple had wed secretly three months before, that marrying Darsie would mean years of adventure in mining camps and towns throughout the West, far from the settled, elegant future she'd been brought up to expect?

Butte was called the richest hill on earth. Beneath it, tunnels teemed with miners extracting ore. The wealth was mostly copper, deposited in massive chunks—called bodies, not veins—as large as twelve-story buildings. The city's residents were blasting and sifting its very foundation. The activity underground was the exact opposite of building a city.

Butte was remarkably diverse. Many immigrants were Irish or Cornish, but so varied were the ethnicities of their workers that mines posted "No Smoking" signs in as many as sixteen languages. For the immigrants, it was Butte, America. The draw was mining and the many industries, legal and illegal, that supported it. The city was intensely industrial and densely urban.

When Sydney arrived, Butte boasted 275 saloons and the largest red-light district in the West, with entertainment available twenty-four hours a day to accommodate the miners who worked shifts around the clock. Mine whistles set the town's rhythm. The smelter, some twenty miles west in Anaconda, glowed red and belched smoke all night. The Butte Miners' Union was the largest union local in the world, and Butte's mines were statistically the world's most dangerous. Funeral processions for miners seemed never-ending. Someone in Butte was always dying in the mines.

For Sydney Bard, the contrast between Butte and her genteel Eastern upbringing was staggering. Before her marriage, Sydney had been Elsie Thalimer Sanderson.[2] Born in Elizabeth, New Jersey, in 1878, she had trained as an illustrator at the Eric Pape School of Art in Boston. Darsie Bard entered her life as a tutor to her younger brother, Jim. Darsie was working his way through Harvard. Bard family lore has it that Elsie Sanderson interviewed Darsie for the tutoring job, and, after stumbling back to his boarding house in a daze, he swore to his roommate that he had just met the girl he was going to marry.

Darsie Campbell Bard was not from the East, although he'd adjusted to Cambridge life, rowing varsity crew and earning respect for his quiet studiousness. He was born in Hannibal, Missouri, in 1878, and spent his teenage years in Portland, Oregon.[3] He attended Portland High School and Portland Academy, achieving what the *Oregonian* called "a brilliant record as a student."[4] He continued to succeed academically at Harvard, where he had been accepted on his merit, not on his name.

Like most of the all-male student body at Harvard, Darsie was a white Protestant. As a Westerner, however, Darsie was in a minority: most of the students were from New England. Moreover, Harvard students were defined by wealth and social class, and Darsie had neither. He earned his tuition and living expenses by tutoring and by working in Harvard's astronomical observatory.[5]

Darsie was raised primarily by his mother, Anne Elizabeth Campbell Bard. She was tiny, with large blue eyes and curly hair, one of the beautiful Campbell sisters of Wheeling, West Virginia. Anne Elizabeth survived a difficult marriage by virtue of her own tenacious grit. This life rendered her both pragmatic and eccentric. We will call Anne Elizabeth Gammy, as she was eventually known to her grandchildren. This family abounds with members who share names—Bard, Cleveland, Anne, Mary, Betsy, Alison, Heidi, Darsie—so, best to simplify.

Darsie's father, James Bard, was a fairly successful business agent when he and Gammy married, but in 1880, when the couple was living in Denver, he began to gamble, funding the habit with money embezzled from the insurance agency that employed him.[6] He went to jail. Gammy supported herself and Darsie by taking in sewing, teaching school, and working as a clerk. When James was released, the family moved to Portland, but James continued unrepentant, eventually abandoning his wife and son. Gammy filed for divorce.

Betty later wrote that her paternal grandfather "took his wife out West, played Faro with his money, his wife's money and even some of his company's money and then tactfully disappeared and was always spoken of as dead."[7] Gammy was granted a divorce on the grounds of desertion and cruelty in 1901, Darsie's junior year at Harvard.

Although divorce rates in America had been climbing since the Civil War, divorce still carried a considerable stigma. Betty's sarcastic observation that James "tactfully disappeared" was apt. With James absent, Gammy could pass as widowed, not divorced, a common tactic at the time. Although James Bard actually lived for two more decades, to Gammy, he was as good as dead.[8]

Having spent his childhood in the shadow of his father's failings, Darsie was determined to succeed. During his final months at Harvard, he filled out an exit questionnaire listing his memberships (Mining Club, Natural History Society), declaring a preference for geology classes over Greek or fine arts, stating his ability to play piano, and offering that he'd been published in the *Oregon Naturalist*. Asked, "What advantages do you think you ought to have found at Harvard which you have failed to find?" Darsie responded, "Fellowship." With Elsie Sanderson, Darsie found fellowship.[9]

Raised with patrician values, but without great wealth, Elsie chose a man of quick intellect and obvious promise, but with no financial cushion. She and Darsie were well suited temperamentally. They became engaged during Darsie's junior year, against Elsie's mother's wishes, and were married secretly in Boston on December 15, 1902, shortly before Darsie graduated. A few weeks later, Darsie departed for Butte, where he worked briefly for the Bell and Diamond mines before being hired by the Amalgamated Copper Mining Company (ACM) as a field geologist.[10] A few months after Darsie's departure, Elsie disclosed her marriage to her parents and younger brother. Days later, she boarded the train to Butte.

Neither Elsie nor Darsie cared for her given name, and after they married, she began using the name Sydney. The name honored her elder brother, Sidney Cleveland Sanderson, who had died in childhood.[11] Sidney was also her father's name and her grandfather's.

Sydney's mother, aspiring to see her only daughter rise in society, had taught her to manage servants, prepare fine cuisine, and hold her own in polite company.[12] This set of skills was not in high demand in

Butte, where social classes mixed together and where all wealth was new. There, Sydney's strongest asset was her willingness. Once in the West, she pushed her sleeves up and set about making the place a home.

Throughout her marriage, Sydney managed to be with Darsie under highly adverse conditions. As newlyweds, using Butte as their home base, the couple moved among remote mining camps, with Darsie inspecting mines, analyzing their potential, and suggesting ways to improve yields, and Sydney keeping house—sometimes in a tent. Sydney, ever sanguine, brought happiness, family life, and deep fellowship to their marriage. She was an excellent wife by all the standards of the time.

Mining engineers were almost invariably male during these years, and their wives were expected to accompany them on their travels. Frequently living in remote locales away from women of their own socioeconomic class, the wives formed a supportive, if long-distance, sisterhood.

Several of these women published accounts of their adventures. Josephine Hoeppner Woods was the first woman to earn a graduate degree from the State College of Washington (now Washington State University). When she was preparing to join her husband in the Peruvian Andes, Woods learned that the mining company required wives to obtain a doctor's note certifying that they could endure high altitude. Before Lou Henry Hoover's husband was elected the thirty-first president of the United States, she accompanied him worldwide on mine inspection trips, with babies as young as one month in tow; like her husband, she held a degree in geology from Stanford University. If these women wanted to see their husbands, they went along or (as when pinned down by advanced pregnancy or small children) visited as often as they could.

When Darsie's work extended for a long stretch, Sydney used a hotel room or rented house in the vicinity as a base camp while Darsie and his mining partners went farther afield. Darsie found the life exhilarating: locating rich areas of ore, attempting to buy out the prospector who had staked them, traveling across the country looking for undiscovered mineral wealth. Darsie was rugged, and his skill analyzing the soil—essentially, reading the ground—made him valuable.

Four decades later, a mining partner of Darsie's who had traveled with him in Nevada around 1906 remembered that the two had

> lived and breathed geology. . . . We had a team of horses that could be driven or ridden, and a Studebaker buckboard with our 1500 pound load of hay and grain, water, food, text books, working tools, and good clothes, etc. We went wherever we thought there was a chance for a mine, and we could camp anywhere on the bare ground and be at home. . . . We covered many hundreds of miles in Nevada and we examined hundreds of prospects. We climbed mountains—explored abandoned and unsafe mines—climbed around in stopes on all fours. Our lives depended on a rickety ladder. . . . We learned about mining engineering in these years, namely, the hard way.[13]

This tale is romantic in its retelling—a formative Western myth sprung to life. Darsie was living it—willingly, eagerly—and so was Sydney.

A little more than a year after she joined Darsie in Butte, Sydney was pregnant. The couple's home base was a rented cottage on West Granite Street, two blocks from the hulking redbrick mansion built by the copper king William Clark for his first wife, Katherine. After her death in 1893, Clark had remarried and lived mainly abroad, but the mansion still visually dominated the neighborhood.

By autumn 1904, Gammy had joined her son and daughter-in-law in the small house. On November 21, 1904, Sydney gave birth to a daughter, Mary Ten Eyck Bard, whose middle name honored Sydney's Dutch ancestors. Eight months later, the Reverend Slator Clay Blackiston baptized Mary at St. John's Episcopal Church. Grace Cahoon, the physician who had delivered Mary, served as one of her baptismal sponsors.[14]

Less than six months after Mary's birth, Darsie was prospecting in Utah and Nevada, although Butte was still home. Having given up their first house, the family briefly rented a shingled cottage on West

Copper Street, nudging the foothills of Big Butte, the weathered outcrop from which the town took its name.

Darsie operated a copper mine in Ely, Nevada, helping to form first the Western Development Company and then the Butte & Ely Company. Sydney, Gammy, and baby Mary joined Darsie there, living for a few weeks on the Agee Ranch atop Spruce Mountain in Elko County, Nevada, "in a very small shack but [with] an air of happiness and good tolerance of the frontier conditions on the part of all concerned," according to Darsie's mining partner, who was also staying there.[15] By early 1907, the Bards had rented a house in the Mapleton Hill neighborhood of Boulder, Colorado.[16] Mary was two, and Sydney was pregnant again.

Boulder prided itself on being a healthful, civilized, scholarly community. It was home to the University of Colorado and to a lively and extensive Chautauqua Assembly—a mass cultural movement whose proponents believed in self-improvement through education.[17] Ringed by mining towns and camps producing gold, silver, tungsten, and coal, Boulder dedicated itself to higher culture. Sydney and Gammy spent time with Gammy's three sisters, who had settled there. Sydney joined the Friday Musical Club, which gave monthly afternoon recitals.

On March 26, 1907, Anne Elizabeth Campbell Bard was born. The family called her Betsy, a nickname she would use throughout her childhood. Darsie, as usual, was away on a mining trip. Betty's account of her own birth has Gammy dashing, scatterbrained and panicky, to summon a veterinarian neighbor to help. Sydney sent the vet home, cut and tied the umbilical cord herself, and named her newborn daughter in Gammy's honor.[18]

Betsy was born into the inadvertent matriarchy created by her father's nearly constant absence. At its head was the grandmother whose name she shared. Despite Gammy's belle-like youth and delicate features, her central attribute was the core strength that fueled her steely perseverance. Then came Sydney, who had chosen adventure over security and would continue to do so, compelled first by her husband and later by the dreams, whims, needs, and demands of her children. And, most important, there was Betsy's big sister, Mary.

With the dogged determination and born leadership of the classic eldest child, Mary Bard would set the path for Betsy throughout her life. This sister was a force of nature, at least to her siblings. When she made a plan (and Mary always had a plan), resisting it was nearly impossible. Veering away from her sister's plan was a skill Betsy eventually learned but seldom practiced. Whether traveling in Mary's protective wake or pushed ahead by one of Mary's stubborn schemes, Betsy's dance with this sometimes maddening but intensely beloved sister would be her most defining relationship.

The Reverend Eleazer Sibbald baptized Betsy at St. John's Episcopal Church in Boulder on May 12, 1907.[19] The date of the baptism matters, because later in her life, for reasons unclear, Betty MacDonald shaved a year off of her age. By the time she became famous, her birth year was recorded as 1908, but this was physically impossible: by March 26, 1908, Sydney was pregnant with her third child. Boulder County did not register births in 1907, but the baptismal record tells the tale.[20]

Darsie was on the move constantly, with and without his family. On April 14, 1907, the *Anaconda Standard* reported, "Darcy [*sic*] Campbell Bard is in the city from Nevada and will leave in a few days for Arizona." His daughter Betsy was just a few weeks old—he was likely in Nevada when she was born—and he had almost certainly not yet seen her. After the Arizona trip, he made it back to Boulder in time for Betsy's christening but departed again almost immediately. By June, Darsie was in Missoula, Montana, on business.

"When I was a few months old," Betty wrote, "Mother received the following wire from Daddy: 'Leaving for Mexico City for two years Thursday—be ready if you want to come along.' This was Monday. Mother wired: 'Will be ready' and she was."[21] In the event, the Bards remained in Mexico less than one year.

The Bards' next home was in Placerville, Idaho. Of all the places the Bards lived for any length of time, Placerville was the most remote. They must have understood that it was a necessary stop on Darsie's climb up the business ladder, a place for him to gain managerial experience.

In Betsy's day, mule trains packed supplies from Boise to Placerville, picking their way through Ponderosa pines and fir trees across the weathered hills that surround the town. The dirt was flecked with bits of gold and mica. Founded in 1863 during the Boise Basin gold rush, Placerville was home to some five thousand people in its early days. Fewer than two hundred remained during the Bards' two years there. "The snow was fifteen feet deep on the level in winter and mother bought a year's supply of food at a time. Our closest neighbor was a kind woman who had been a very successful prostitute in Alaska and wore a chain of large gold nuggets which reached below her knees. She was very fond of me," Betty wrote.[22]

In Placerville, Sydney had limited choices in forming friendships. A genial former prostitute must have had interesting stories to share over the tea table, at least. Unlike her own mother, who cared about social niceties, Sydney seems to have taken in stride the less controllable aspects of her life with Darsie, such as whose company she might keep. Spending their early years amid a panoply of multifaceted, colorful adults who'd had outrageous adventures and spun them into stories was perhaps the germ of the Bards' fascination with unusual characters.

Darsie had come to Placerville to supervise his first placer mining project.[23] Sydney—pregnant again—managed the snow, the tiny house, the relative isolation, and her two small daughters with Gammy's help. Sidney Cleveland Bard—always called Cleve—was born in Placerville on November 29, 1908, and the 1910 federal census records the family as still living there, on Star Ranch Road.[24]

Betsy was about three and a half years old when her family left Placerville. In June 1910, Darsie was elected to fill the chair of mineralogy and geology at the Montana School of Mines back in Butte. Mary was nearing school age, and it was time for a more stable living situation.

The Montana School of Mines was founded in 1900 to train geological, metallurgical, and mining engineers. The location, an area rich in mineral resources and honeycombed with mines, allowed students to move directly from books to picks and shovels. The School of Mines anchored Butte's Westside neighborhood, which was populated mainly by the town's wealthier citizens. Irrespective of their financial status, however, no one in Butte lived isolated from the mining industry. During his years as a professor, Darsie also continued to work as a consulting mining engineer. This work brought in extra income and allowed him to build both a reputation and a stable of clients.

Before returning to Butte, Sydney took her children back East, to her maternal grandparents' home in Auburn, New York, to meet her family. It was apparently her first trip home since her elopement.[25] Sydney's mother insisted that the Bard children call her Deargrandmother, and she attempted to refine their manners. "She tried hard," Betty recalled, "to scrape the West off these little nuggets."[26]

On their return to Butte, the family settled into a modest gabled clapboard house at 1039 West Granite Street, on a corner three blocks from the School of Mines. The new house sat high above the street. A tiny turret rose from the center of its shingled roof, resembling an upside-down ice cream cone. The house was two blocks south of the Butte, Anaconda & Pacific mining railroad, which carried ore from Butte mines to the smelter in Anaconda. The rattling ore cars screeching over constantly busy rails and the rumble of dynamite blasting far below the town provided background accompaniment to all neighborhood activities. Darsie crossed the railroad tracks on his way to and from the School of Mines each day. The Bard children could watch from their front porch as the Butte Electric Railway's yellow streetcar clacked slowly past their house and turned south onto Emmet Avenue toward the central business district, called Uptown.

By the time the family returned to Butte, the nation's appetite for electricity had surged. Generating and transmitting electric power required copper wire as a conductor, and America depended on the Butte mines for this crucial material. Mining copper necessitated a city under the city: an ever-expanding maze of shafts and tunnels, teeming with constant activity, backfilled as their ore was exhausted. Below all of the ordinary life on Butte's surface teemed this mining hive. Except during strikes, the mines operated ceaselessly. Against this backdrop, Betsy and her siblings grew.

Headframes (also called gallus or gallows frames) resembling giant oil derricks dominated every view in Butte. Essentially huge elevators, they moved men, equipment, and supplies into and out of the sweltering mines. They also transported the mules that pulled the ore cars in the tunnels, lowering the animals underground in special trusses. Headframes were high-tech wonders in their day, their construction akin to building skyscrapers. The headframe of the Anselmo mine loomed two blocks northeast of the Bards' house. The Orphan Girl mine headframe stood half a mile west, beyond the School of Mines. Big Butte hovered protectively nearby, marked proprietarily with whitewashed rocks forming a letter M, for the Montana School of Mines.

Although the Bards were now settled, Darsie was still gone for extended periods, hired by private clients or leading school trips. "Points of geological interest are not always the most accessible," stated the Montana School of Mines 1912 senior class book: visiting them sometimes required a journey of weeks or months. Darsie led groups of students on horseback to Bridger Canyon in Utah or Yellowstone in Wyoming for field geology classes, trailed by a horse-drawn chuck wagon.

Sometimes Sydney accompanied Darsie on these trips, and sometimes the whole family went along, camping throughout the Western states. One family member recalled hearing that to keep her small children from wandering into danger while she attended to camp duties, Sydney would tie a rope around each child's waist and attach the other end to a stake driven into the ground. The children had food and water and were close enough to one another to play, but their tethers kept them from straying.

Sylvia Remsen Bard, Sydney's fourth child, was born on December 31, 1912.[27] Her life was short: on May 18, 1913, a dismal day of drizzling rain mixed with snow, Sylvia died of pertussis, or whooping cough. Thanks to a vaccine developed in the 1950s, most parents today are unfamiliar with the desperate sound from which the disease takes its common name. Patients with pertussis cough and cough and cough, then suck in a breath with a loud whoop, then cough again. To hear a baby cough so convulsively is terrifying, as is the fact that the whoop confers the desperate hunger for air. Pertussis is one of the most contagious human diseases, and it is most dangerous for babies and children under the age of five. Their small windpipes are more easily obstructed by mucus, and the prolonged struggle for breath quickly weakens the young, especially babies, and deprives them of the strength to take in nourishment.

Sylvia Bard was one of eleven children under five (and one of seven infants) to die of pertussis in Butte in 1913. Her death certificate—signed by Dr. Thomas Moore, who had delivered Sylvia at home just four and a half months earlier—states that the onset of the disease occurred one month and thirteen days before death. This annotation speaks of six weeks of struggle—struggle to nurse her, struggle to keep her alive.

It is difficult to know how this sister's death affected Betsy, who was six when Sylvia died, although the Bard home must have been saturated by grief. It was the first great loss Sydney and Darsie had faced together.[28] Betty MacDonald never mentioned Sylvia in her books.[29]

The Reverend Blackiston (who had baptized Cleve, then three years old, on the family's return to Butte, but not yet Sylvia) officiated at a brief private funeral held at the house.[30] Sylvia's tiny coffin was buried at Mount Moriah Cemetery on Butte's southern edge. If there was a grave marker, it did not endure, leaving only a slight indentation in the sparsely covered ground. As the seasons passed, all traces of Sylvia Bard's brief existence dissolved into Butte's coppery, implacable soil.[31]

One reason the family had settled in Butte was so that the children could be educated. Mary attended McKinley School, a two-story redbrick building two blocks from the Bards' house.[32] First Betsy and then Cleve joined her there, climbing the school's wide interior steps, their hands sliding over the thick brass rail. During Butte's icy winters—the town averages 223 days a year of below-freezing temperatures—the children coasted down Montana Street on their sleds after school, and in the evenings, Darsie took his bundled brood bobsledding.

The bitterly cold mornings, Betty remembered, did not deter her father's determination to test and toughen his children physically. Intent on fostering vigor and good health, he insisted they start the day by running around the block. Gammy "would stand by the door waving her 'apern' and wailing, 'Darsie Bard, how can you drive those poor little cheeldrun out into this bitter cold?' We'd hang around the steps blowing our hot breaths into the freezing air and watching them smoke and hoping that Gammy would soften Daddy, but he only laughed at Gammy and shut the door firmly and finally."[33]

Darsie set high standards for his children, provided structure in their lives, and, on occasions, meted out punishment, encouraging Betsy, Mary, and Cleve to learn self-discipline. We have only Betty's reports on which to rely, but these paint a consistent picture: Darsie was a kind and traditional father, a man who enacted this role not just by providing for his family's financial needs but also by making a secure home for them with Sydney. Darsie seems to have accepted high spirits in his children, but he expected them to obey him, believing that under his moral and intellectual guidance, they would grow strong.

Despite their parents' influence, Mary was the dominant force in Betsy's life from early childhood. Betty's books describe a big sister who is always in complete control, a geyser of plans and ideas into which she drags, pushes, or cajoles her sidekick, Betsy. The Mary of these stories bubbles with enthusiasm and self-confidence.

Like many strong-willed children, Mary possessed qualities that were considered faults in childhood and virtues in adulthood. In the retelling, though, playing Trilby to Mary's Svengali often brought Betsy to the edge of peril—once nearly plunging her into an abandoned mine shaft and another time accidentally impaling her small foot on the tines of a rake.

Although their father warned them of the dangers, cautioning them to watch for abandoned mine shafts and forbidding them from playing on flumes, Mary, Betsy, and Cleve were Butte children, and the mines were part of their childhood play. The cultural anthropologist Janet L. Finn describes life for children in Butte: "Year-round, Butte children honed their risk-taking skills in and around the workings of the mines, incorporating the gallows frames, slag heaps, settling ponds, and train tracks into their social worlds. In contrast to expert calls for safe, designated sites for child's play, Butte youngsters preferred the allure of the mine yard. They built forts from pilfered mine materials, organized potato roasts behind slag heaps, and dangled from ropes suspended from ore train trestles."[34] This sort of unsupervised, daring play encouraged the Bard children's imaginations to flourish.

This risky behavior among children took place against the equally dangerous backdrop of adult existence. Violence was a fact of life in Butte, especially during 1914, when conflict between the conservative Butte Miners' Union and the more progressive or radical Butte Mine Workers' Union resulted in the dynamiting of the Butte Miners' Union Hall, less than a mile from the Bards' house. Two National Guard battalions were deployed to Butte, and Silver Bow County was briefly placed under martial law. Newspaper stories claimed that 1,500 members of the IWW (Industrial Workers of the World, called Wobblies) were en route to terrorize Butte citizens. Although this rumor was false, it increased the residents' fears.

Work stoppages in the mines brought violent demonstrations, and this violence sometimes extended beyond the mines. Butte history includes scenarios in which angry strikers lashed out against mine company officials' families: wives and children had to flee as their homes were set ablaze, and grocers showed their support for striking miners by refusing to trade with these families. Darsie was much more closely allied with the mine managers than with the workers, and although there is no evidence that the Bards were ever overtly threatened, they held a somewhat ambiguous position in Butte's strata of alliances.

On January 16, 1915, Sydney gave birth to a daughter, Dorothea Darsie Bard, called Dede. In her books, Betty described this sister as differing both in appearance and temperament from the rest of the Bard siblings. Family lore recorded Darsie Bard's special closeness with Dede, whose birth less than two years after Sylvia's death may have been a kind of balm.

The unpretentious Bard house must have felt increasingly cramped: three growing children; baby Dede; Darsie, Sydney, and Gammy; and always at least one live-in hired girl. Life for the Bards was also difficult in other ways. The winter of 1915–16 was brutally cold. Betsy fell ill with scarlet fever. Mary and Cleve were sent to stay with friends to spare them from exposure to the disease.

World War I further increased the worldwide demand for copper. By 1916, there were some 14,500 miners working in rotating shifts in Butte, descending with picks and dinner buckets and ascending eight hours later, filthy, tired, and hungry for the open air—even the sulfur-laden air of Butte. The city, already rough, was getting rougher. Establishments catering to single men—saloons, boardinghouses, brothels—boomed. But many other miners were married and had families, which meant more children elbowing each other in the shared desks at McKinley School, where Mary, Betsy, and Cleve stair-stepped their way through the grades.

The punishing weather, the overcrowded conditions, and Butte's inherent danger probably influenced Darsie and Sydney to begin planning their next move, considering life in a warmer, calmer place. Although Sydney loved the West and Westerners, she and Darsie aimed to raise children who were not just resilient but also refined. The constant struggle to protect her children's manners, language, and social skills must have been exhausting. Betty wrote that her mother dosed the children with bitter cascara as punishment when they swore and that they wondered why the family's hired girls, who swore constantly, were not similarly dosed.

Then, too, Mary, with her flamboyant red hair and live-wire personality, was nearing young womanhood, in greater need of supervision and protection from a population of rough men. Betty remembered that the children's forays into Uptown were strictly chaperoned. Gammy insisted that they close their eyes when walking Butte's raucous streets, but such restrictions could not be enforced forever. Butte was no place to let daughters roam—or a son, for that matter. Perhaps Darsie and Sydney did not want their children to come of age in Butte.

Darsie and Sydney envisioned more for their four surviving children, and for themselves. Darsie had proved his skills by demonstrating leadership and scholarship at the School of Mines. He had amassed enough private clients to feel confident about earning a steady income from consulting work. He was a Mason and a member of Butte's prestigious Silver Bow Club. He knew the major players in the mining business well. The time had come to step into the role of businessman.

A mining trip took Darsie to Mount Baker in northwest Washington. Sydney was with him, and en route they visited Seattle.[35] Although Darsie had grown up in Portland, he had apparently never been to Puget Sound, and he was immediately captivated. Seattle was near enough to mineral riches for Darsie to pursue his work, an important business nexus, and far less rough than Butte. A move to Seattle would give Darsie and Sydney the opportunity to raise their family in a permanent and cultured place.

In the late summer of 1916, Darsie resigned his position at the Montana School of Mines. Sydney and Gammy packed up the household. Mary and Betsy and Cleve said goodbye to their friends. Accustomed as they were to moving, the Bard children had never ventured to such a cosmopolitan new city. They traded up: modest Big Butte for towering Mount Rainier.[36]

Montana is stark, lushly tinted but sparse in vegetation. In Butte's decomposed granite soil, rich in minerals, sagebrush grew, but not much more. No trees, no vegetable gardens, no rows of hollyhocks softened the fences of the miners' cottages. Young Betsy's front yard had one tiny square of grass that struggled to survive in the hostile environment. Betsy treasured it, protected it, and played on it, laying her dolls on the tenacious green patch.

When the wind blew from the direction of the Anaconda smelter, Butte's air was fumed with toxic smoke, yielding stunning sunsets that were likely taken for granted. The Bards were bound for a completely different environment, where sunsets were obscured by rain clouds and the landscape was lush and green. Betsy Bard was plucked from her familiar smoky-aired, smelter-glowing, bruise-colored landscape and transplanted to taciturn Seattle—wet, gray-skied, with towering trees and mountains, and birdsong that was not drowned out by blasting dynamite.

Everything Betty MacDonald wrote about the verdant, wanton, overwhelming Pacific Northwest landscape was written not only through observation but in implicit contrast to Butte, where she formed her earliest memories, where she learned to observe people's foibles and to take the measure of the world. Butte was frantic with industry under her feet; its multiethnic citizenry embraced the outlandish and eccentric. The whores, the miners, the housemaids, and the millionaires formed the fabric of Betty's early life. Butte was her measuring stick.

Betty would mine her rich memories of childhood as inspiration for her stories. Whether or not the Bards were seen as eccentric in Butte, that city sowed eccentricity in them. In time, the family would be perceived by acquaintances as deeply unconventional, and by the world at large—because of Betty's books—as characters both familiar and unique.

Perhaps Betsy had seen postcards of Seattle's Smith Tower. The 462-foot marvel was the tallest building west of the Mississippi river and boasted an observation deck from which visitors could gaze across Puget Sound toward the mountains on the wild Olympic Peninsula. Nine-year-old Anne Elizabeth Campbell Bard could not have dreamed that she would someday sit down at a typewriter made by L. C. Smith—whose son built the tower—and compose a tale based on her own life on that wild peninsula, a story that would be read around the globe.

CHAPTER TWO

Fate Alters the Plot

I n autumn 1916, the Bard family arrived in a Seattle that was full of promise. William Boeing was in the earliest stages of developing the aircraft company that would bear his name and become synonymous with his city. The Lake Washington Ship Canal, connecting Lakes Union and Washington with Puget Sound, was nearing completion. The business community was robust. The city had a symphony orchestra, a Fine Arts Society, theaters, and a well-stocked public library with branches throughout the city. Nellie Cornish's school taught classical music, dancing, painting, and singing. Seattle's parks offered ready outdoor recreation, and nature was within easy reach.

The move to Seattle meant, Betty wrote, that "pioneering days were over and preparedness for the future began."[1] Sydney enrolled Betsy and Mary in singing, piano, folk dancing, ballet, French, and drama lessons, readying them for a future as refined ladies. Saturday mornings were reserved for gym class followed by swimming at the YWCA in downtown Seattle.

While Darsie and Sydney explored the neighborhoods of their new city in search of their ideal permanent home, the family rented a house in the area called Capitol Hill. Previously the residence of the Danish consul, the place was grand, three times as large as the Butte house. The Bards enjoyed territorial views, three floors of airy rooms, and a basement large enough to serve as a ballroom or a gymnasium.

Darsie and his business partner, J. C. Johnson—operating as Bard & Johnson, consulting geological engineers—leased office space on the twenty-first floor of the Smith Tower.[2] With Darsie's existing clients as their base, the new firm soon amassed an impressive client roster, including the Milwaukee Railroad, the Ladysmith Smelters of Vancouver Island, and the Butte & Superior mining consortium.

Darsie joined Seattle's University Club and Arctic Club. Founded in 1907, the Arctic Club's charter members included more than two hundred men from mineral-rich Alaska. Many of the Northwest's most active and important businessmen belonged to the club, and their grand clubhouse at Third Avenue and Jefferson Street provided reading, dining, billiard, and assembly rooms, as well as 120 sleeping rooms—about six times more rooms than the Silver Bow Club, Butte's equivalent facility. The University Club, founded in 1900, encouraged social interaction among Seattle men who had graduated from college or university.[3] Its members could use the private dining room and squash courts and participate in frequent social gatherings. Both of these clubs afforded Darsie opportunities for networking among Seattle's social and business elite. The memberships also boosted his family's social opportunities.

Betsy, Mary, and Cleve were enrolled briefly in Lowell Elementary, the public school nearest their rented house.[4] In fall 1917, Betsy and Mary were transferred to St. Nicholas School, a private institution whose mission was to prepare girls for college or university and for leading roles in Seattle society. The school was housed in a three-story building at 712 Broadway North (now East), a short streetcar hop from the Bards' Capitol Hill home.[5]

St. Nicholas students were the daughters of Seattle's male business community and their wives, who led, facilitated, and funded the city's cultural and benevolent enterprises. Young women educated at St. Nicholas were encouraged to use their wealth for good rather than to rely on it for privilege. The school stressed academics, proper behavior, and helping the less fortunate. St. Nicholas students "adopted" a ten-year-old French girl during World War I (Mary Bard was among the young patronesses) and performed interpretive dances at a fundraising luncheon for the Seattle Day Nursery, which provided care for the children of low-income working mothers (Misses Elizabeth and Mary Bard, among others, frolicked in the "Dance of Joy").[6] For

St. Nicholas girls, rolling bandages for the Red Cross and raising funds for the Children's Orthopedic Hospital went hand in hand with learning to host teas and formal dinner parties. These lessons were firmly reinforced at home.

Betsy and Mary studied dancing at Nellie Cornish's school. "'One, two, three, LEAP!' shouted our ballet teacher, as she pounded her stick on the floor. Mary leaped so high they had to pull her down off the ceiling but I, who had also seen Pavlova and the Duncan Dancers, rubbed my ballet slippers in the rosin and dreaded my turn," Betty wrote of these lessons.[7]

The Bards seem hopeful in 1917, their new life freshly begun. It was a long way from Butte's clattering ore cars and shrieking mine whistles to Seattle's pattering raindrops and lush front lawns. Confident Mary quickly took root in the Bards' fertile new environment: she had no trouble learning to be grand. Betsy—whose grades were better than her sister's—picked her way through the St. Nicholas social scene more shyly.

Darsie and Sydney settled on the idea of a country environment for their children. In autumn 1918, they found a comfortable, gracious house in Seattle's Laurelhurst District.[8] The house was warm and welcoming, painted light gray and wrapped in a broad wooden porch. Climbing the steep steps to this porch brought the expanse of Lake Washington into view, offering prospects of refreshment, exploration, and adventure.

The house was built in 1900, and stood alone on land homesteaded by some of the first settlers to the area, which was not yet called Laurelhurst.[9] The land was sold to developers in 1907 and divided into large lots. In 1910, it was annexed by the city of Seattle. Over time, the empty lots around the Bards' house would slowly fill with other homes. When the Bards had lived in the house nearly a year, Darsie and Sydney purchased two adjoining lots and Gammy a further two, giving the family a sizeable compound.[10]

When the Bards moved to Laurelhurst, it was much more like the country than the city. It was about six miles from Seattle's central business district—just close enough to be accessible over the bumpy roads by automobile, but far enough away to offer respite. Unlike other Seattle neighborhoods, whose fortunes have waxed and waned, Laurelhurst has been steadily posh. For a short time during early 1900s, the land adjacent to the property Darsie and Sydney bought was Seattle's first golf club. The club was gone, but the pastoral feel that had attracted its developers remained. Despite Laurelhurst's distance from the city, grocers, ice men, and a fishmonger happily called for orders and made deliveries.

After the move, Betsy and Mary continued at St. Nicholas. Darsie dropped his daughters at school on his way downtown, or they caught the Laurelhurst jitney. This vehicle —an elongated Ford touring car— was purchased jointly by Laurelhurst families frustrated by the fact that Seattle's public transportation network ended far from their neighborhood. The jitney ride could be terrifying: after meandering its way through the neighborhood, the unwieldy vehicle had to charge up a steep, one-lane wooden trestle bridge that carried traffic over a marsh, finally reaching the University District and the city streetcar line.[11]

In Laurelhurst, the sense of nature, space, and calm was palpable. A quick bushwhack from the porch brought the Bards to Lake Washington, where they hosted beach parties. Long woolen bathing suits were the accepted attire for women and girls at the time, but Mary and Betsy's friends recalled the sisters' habit of swimming nude if not in mixed company.

Mary's lifelong friend Margaret Bundy Callahan remembered, "The Laurelhurst home was surrounded by knobby old fruit trees, pasture and woodland. It sat high on a bluff above the water and its unpretentious, spacious rooms rang always with the voices of many children. A horse, a cow, chickens, dogs, cats were added quickly to the family group. Mrs. Bard always loved animals and gardening. Life was very full and very happy."[12]

The heart of the house was its large, high-ceilinged dining room. The Bards' table was accommodating, and Sydney's excellent cooking and ready welcome drew many visitors for food and conversation. There was a partial basement where the children could play on rainy days, bedrooms upstairs —Betsy and Mary shared a bed —and an attic, where treasures and collections could be squirreled away. Eleven-year-old Betsy began to make up stories to amuse her siblings, especially Mary, for whom she spooled out the adventures of two orphan sisters, Nancy and Plum. If Betsy flagged, Mary would plant her icy feet on Betsy's back, refusing to take them off until she continued the tale.[13]

With the Laurelhurst house, Darsie and Sydney put down permanent roots and began a more social chapter of their lives together, fulfilling aspirations that Butte could not satisfy. The Laurelhurst house was both a home and a showplace for entertaining. Darsie was making good on his determination to be a better man than his own father.

Betty's books describe Darsie as a man whose love for his children was expressed in part by a desire to help them develop self-discipline. He required them to rise early, take cold baths, drink no water with their meals, forgo salt, use the gymnastic equipment at the YWCA and YMCA, and play sports. He prescribed healthy after-school snacks: fresh vegetables, apples, smoked herring, and hardtack. At their father's insistence, the siblings performed exercise routines to instructions from a record played on the Victrola. He taught them tennis, playing doubles on a public court on Saturday mornings.

To become self-reliant and gain useful skills, the girls learned to cook from Sydney. Darsie taught Cleve archery. The siblings were given complicated chores, including painting the house's steep roof. Darsie took them on birding hikes along Lake Washington Boulevard near the lake's then-wild shore, guidebooks in hand, insisting that they learn to identify birds and their calls.

From birth, Betty wrote, her father helped her and her siblings to develop their intellectual abilities. He quizzed them with intelligence tests, played mental games with them, tossed them math questions, and demanded rapid-fire lists of synonyms and antonyms. Darsie ensured the Bards' financial security, but more than that, he provided the family's structure, direction, and discipline.

Sydney was perhaps less Darsie's co-captain or first mate than a favorite passenger. Betty's books and the accounts of family friends portray Sydney as an indulgent mother, quick to accommodate her children's whims, and quite ready to abandon the health and discipline regimens her husband established for their children once his back was turned.

Darsie Bard published frequently and was considered a leader in the field of mineralogy. Visiting mining sites was still a part of his consulting business, but another lucrative aspect of it was serving as an expert witness in court cases. Many minerals cases were tried in Butte, and Darsie traveled there frequently to testify.

In January 1920, temperatures in Seattle hovered just above freezing. Sydney, at age forty-two, was four months pregnant. Dede, remembered in family accounts as her father's little shadow, had just turned five. The family celebrated Dede's birthday without Darsie, who had taken the train to Butte to testify in a case at the Silver Bow County Courthouse.

The news arrived from Butte by telegram, sent by Dr. Tom Moore, long the Bards' family physician: Darsie was ill, and Sydney should come at once. She packed a bag, rushed to King Street Station in downtown Seattle, and boarded the Northern Pacific train for the twenty-one-hour journey east toward Butte. Darsie lay in Murray Hospital, his breathing labored. Old friends met Sydney's train and drove her to Darsie.[14]

Darsie Bard died in the early hours of Saturday, January 24, 1920, with Sydney at his side.[15] He was forty-one years old. "Acute double lobar pneumonia," Dr. Moore's pen scratched across the death certificate.[16] The *Anaconda Standard* headlined the news of Darsie's death, calling him "one of the foremost geologists and mineralogists in the United States," and accompanying the obituary with a large etching.[17] The paper, printed daily in Anaconda, was delivered to Butte on the Butte, Anaconda & Pacific Railroad, clacking down the tracks that ran directly behind the Bards' old house on Granite Street—taking Darsie's handsome, thoughtful face past the house once more. That evening, the Butte Masonic Lodge conducted services in Darsie's memory, while Sydney brought her husband's body back to Seattle for cremation. Butte had been Darsie's home, off and on, longer than anyplace else, and many friends and former students there mourned him.

Darsie's funeral was held in Seattle on the afternoon of January 26, at Bonney-Watson funeral parlor. Seattle newspapers scarcely mentioned the event: Bard & Johnson was a new company, and Darsie had only just begun to integrate with the large business community.

The Bard siblings now faced a tenuous future. They were poised on the brink of the boom times of the 1920s, and it seems likely that their fortunes would have been different if Darsie had lived. All of Betty MacDonald's recorded memories of him suggest that Darsie had steered the family. It is impossible to imagine Betty experiencing the events recorded in *The Egg and I* had her father lived.

Sydney was well prepared to be a wife but ill prepared to be a widow. In some deep way, the blow of Darsie's death unmoored her, perhaps because Darsie himself had been her mooring. Without him, Sydney was adrift, rendered incapable of plotting her own destiny. She became a pawn, especially to her children. The shock of Darsie's death wore off in time, but some essential part of Sydney's ability to function remained flaccid.

Darsie's death created unexpected financial difficulties. Despite her grief, Sydney had to address these immediately. Because of a technicality in his will, which had not been properly witnessed, the family was left completely without income.[18] To access funds from his estate to cover the expenses of daily living, Sydney had to go to court.

Trying her best to cope with settling the estate and with the sudden lack of funds, Sydney moved thickly through the final months of her pregnancy. She petitioned the court for the release of almost all of Darsie's estate, to be invested in first mortgage bonds in the Carnation Company. Carnation produced canned evaporated milk, which could be stored and be shipped unrefrigerated. The bonds would draw interest at the rate of 7 percent per annum and would mature five years after purchase. The reasons behind Sydney's investment decision are unclear. Carnation was headquartered in Seattle, and it is possible that she knew executives from the company, or their wives. Just as likely, she had read about the bonds on the stock pages of Seattle newspapers, which frequently advertised Carnation's investment opportunities with hooks like "You can do without an automobile but can you do without milk?"[19] The judge authorized the expenditure.[20]

On June 25, 1920, a rainy Friday in an extraordinarily rainy month, Alison Cleveland Bard was born in the family home. She shared a middle name with her older brother, Sidney. Her birth and Darsie's death left Cleve as the lone male in a family of women. Besides her mother, Alison had Mary, Betty, and Gammy to rear her.

In autumn 1920, Sydney learned of a possible source of income for the family: an undeveloped mineral property, a potential source of gypsum, in Lewiston, Montana. Darsie had co-owned the property with Raymond Calkins, a longtime friend who had risen through the ranks of the Chicago, Milwaukee, St. Paul & Pacific Railway, becoming president of the line in 1919. Calkins told Sydney that he thought that if the property were developed, it could support Sydney and her children. Sydney asked him to handle the transactions for her, so Calkins found a tenant who was interested in leasing the property and developing the gypsum mine.[21] Their agreement stipulated that the lessee would pay royalties to Calkins, Sydney, and Sydney's children of not less than two thousand dollars twice yearly, plus an advance royalty of four thousand dollars, due by March 1921.

There was one hitch: the developer was unwilling to enter into an agreement with minor children. To circumvent this difficulty, Calkins told Sydney he would set up a corporation that would lease the property on behalf of the owners. Calkins then organized the Northwest Gypsum Products Company, sold his own mining rights to the new corporation for ten thousand dollars, and proceeded under that company's name to mine gypsum.

Meanwhile, Darsie's Montana estate, consisting solely of the gypsum property, went through probate, and Lewiston National Bank sold the Bards' portion of the property to Calkins for its appraised value of $1,800. Thereafter, Calkins held title to the entire property. Sydney received an initial payment and was at first content with the transaction. It was only years later, when she learned that Calkins was profiting heartily from the mine, that she smelled a rat. She had sold the land, she realized, but not the mineral rights. There was also the question of whether that land had been fairly appraised. The murky financial deal with Calkins was a warning that the Bards' fiscal security blanket was starting to fray.

With Darsie's death, his daughters lost their foothold in Seattle's junior elite: Betsy and Mary Bard disappear from the St. Nicholas School roster after the spring of 1920. Eliminating school fees was an obvious economy. Autumn found the sisters—Betsy a freshman, Mary a junior, both still wearing their St. Nicholas uniforms—enrolled at the public Lincoln High School, a large, Jacobean-style brick building in Seattle's bungalow-filled Wallingford neighborhood. The following year, studious Betsy was secretary of the sophomore class. Gregarious Mary appeared in the senior play and in the school's opera, sang in the Glee Club, and chaired the Football Dance and the Girls' Club social committee.

Despite increasingly shaky finances, the Bards maintained the same happy, open household as they had before Darsie's death. Margaret Bundy Callahan remembered, "At Lincoln High they made many new friends instantly and the Laurelhurst house was more full than ever of young people. Sunday evening open house at the Bards became an institution: phonograph music, the creaking of a hammock on summer evenings, the shuffle of dancing feet, lake-bathing and beach fire parties, waffles and hot chocolate and always the sound of young laughter. Sydney, or simply 'Syd,' became a trusted second mother to her children's friends, the repository of innumerable youthful confidences."[22]

Among the Bard sisters' new friends was Blanche Hamilton, a tiny girl who captivated Betsy with her ability to tell stories. She would become a lifelong friend. The youngest daughter of a mother who valued reading above almost anything, Blanche lived in a modest home in the Green Lake neighborhood. When Betsy invited Blanche home to meet her family, Blanche was awed at the prospect of visiting Laurelhurst.

Blanche recalled her first impression of visiting Betsy's home and meeting her mother: "As we entered the front door, Betsy's mother, Mrs. Bard—or Sydney, as she asked both young and old to call her— met us. She was tall and thin, with patrician features, smartly plain in dress, and extremely warm and charming."[23] Sydney is present—in Blanche's recollections as in Margaret's—more as a friend than as a mother. Blanche joined the midnight waffle and cocoa parties that followed nighttime skinny-dipping sessions in icy Lake Washington. She remembered her first encounter with Betsy's little sisters, "dressed in long white nighties with their little pink toes peeking out from under the bottom ruffle. Dede . . . was about five years old and had round, shiny gray eyes and dark brown hair. I wanted to reach over and pat her smooth ivory skin. . . . Alty [Alison], a little over two years old, had reddish hair, gorgeous amber-colored eyes, and the same lovely satin skin as Dede's."[24] The girlhood Blanche Hamilton describes sharing with Betsy sounds carefree. Blanche remembered that Betsy and Mary, in stark contrast with most of their peers, were completely unafraid of teachers, the school principal, and other authority figures. This egalitarian attitude seems likely to have stemmed from Sydney's anti-authoritarian approach to childrearing.

Despite the outward suggestions that the Bards continued to lead a carefree, happy existence, Darsie's death had left a void that Sydney would not or could not fill. Margaret Bundy Callahan is an important source on the Bards' family life during this period. She grew close enough to the family to learn that Mary had always had tantrums, and that Darsie had disciplined her, handled her temper, and tried to rein her in. Sydney, in contrast, wanted her children and their friends to like her. She smoked and drank with her teenage children, for example, rather than setting limits or forbidding these activities. The Bard children, who had called Sydney "Mother" prior to their father's death, now called her by her name. This change was indicative of a loosening of family discipline.

Mary had her own ideas and more self-confidence than was sometimes prudent, and she took advantage of her mother's leniency to exercise her independence. During the years immediately following her father's death, Mary apparently realized that she could now set her course, and her family's course, with little opposition. Sydney offered opinions but not rules. Life at the Bards' lacked structure, perhaps almost as if no adult were present, so welcoming and eager was Sydney for the friendship of her children and their friends. "Everybody in this house does just as he pleases," Betty credited Gammy as saying, and that statement seems to have been largely true.[25]

Mary's interests during these years tended less toward Seattle's high society and more toward intellectual and cultural pursuits. "I have often wondered whether Mary would not have broken away, anyhow, had her father remained alive," Margaret Bundy Callahan reflected. "There was a wayward streak in her nature that would probably have carried her off the beaten track, regardless of the fetters of circumstance."[26]

Margaret noted both the pleasant and the unpleasant sides of Mary, whose well-intentioned bossiness Betty would later credit with her own success. Margaret reflected, "Mary is surely a paradox if ever there was one. She is fundamentally so honest, yet with so much deception streaking her nature; at once so conventional and so scoffing at convention; so onto the imbecilities of the social world and so duped by them; so warm and giving in her responses to other human beings about her, yet at times so coldly selfish and cruel."[27] One of Mary's notable qualities was her refusal to back down. If she decided someone should do something, she pushed and pestered until she prevailed.

Mary graduated from high school in 1922. Her photograph in the Lincoln *Totem* yearbook shows a vivacious young woman. Her motto reads, "Torchy is the girl who put the pep in 'pepper'!"[28] That fall, Mary matriculated at the University of Washington, pledging the Alpha Phi sorority. As active in college as she'd been in high school, Mary served on the YWCA executive council and on the class social committee. In the four quarters she completed, she took courses in music, English, French, public speaking, and business administration.

The University of Washington was even closer to the Bards' Laurelhurst home than Lincoln High School. The university had moved from its original location in downtown Seattle to what was then freshly logged land between Lakes Washington and Union in 1895. The southern portion of the campus was developed with both permanent and temporary structures created for the 1909 Alaska-Yukon-Pacific Exposition. Many of the exposition buildings were used for classes during Mary's time on campus.[29]

In the fall of 1922, Betsy was assigned to attend the new Roosevelt High School, named for President Theodore Roosevelt, in northeast Seattle. Seattleites dubbed the building the "million-dollar school." It boasted a 1,500-seat auditorium with a stage that was at the time one of the largest on the West Coast, separate gymnasiums for boys and girls, and modern brick and reinforced-concrete construction. Black walnut trees transplanted from Theodore Roosevelt's Oyster Bay estate in New York graced the school's front lawn.

Betsy and Blanche Hamilton (who lived only a few blocks from the new school) entered as juniors. Betsy sang in the Glee Club and served on the school's Improvement and Good Cheer committees. She was a member of the Honor Society. Her aspiration, according to Roosevelt's *Strenuous Life* yearbook: "To be an illustrator."[30]

Betsy and Blanche graduated from Roosevelt in 1924, as members of the school's second graduating class. Following Mary's footsteps, Betsy matriculated at the University of Washington, eschewing her soft childhood nickname for the brisker name of Betty, which she thought sounded more sophisticated. Betty took mainly design and drawing courses, along with English, Spanish, and physical education. Like Mary, she pledged Alpha Phi. Betty completed three quarters: fall 1924 and winter and fall 1925.

Betty did not know how to drive. Mary used the family car, an old Franklin, to ferry family and friends between Laurelhurst and the University District. She was nearsighted and a poor driver, Margaret Bundy Callahan observed, and while behind the wheel she was uncharacteristically silent as she concentrated on keeping the Franklin on the road.

At home, money was going out, but little was coming in. Widows in Butte (who were numerous because of frequent mine accidents) often took in paying boarders after their husbands died, but in Seattle, Sydney didn't. The family could also have moved to a more modest home in a less expensive part of town, but with all five of her children still at home, plus Gammy, Sydney perhaps felt she needed a house with some space. The Bards cut back in some ways, but Blanche Hamilton and Margaret Bundy Callahan report a font of delicacies, including items delivered from Seattle's most exclusive food store, Augustine and Kyer. Sydney apparently refused to economize on food for her children and their hordes of friends.

What Sydney did try as a means of bringing in money was operating a tearoom in the University District. It might have been her idea, but more likely it was Mary's. Tearooms were popular in the late 1910s and 1920s, providing places where respectable women could dine alone or with other women, and running a tearoom was considered a genteel female enterprise. The city already boasted several popular establishments downtown. Moreover, Sydney had some experience to draw on: she, Mary, and Betty had all volunteered in the Children's Orthopedic Hospital Tearoom, one of the hospital's fund-raising enterprises. For an inveterate hostess and marvelous cook like Sydney Bard, the tearoom venture must have seemed like a pretty good bet.

Sydney called her shop the Mandarin. All the Bards pitched in to help run it. Betty waited tables or minded Alison and Dede, Mary was the hostess, and Sydney cooked. Home-cooked food was de rigueur in tearooms, with an emphasis on delicate, ladylike dishes such as finger sandwiches, crab salad with cheese crackers, toasted cheese, waffles, chicken salad, deep-dish apple pie, and warm gingerbread.

The Mandarin received frequent mention in the *Gossip of the Shops* column of the *Seattle Times*, written by "Jean"—who may have been a family friend. Jean effused, "With its dear little tables all painted a cool, cool green, and bright splashes of lacquer red about the cozy room, it is quite the most delightful place I've seen in a long time. And the food is wonderful! You all know Mrs. Darsie Bard, of course. Luncheon, tea, and dinner."[31] In winter, Jean raved about the Mandarin's blazing fireplace and "homey" atmosphere. In summer, she advised her readers, "The special ice tea Mrs. Bard makes is the best in the city and her salads and sandwiches—yum! Yum! The delicious evening dinners are drawing more and more University District folk to The Mandarin!"[32]

But this assessment was overly optimistic. Part of the tearoom's problem may have been its multiple changes of location. The first location, 4515 15th Avenue Northeast, was on the ground floor of a small apartment building.[33] This was slightly off the University District's main thoroughfare, although it was on the Cowen Park–University District streetcar route. After less than a year, the Mandarin moved to 4530 University Way Northeast, more central to off-campus student activities. The building had been the University Way Club and was also at some point used as the Beta fraternity house.[34] This location, too, Jean found homey: "One you can lounge around in, or play the piano."[35]

Less than a year later, the Mandarin moved to 4311 15th Avenue Northeast, where it occupied the ground floor of an aging rooming house.[36] This, Jean told her readers, was "its permanent location—a spacious, homelike place, so comfortable and somehow just like we've read about in story books. Everyone who enjoys Mrs. Bard's home cooking gathers there, from school children to grown-ups."[37]

They may have gathered, but they didn't pay. Blanche Hamilton summed it up: Sydney "was no business woman as she had too much heart. Her friends and those of her children would go in to eat, and when they tried to pay the check, Sydney was apt to say, 'Oh, Joe, let's make this one on me.' She had been the hospitable hostess in her own home too long. She could not make the transition, and the tearoom did not pay."[38]

The Bards' Mandarin adventure ended poorly. The University Provision Company, a meat market that supplied The Mandarin, filed a complaint against Sydney in King County Superior Court demanding past-due payment.[39] They filed a writ of attachment on Sydney's car—the 1917 Franklin Touring automobile—which the King County sheriff impounded. In January 1925, Sydney settled the bill by signing the car over to University Provision, and the action was dismissed.

In this crisis, as in most other matters on which family members or friends noted their impressions, Sydney appeared unflappable. Maybe the worst possible thing had already happened to her: losing her husband. Blanche Hamilton recalled hearing that after Darsie died, Sydney collapsed completely. "You have to get up, Sydney, you have to!" Mary had pleaded with her mother. Perhaps, having endured that loss, Sydney Bard figured nothing in the world could ever take her that far down again.

Her financial difficulties, however, would persist. From 1924 on-ward, the public record shows a trail of Sydney's real-estate troubles. King County and Jefferson County property transfer records, the many deeds, mortgages, and quit-claims bearing Sydney's name, and the civil case files tell a sorry story.[40]

When Darsie died, the Bards owned the Laurelhurst property free and clear. This property's legal description—which matters here be-cause of Sydney's subsequent actions—was The Palisades Addition to the City of Seattle, block 4, lots 1–4. Lot 3, on which the house stood, was the most valuable. Sydney mortgaged lots 3 and 4 to the State Savings and Loan Corporation. Her monthly mortgage payments were set at forty-eight dollars. Sydney traded her equity for cash and then, as court documents later stated, "utterly failed" to make any mortgage payments. This established a pattern, a real-estate shell game of mort-gage and remortgage that Sydney would continue for the next two decades, no matter where she and her family lived.

Sydney's actions indicate that she was suggestible, especially to the ideas of her children. If the tearoom was Mary's idea, now it was Cleve's turn. "On a drive to the Olympic Peninsula, the Bard family was attracted to a picturesque farm," Blanche Hamilton remembered. "Although Betty's younger brother, Cleve, was only seventeen and had no farming experience, he thought farm life would be wonderful. Prac-ticality was swallowed up in romanticism. They bought the farm."[41]

"She's not like a mother a bit," Margaret Bundy Callahan re-membered Mary's telling her about Sydney.[42] Nothing demonstrates Sydney's lack of maternal wisdom quite as much as her decision to purchase a large dairy farm in Jefferson County for her completely inexperienced teenage son to run. What was she thinking?

Maybe Sydney believed the family had exhausted the promise of Seattle. She was teetering on the brink of insolvency, and the Manda-rin enterprise—even if spun to their friends as madcap fun—had been a failure. Funds for Betty's and Mary's college tuition had dwindled. And Cleve, the only son of a Harvard man, refused to attend high school. His Roosevelt High School attendance record shows a string of poor marks, followed by the harsh rubber stamp "On Probation" and—as of spring 1925—"Dropped for Scholarship." Cleve, more than anyone, needed a fresh start.

And things might have worked out: Cleve might have shaped himself into a dairyman if only Sydney—who, in her defense, had never handled a property purchase on her own—had thought to investigate the farm's chain of title.

About the time Sydney was slipping into arrears on the Laurelhurst house's mortgage, a gentleman named T. C. MacNamara sold the dairy farm—in Chimacum, Jefferson County—to a man named H. K. Blonde. Back in 1923, MacNamara had mortgaged this property to the Washington Mutual Bank. Blonde was supposed to take over MacNamara's mortgage payments. Instead, in late 1925, Blonde sold the property to Sydney, who was now supposed to make mortgage payments on the dairy farm to Blonde. A well-respected farmer, Percy Wright, owned the adjoining property and would eventually become directly involved in the Bards' real estate affairs.

The Chimacum property purchase included a large herd of cows, a flock of chickens, horses, pigs, and goats. The Bards—all but Mary, who had a job and an apartment in Seattle—moved there to take up dairy farming, with Cleve in charge.[43] Cleve had never farmed or cared for livestock: a hired boy handled the domestic animals in Laurelhurst, and the family had almost certainly never owned anything more than cats and dogs in Butte. It was, to say the least, a risky decision.

But for the Bards, the new undertaking was an exciting adventure. Like many of their past experiences—in Boulder, Placerville, and even Butte—Chimacum might have become simply another chapter in the family's story. But for Betty, it would be more. The Sunday drive, the farm for sale, and her mother's willing acquiescence to Cleve's whim gave rise to the most significant and enduring experience of her life: the three years she would recount in *The Egg and I*. Although the process of distilling that experience into narrative would take decades, the move to Chimacum was like a key sliding smoothly into the lock that opened Betty Bard MacDonald's destiny.

CHAPTER THREE

Child Bride

THE Bards decamped from their Laurelhurst house primed for a
fresh start, but from the very beginning, the dairy farm venture
was doomed, for several reasons. First, life in Chimacum was far
more primitive than the life the Bards had become used to in Seattle.
Although they'd sometimes lived rough when Darsie was alive, they
were not prepared for the daily dawn-to-dusk hard work of running a
commercial dairy farm.

Second, their new home's location required the vivacious Bards to
endure isolation, offering few of the amenities and distractions they
had grown fond of in bustling Seattle. Jefferson County is situated
on Washington's lush Olympic Peninsula. Non-Native settlement in
the area began in 1850, on Chimacum Creek, about ten miles south
of the region's most important early port of entry, Port Townsend.
When the Bards moved there in 1926, the combined population of the
neighboring areas called Chimacum and Center hovered around 275.

Third, Chimacum was a difficult place to be a newcomer. The
Bards had chosen a community populated by families that had worked
their land for decades, whose bloodlines were repeatedly intertwined
by marriage. In Chimacum, the Bards knew no one. And finally, although the Bards remained ignorant of this for many months, there
was the looming disaster of their property's broken chain of title.

Far from Jazz Age Seattle, life in Jefferson County moved at a
slow pace. Many men worked in logging and lumbering. Hauling,
transportation, and heavy farm work were still done with horses. The
roads were mostly dirt and often pocked with chuckholes, although

the county was working to improve them. Except for those few who owned small generators, Chimacum residents would not have electricity until the late 1940s.

Chimacum featured a garage, a hotel, and a small general store and post office. Major shopping trips required a journey to the mill-owned store in Port Ludlow, a few miles away. Journeys from Chimacum to Port Townsend—where the Rose Theater played silent movies, and confectionery stores and cafes beckoned—were all-day affairs because of the poor roads, and so they were a rare treat.[1]

Little is known of this period of the Bards' life. Their friends Margaret Bundy Callahan and Blanche Hamilton left few recollections of the family in Chimacum. Blanche was studying to be a teacher and never visited them there. Margaret was working on the editorial staff at the *Seattle Star* and saw them rarely. It is especially difficult to know exactly what life during the first year or so in Chimacum was like for Betty. We do not know, for example, if she was sorry to leave college, what her daily life on the farm entailed, or whether she held a job away from the farm.

Although automobiles were still rare in Chimacum in the 1920s, Cleve always had a car, and this would have increased the Bards' chances to take part in social life and recreation, if they wanted to. Whether they mixed with them socially or not, the Bards took the measure of their neighbors. The culture shock Betty described in *The Egg and I* probably reflects her first months in Chimacum: in this insular rural community on the Olympic Peninsula, the Bards were a poor fit.

After Darsie's death, the Bards had increasingly defined themselves as an exclusive society. They ruthlessly criticized but also enjoyed other people's foibles, blurring the line between appreciation and mockery. The less money they had, the more comfort they may have drawn from feeling intellectually and socially superior to their neighbors. To Jefferson County old-timers, the Bards' attitude would have been obvious, and off-putting.

Not all the Bards were snobbish. At Chimacum High School, Dede edited the paper and was remembered warmly decades later by classmates who rode the school bus with her. Stories that circulated later had Cleve cutting a wide swath through the population of young women in the area. He went to dances and sometimes strong-armed Betty into going along so she that would not be considered snooty. But Cleve seems always to have stood alone, coming and going when and where he wanted to, only loosely connected to the female household, an independent agent.

Mary visited frequently from Seattle, often bringing friends who helped sustain the old open-house tradition, if in a more rural style. Betty acted as hostess. Mary sometimes stayed with her family for longer stretches during this period: one story has her teaching tap dancing classes in Port Townsend, and she once performed a dance at a Chimacum High School evening gathering, as documented in the *Port Townsend Leader*.[2] Mary's experience of living independently and starting to build a work history would be important to the Bards during the next decade.

Meanwhile Betty, in Chimacum, tumbled into romance. Blanche Hamilton describes how Betty encountered the dashing Robert Heskett, the older man who swept her off her feet:

> One time when Cleve was in Seattle he bumped into an old friend, Bob Heskett, and brought him home to the farm. Both Mary and Betty thought Bob was a beautiful man. He was tall and well-built, with uniform white teeth, dark hair, and blue eyes. In his late twenties, he appeared very smooth indeed to a girl of eighteen. He began to notice Betty rather than Mary, which was most unusual as most of the guys who came to the house were more attracted to Mary. Before the summer was over, the romance had gathered great momentum and Betty confided in me that Bob had finally seduced her in the strawberry patch.[3]

Betty later described how thrilled she was to best Mary, and the strawberry-patch seduction (presumably in June) might be the reason that Betty subsequently wed in haste.

Mary thought Robert Heskett looked almost exactly like the film heartthrob Gary Cooper.[4] Heskett was born in Cedar Falls, Iowa, and raised mainly in Fargo, North Dakota. When Bob was a young man, he and his father worked homestead claims in Montana. During World War I, Bob fought in France as a private in the U.S. Marines. In 1920, Bob's sister Katherine, who was nearest him in age, died, and the Hesketts left Montana soon afterward. By 1923, Bob was living in Seattle with his parents, Otis and Florence, and two younger sisters. After Bob's mother died in 1925, his father quickly remarried. By the time Bob and Betty met, both he and his father worked for Mutual Life Insurance.

Betty MacDonald was not a romantic writer, but her description of her whirlwind courtship with Bob takes her as close to that label as she would get: "He liked me. I still cannot understand why unless it was that he was overcome by so much untrammeled girlishness. He took me to dinner, dancing and the movies and I fell head over heels in love, to his evident delight."[5]

The King County document certifying the legal marriage of Robert E. Heskett and Anne Elizabeth C. Bard reveals that Betty and Bob were married by the Reverend Herbert Gowen on July 10, 1927.[6] The wedding took place in the Gowen home.[7] The witnesses were Bob's father and stepmother—not Mary, not Sydney, not Dede, not even Cleve. Their absence suggests that the marriage was an elopement. If Betty's family had been present, it seems likely that they would have stood as witnesses.

Family lore holds that despite his good looks, Mary Bard loathed Robert Heskett. Whether this was because he failed to favor her over Betty or for other reasons is hard to know. In marrying Bob, Betty made a stand against her sister, perhaps the first time she had done so in any significant way.

Sydney announced her daughter's marriage in the *Seattle Times* the following week. After a short stay in Victoria, British Columbia, the notice stated, "they will return to Chimacum, Wash., where they will be at home."[8] Home at the time would have meant living with Sydney on the dairy farm. After Betty wed, her maternal grandmother—she who preferred to be addressed as "Deargrandmother"—commenced her letters to Betty, then twenty, with "Dear Child Bride."[9]

Bob was gentle, Betty wrote, and smitten by her girlish naïveté. Sydney had taught Betty housewifely skills: how to make up a bed with mitered corners, how to cook and arrange flowers and set a sparkling table. She had learned to control small details whether or not she could control the large ones. Betty had also been raised by Gammy, who was (at least in the retelling) a droll, fatalistic skeptic. Betty brought her mother's and grandmother's somewhat disparate views to her married life. Having observed her parents' strong union, Betty also came to her marriage with that ideal in mind.

The marriage likely began with several romantic weeks or months. The couple had something to look forward to: just before their marriage, or perhaps immediately after exchanging vows, Betty had become pregnant. On February 23, 1928, she gave birth to Anne Elizabeth Heskett at Seattle General Hospital.[10] By the time Anne was born in Seattle, Betty and Bob were no longer living with Sydney in Chimacum. Whether or not Sydney had been making her payments to H. K. Blonde for the property, Blonde was certainly not making his required payments on MacNamara's mortgage to Washington Mutual. In August 1927, shortly after Betty's marriage, Washington Mutual began foreclosure proceedings on the Chimacum farm. In late 1927, Jefferson County Superior Court handed down a judgment against MacNamara, ruling that neither Blonde nor Sydney had any legal interest in the property and ordering that it be auctioned off to pay the debt. In January 1928, the dairy farm was sold on the Jefferson County Courthouse steps.

In later years, the Bards obscured the details of the farm's demise, blaming the loss on a larger-than-expected bill for drainage from the county and the discovery of tuberculosis in their dairy herd, which could have been the case. In order to market milk from the region as guaranteed free of bovine tuberculosis (which can infect humans through consumption of contaminated milk), Jefferson County instituted rigorous testing. The only way to eradicate tuberculosis in a dairy herd is to destroy the herd.

Sydney still had one hope for getting her hands on money: the Bards had learned from old friends that the Montana gypsum mine being worked by Darsie's former partner, Raymond Calkins, was much more profitable than he had suggested. Sydney started corresponding with Calkins, who repeatedly promised her royalties but did not pay them. In September 1927, Sydney initiated a suit against him.[11]

While this case moved through the courts, however, Sydney lost her desperate struggle to keep the Laurelhurst property. The State Savings and Loan Association started foreclosure proceedings on lots 3 and 4, which included the house.[12] One week after she lost the Chimacum dairy farm, Sydney sold lots 1 and 2 of the Laurelhurst property to Percy Wright, her former Chimacum neighbor, who had been living with his family in the Bards' Laurelhurst home for over a year.[13]

In March 1928, a few weeks after Anne's birth, the gypsum mine case was settled, with Calkins agreeing to pay each Bard sibling $1,860 (equivalent to about $24,675 today). Sydney safeguarded at least some of Alison's and Dede's portions. Mary, who recognized frugality as one method for controlling destiny, probably put her money in the bank. What Cleve did with his money is impossible to tell. For Betty and Bob, new parents, Betty's money was a godsend, enabling them to purchase the property about which—in a plot twist the young mother would likely have found completely implausible, had some palm reader or Ouija board predicted it—she would later tell the world in *The Egg and I*.

The proceeds from the land sale and the Calkins settlement proved insufficient to save the Laurelhurst house. The King County Superior Court ordered that the property be sold to satisfy Sydney's debt to the State Savings and Loan Association. In December 1928, the large, gracious home into which Darsie and Sydney had confidently moved their family almost exactly ten years before was auctioned on the King County Courthouse steps.

For Sydney, these two losses—her properties sold on the steps of two county courthouses—bracketed the year 1928. At fifty-one, Sydney was now a grandmother. Dede and Alison were youthful aunts. Gathering her younger children and Gammy, Sydney found a place to rent somewhere in Jefferson County.[14] The Bards opted to remain near Betty, Bob, and baby Anne.

Bob's decision to quit selling insurance and take up chicken ranching coincided with Betty's receiving her portion of the Calkins settlement. Bob later claimed that Cleve and Sydney urged him to make the change.[15] The notion that Bob should try his hand with chickens was not completely bizarre: egg ranching was a popular occupation in Washington during the 1920s. Alderwood Manor, a planned community about twenty miles north of Seattle, included a huge demonstration farm designed to show potential homeowners how to make egg ranching pay. By the time Betty and Bob went into the egg business, Alderwood Manor was one of the largest egg-producing operations in the nation.[16] In Jefferson County, egg ranches were all the rage. The *Port Townsend Weekly Leader* carried frequent stories about home egg-laying contests, and participants received advice on the care and feeding of their flocks. County residents held what the paper called "poultry meetings," inviting visiting experts to lecture. The paper's classified section advertised chicks, priced as low as $130 per thousand.

The property Betty and Bob bought to begin this venture was in Center, which bordered Chimacum and over time would eventually come to be considered part of Chimacum.[17] Two valleys—Beaver and Center—undulate gently along this finger of the Olympic Peninsula, the ridge between them more like a long, narrow hill than the fierce mountains Betty described in *The Egg and I*. Her forty-acre ranch was known to neighbors as the old Hammargren place, after the pioneer who received the property from the federal government in an 1891 land grant. The road running past the property was designated Road No. 16. In Betty's time, this road—also called Swansonville Road and Winding Road—ran all the way from Discovery Bay to Port Ludlow. Thanks to Betty it would become—first colloquially, then by habit, and finally by county decree—Egg and I Road.[18]

The property's chain of title is a mystery: no record survives of a deed or mortgage confirming the precise day when the Hesketts purchased the property. A Seattle firm held a mortgage and paid the property taxes when Betty and Bob lived there. There were two houses on the land: their farmhouse and a smaller, older dwelling that subsequent owners nicknamed the Pioneer House and which likely stood empty during Betty and Bob's tenancy.

The Hesketts' farmhouse was a cedar-shaked cottage with a rickety porch. The ten acres closest to the house had been logged long before the Hesketts purchased the property, but second-growth forest and mature fruit trees endured scrappily nearby. The cottage's main floor featured tall, narrow windows that seemed to beg the often-murky Northwest sun to find them. An attic tucked under the steeply pitched roof was accessed through an exterior door high up on the outside of the cottage. Using a long ladder, trunks and boxes could be carried up for storage. With the ladder removed, the doorway looked eerily wrong, as if the attic harbored incorporeal beings capable of walking out into midair.

The Hesketts' neighbors to the east were Albert and Susanna Bishop, who lived in their farmhouse with those of their thirteen children who had not started families of their own. To Bob and Betty's west lived Edward and Ilah Bishop and their teenage son, Bud. Edward was Albert and Susanna's eldest son.[19]

Eight months after Anne's birth, Betty was pregnant again. On July 14, 1929, she gave birth to Joan Dorothy Heskett at St. John's Hospital in Port Townsend.[20] Betty did not mention her second daughter's birth in *The Egg and I*. Given her vivid descriptions of her difficulties caring for one baby, a farm, and hundreds of chicks, perhaps she decided that two babies would strain credulity. And yet, two babies were what she had.

By this time, the romance of her marriage to Bob had dissipated. Betty never knew when or why she ceased to charm Bob, or what about her might have irked him. That Bob had been a soldier and endured the horrors of the battlefield may have played into his impatience, but she could do nothing about that except stay out of his way.

Jefferson County lore holds that Bob Heskett, like many of his neighbors, distilled moonshine. Betty's unpublished draft of *The Egg and I* contained a good deal of discussion of this Prohibition-era activity.[21] It seems possible that chicken raising supplemented moonshine manufacturing, or vice versa. Grain for hen feed might have disguised grain for mash.

Betty's marriage to Robert Heskett and her experiences as a young wife and mother in late 1920s rural Jefferson County differed greatly from the version of that marriage that Betty presented in *The Egg and I* in 1945. Years before writing it, almost immediately after living it, Betty started recounting a version of her experiences to entertain her friends. Betty's repeated tellings honed her version of events. Betty selectively reshaped her past, cutting the most disturbing incidents. Her highly curated history eventually—and unexpectedly—won her fame.

Young Bud Bishop, one of the Hesketts' nearest neighbors, pitied Betty and helped her. Seven decades later, near the end of the life he'd spent farming the Chimacum property where he'd lived since birth, Bud gave his oral history to a Jefferson County Historical Society volunteer, who asked him about his now-famous former neighbor. Betty was usually left alone with her two little girls, Bud remembered. "I cut her wood and got bark and stuff off the stumps for her in the wintertime because her husband was a bum. He was either drunk or making moonshine, and she was up there with two little baby girls, and she couldn't get wood so I went up there and got wood for her, to keep them from freezing."[22]

Bud Bishop's memories are an important testament to the life Betty actually lived. *The Egg and I*, as summed up on its cover, recounted "life on a wilderness chicken ranch told with wit and high humor." There was no helpful Bud; there were no over-hasty baby arrivals. And there were no Bards, although in truth Betty's family was never far away. Like many of her other purposeful omissions, Betty's decision to conceal the Bards' presence in Chimacum when she described those years altered the story.[23]

Among her siblings, Dede especially seems to have helped Betty and provided companionship, bringing her groceries and helping with Anne and Joan. As a young teenager, Dede was old enough to help but too young to intervene in what she saw. By contrast, if Mary had witnessed some moments of her sister's deteriorating marriage, she almost certainly would not have permitted Betty to remain with Bob.

But Mary was living in Seattle, and soon the rest of Betty's family would do likewise. By fall 1930, Sydney, Cleve, Dede, and Alison had turned their backs permanently on rural living and headed again for Seattle, indoor plumbing, paved roads, and electricity.[24] Gammy moved to Boulder, where she lived with her sisters for the rest of her life.[25]

While the Bards were failing at dairy farming, losing all their property, and growing ever poorer, the rest of the country was speculating on stock and dancing the Charleston. As Sydney and her family packed their bags to move back to Seattle and to Mary, reverberations from the 1929 stock market crash signaled the beginning of the cruel decade of the Great Depression. The penury it brought to much of the rest of the country was already familiar to the Bards, who hadn't had a dime to spare for years.

With her family gone, Betty found that she could not remain with Bob. Leaving him permanently took at least two tries. The court records of Betty's first attempt to extricate herself from her marriage reveal Mary's helping hand: Betty's attorney, almost certainly working pro bono, was Edward Bundy, the father of Mary's old chum Margaret Bundy Callahan.[26] In Blanche Hamilton's account of the event, Mary drove to Chimacum and took Betty and her tiny daughters—Anne was two and a half, Joan eleven months—back to Seattle. When Betty initiated divorce proceedings in King County on June 27, 1930, she was staying in Mary's apartment.

Betty was twenty when she moved to the Chimacum chicken farm and twenty-three when she abandoned it. When she started writing *The Egg and I*, she was in her mid-thirties and newly married to her second husband. She focused the book on the outrageous foibles of her rural neighbors—including those who lived closest, to whom she gave the surname Kettle—because describing these was easier, safer, more palatable, and much funnier than describing the collapse of her marriage or her husband's cruelty. She was not even trying to describe the real Bob, she later told her literary agent, but rather to endow her first husband with many of her second husband's characteristics.

Betty's divorce petition reveals that she and Bob held no community property. The farm and its flock of seven hundred chickens belonged to Betty alone, since they were purchased with funds she inherited—via the Calkins lawsuit—from her father's estate.

Although Bob was able-bodied, Betty alleged, he had done nothing to support his family other than taking on a small amount of work on the farm.

Betty's petition paints a stark picture of her three years with Bob: "That at all times since said marriage the defendant has treated the plaintiff in a cruel and inhuman manner and subjected her to such personal indignities as to render life burdensome; that the defendant has on numerous occasions violently beaten plaintiff and used towards her other personal violence; and defendant has on many occasions used towards plaintiff violent and abusive language, and subjected her to insults in the presence of members of her family and friends. That during all of said time defendant has been and now is an habitual drunkard."[27]

The judge issued Robert Heskett an order to appear in court, restraining him from disposing of any of the property—the farm and flock—set forth in Betty's petition. The process server located Bob, but either it was already too late or Bob ignored the order, because he sold all of the chickens and what he could of their household goods. He turned over nearly all of the resulting sum of $450 to Betty's attorney. Given Bob's later actions, this seems miraculous. Bob also acknowledged Betty's sole ownership of the property.[28]

Betty was never sure what happened to her possessions after she fled the chicken ranch. Bob left Chimacum soon after. According to Betty's later recollection, sometime during the next year, Bob drove her back to the ranch to retrieve books and some of their wedding presents. Other people were living in the house by then, using Betty and Bob's things.[29]

The legal record gives no account of the outcome of Betty's June 1930 divorce petition. An undated biographical statement Betty prepared for her publisher, J. B. Lippincott, states, "In 1930 I moved back to Seattle with my family, was divorced from my husband, the chickens, and the Indians, and entered into a business career owned and operated by my older sister, Mary."[30] In July 1931, however, Betty filed for divorce a second time.[31] "Said defendant has made plaintiff many promises to do better and relying on said promises, plaintiff has continued to live with said defendant although plaintiff's life has been made very miserable and unhappy by said defendant from the very beginning of said marriage," Betty's second pleading reads.[32] For a little while, and living who knows where, Betty must have gone back to him. No reason other than reconciliation would explain the need to file for divorce a second time.

The Egg and I makes no mention of divorce, perhaps on the principle that it would be unpalatable to readers. Betty would wait five years after *Egg* was published before articulating the rupture in print, with stark brevity: "I hated chickens, I was lonely and I seemed to have married the wrong man."[33] A modern memoir could dwell on Bob Heskett's complexities, but in 1945, describing them would have revealed more than society found acceptable and more than Betty could reveal without mortification. In leaving out the most difficult details of her marriage, Betty showed a discretion that aligned with the expectations of her time.

By the time of her second divorce filing, Betty and her daughters were living with Sydney in Seattle, and Betty had embarked on the desperate series of short-term jobs described in her third memoir, *Anybody Can Do Anything*. Bob was in Seattle, selling insurance again.

In 1931, America experienced just over 17 divorces for every 100 marriages. In Washington, the figure was 22 divorces for every 100 marriages.[34] Many considered divorce shameful, a mark of personal failure, and divorce petitions were often rejected in court. At that time, no state recognized incompatibility as grounds for divorce, and no-fault divorce did not exist.[35] In order to be granted a divorce in Betty's day, one member of the couple had to show proof of being wronged by the other. Betty's accusations, painful as they were, would not have been extraordinary for their time.

Out of nine possible grounds for divorce recognized by Washington in 1931, only three could have applied to the Hesketts: adultery discovered within one year of the divorce filing; cruel treatment or personal indignities rendering life burdensome; and habitual drunkenness or the husband's refusal to make suitable provision for his family. Betty did not allege adultery, but her description of the marriage was grim:

Defendant Robert E. Heskett has been guilty of cruel treatment of plaintiff and heaped upon plaintiff personal indignities rendering her life burdensome. Said defendant has struck and kicked plaintiff on a number of occasions and has threatened to shoot plaintiff and the children. At one time said defendant poured coal oil on the side of the house and set it afire and it was only by timely discovery by plaintiff and her younger sister that destruction of the house and injury to the family was prevented. Without justification or cause by plaintiff, said defendant has repeatedly called plaintiff vile names and has threatened to disfigure plaintiff so that no one else would ever care for her. Said defendant has become addicted to the use of intoxicating liquors and frequently during the said marriage has become drunken and abusive toward plaintiff and just before plaintiff's first child was born defendant struck and kicked her. And during all of the said married life said defendant has been brutal with, and abusive of, plaintiff.[36]

The estranged couple fought over the terms of Bob's financial obligations to his wife and children. Bob claimed that during the marriage, he had continued to receive renewal commissions on insurance policies he had previously sold and that he had used that money for their support. Besides, "She and our children are living with her parents in Seattle and are well provided for."[37]

"Affiant's father is dead and her mother a widow, without means of support," Betty's answering affidavit states. She and Mary, it continues, were the sole sources of support for her two infant children, her mother, her sisters ages sixteen and eleven, and themselves.

When the judge ordered Bob to pay child support, Bob demanded custody of Anne and Joan.[38] "Defendant further avers that he is a fit and proper person and is willing, able, and anxious to assure the obligations and duties incident to such care, custody and control." Betty, of course, denied this assertion.[39] From then on, Bob paid child support irregularly and eventually refused to pay it at all. The judge issued a bench warrant for his arrest. Taken before the court commissioner, Bob was held in contempt and ordered to pay Betty what he owed her or else be committed to the King County Stockade. Soon after, Bob's attorney withdrew counsel.

Betty was granted an interlocutory decree on April 30, 1932, entitling her to an absolute divorce to be finalized by either party in six months. She received custody of Anne and Joan, subject to reasonable visitation by Bob. Bob was to pay Betty child support, to pay her attorney's fees, and to pay court costs. When he failed to do so, he served a thirty-day jail sentence, which made the newspaper.[40] About this time, Bob's second attorney quit the case.

On March 8, 1935, the divorce became final.[41] Many years later, Joan (Heskett) MacDonald Keil was asked if she ever saw her father after her parents divorced. "I never saw him ever again," Joan replied.[42] Robert Heskett's father and stepmother lived about a dozen blocks from Sydney's house, but possibly Bob never asked to see his daughters, or else Betty prevented him from visiting.

Nearly a decade after the divorce, Betty was still trying to extract the money Bob owed her. Bob was long gone from King County by then, but Betty, believing that he had left personal property with his sister, filed an affidavit for garnishment. King County Superior Court granted Betty a judgment against Bob, but Betty collected nothing. The affidavit of the service of Bob's writ of garnishment is the final item in Betty and Bob's extensive divorce case file.[43]

Betty's 1931 foray to Chimacum with Bob to reclaim belongings was her final visit to that area. After *The Egg and I* was published, the lonely farm property remained a silent witness, a painting upon whose canvas the real Betty and Bob flickered beneath the book's coat of whitewash, a ghostly but insistent presence. Betty's neighbors also remembered her real story, and when Betty next encountered the Bishop family, she would be facing their accusations of libel in a court of law.

When she left Bob, Betty and her children joined Sydney, Mary, Dede, and Alison in a modest house in Seattle's Roosevelt District.[44] This would be their home for more than a decade. Four bedrooms held the seven of them and sometimes more. In the beginning, and periodically thereafter, Mary held the only job.

Under that roof Betty would struggle to provide for her daughters, and she would slowly work through the trauma of her life with Bob. She would tell stories about the chickens, the moonshine, and her neighbors. She would immerse herself in her family, becoming once again fully a Bard, shedding her married name as she sloughed off the most harrowing details of her marriage. Under her mother's roof, Betty again embraced her family's disregard for social propriety, their sharp-tongued humor, their slavish adherence to the niceties of food and table, and their unconventional but united front against the world. Artistic and eccentric friends and strangers flowed in and out, with Sydney a placid constant, Mary the ringmaster. In this stimulating, financially precarious, and unguarded habitat Anne and Joan grew up. And from this idiosyncratic refuge, Betty Bard faced the 1930s.

CHAPTER FOUR

Especially Betty

T HE house Sydney found on 15th Avenue Northeast in Seattle was modest but conveniently located: blocks from Roosevelt High School, in a neighborhood with the small amenities—butcher shop, grocery, cafes, shoe repair—that rural life had taught the Bards to appreciate. Betty's memories of life in the unassuming dwelling never faded. She wrote:

> From two o'clock Saturday afternoon until two o'clock Monday morning, the house was filled with people. Mary, who was very popular, was being intellectual so her friends were mostly musicians, composers, writers, painters. . . . [T]hey sat on the floor and read aloud the poems of Baudelaire, John Donne, and Rupert Brooke, they put loud symphonies on the record player and talked over them, they discussed politics and the state of the world. . . . I loved the tight expectant feeling I had as I opened the front door and wondered who would be there. I loved Saturday's dusk with the street lights as soft as breath in the fog or rain . . . the firm thudding comforting sound of front doors closing and shutting families in, the world out.[1]

The evening air carried that era's aromas: wood smoke, wet asphalt pavement, the resinous coal-oil odor of the Seattle Light Company's gasworks, and dinner cooking—the deeply enticing scent of crisping meat wafting on frosty air. A city streetcar line ran directly past the house, and with this convenience came the loss of quietude: streetcars regularly clanked and screeched along the rails.

Sydney's reason for choosing the house was purely practical: she could (just barely) afford it. The small house told of a family living in tight conditions, without a fallback. It offered a precarious respite, a thin cloth coat. The Bards were penniless, if still proud, and everyone knew it. Of course, the Bards were not the only Americans in 1930 who had slipped down the economic and social ladder. The crash of 1929 and the Great Depression lowered their neighbors' boats to meet theirs: bobbing unsteadily, taking on water, more patch than hull.

Sydney purchased the house from a Seattle matron, Vida Pixley, in Dede's and Alison's names, listing herself as guardian. This arrangement suggests that she financed the down payment using the girls' portion of the Calkins settlement. Holding on to this house required the same sort of shell game Sydney had played with the Laurelhurst and Chimacum properties. Vida Pixley was carrying the mortgage, a common purchase arrangement at the time, but Sydney took out a second, third, and finally a fourth mortgage on the property.

All this was serious but framed with humor in the retelling. Blanche Hamilton remembered hearing about a visit Betty and Mary made to a posh Seattle banker to try to obtain one of these mortgages. Asked for collateral, Mary was said to have told the banker, "All we have are our two white bodies to offer for that."[2]

Margaret Bundy Callahan recalled Vida Pixley's irritation whenever Mary's name was mentioned: "Mrs. Pixley had sold her house on 15th in the University District to the Bards and they'd never paid her any money because they were so poor, and Mrs. Pixley used to look at [artist Orre Noble] with a glare and snap, '*your* friend, Mary Bard!' "[3]

Once the Bards moved to the 15th Avenue house, Mary took charge of the family's finances. Relieved of personally paying for groceries and coal, Sydney kept house, cooked, gardened, tended children, painted occasional landscapes, and, as Betty later recounted, read a book a day. Over the next decade, Sydney's elder daughters would share the daunting duty of providing for the household. Grateful as they were that their mother could conjure meals from next to nothing and provide a kind of equable stability, Sydney's utter daffiness with things financial tested their patience.

Mary was certain that if her mother and siblings simply bent to her formidable will, financial stability would follow. Margaret Bundy Callahan reflected on Mary's vehement convictions: "Her decisiveness never failed her in a crisis. That decisiveness led her into all sorts of complications, but she never faltered. She enjoyed being decisive about other people's lives as well."[4]

As Betty would later describe, Mary took on the Great Depression as a personal challenge, refusing to allow the economy to best her—or any Bard. After holding several secretarial positions, Mary settled into a career selling advertising. She then became a font of employment leads for others, especially for Betty. But once Mary had found a job for her, Betty still had to keep it, a difficult task during years when workplaces closed abruptly and bosses skipped town without paying, or simply gave up.

In March 1931, Mary found Betty—who had dropped the Heskett, becoming once again Betty Bard—work as a secretary at the American Smelting and Engineering Company.[5] When this job ended after only three months, Betty took a secretarial position at Lumber Research, Inc., in Seattle's Alaska Building. The job ended a little more than a year later, when the office closed. She then embarked on a string of short-term jobs: raising rabbits, modeling furs, tinting photographs, selling direct-mail advertising. The sisters pooled their money, but it was, Betty wrote, "a losing game. Like climbing up a rock slide. We'd just get to the top and the front porch would sag, or the toilet would overflow or the downspouts would leak or Christmas would come and down we'd go to the bottom again."[6]

The Bards, their friends, and the city hunkered down. Money was tight, but some restaurants offered meals worth the pinched pennies. Margaret Bundy Callahan wrote the "Around the Town" column for the weekly *Town Crier*, including restaurant suggestions:

The Open Kitchen at the Public Market: A hole in the wall jernt [joint], and absolutely the cheapest in town. Dinners, believe it or not, for 15-cents—steak. Good cooking. . . . Mannings (All over town, but preferable in the Pike Place Market): Small cafeteria counter, good food and couldn't be cheaper. Sandwiches and salads for 5-cents upstairs in the Pike Place Market. If you get there a little off the noon hour early or late, you can get a table by the window and look out over the waterfront, with no extra charge for the swell view.[7]

The Bards were in solidarity with many fellow Seattleites who were trying to spark fun and comfort without much financial flint.

Regardless of their economic standing, the Bards retained qualities that attracted artistic, unusual, intellectual people. They were intelligent and well-read but never took themselves too seriously. They punctured signs of boastfulness in one another and in anyone else.

The Bards battled their poverty by ignoring it. They were cash-poor but rich in wit and in each other. And they were proud. "Mary still had the makings of a snob, as did all the Bard women," Margaret Bundy Callahan recalled.

> Not the usual type of snob at all, but a peculiar type all their own. Social position and wealth meant nothing to the Bards, except in the most naïve, make-believe sort of way. Theirs was a snobbery based on personal attraction, and they were merciless towards those they regarded as uninteresting. This I believe was a hang-over from when Mr. Bard was alive. Before he died their lives may have been governed very largely by conventional class distinction—they spoke at times with an amusing wistful note in their voices of parties at the D. Whitney Huntingtons. Of course, after Mr. Bard's death there wasn't any money to keep up such associations, so they turned with insouciance that was to mark their attitude towards every change in their fates, to what illusions they could afford.[8]

A family member recalled Sydney's cooking in the fireplace when the electricity had been cut off because of unpaid bills and noted that the Bards' joie de vivre was undimmed. The Bard sisters seemed to be channeling wisecracking heroines of screwball comedies: Jean Arthur, Barbara Stanwyck, Katharine Hepburn. They were witty, sarcastic, and droll, navigating briskly through difficulties, as if directed by Frank Capra or Preston Sturges. Blanche Hamilton said the Bard house had a *You Can't Take It with You* feel, and that Sydney was akin to Penny Sycamore, the mother in that 1934 play by George S. Kaufman and Moss Hart. "Sydney was usually sitting in the corner of the sofa with a book in one hand, a cigarette in the other, a coffee cup on the table, and a couple of dogs at her feet," Blanche recalled. "She made me feel as though she had been sitting there just waiting for me to come and visit."[9]

The family remained impervious to the despair that gripped so many Americans during the Dirty Thirties. On an essential level, in a way that could be perceived as beguilingly attractive during such desperate times, the Bard family didn't give a damn. Not everyone found this quality endearing. To some, the Bards' "so what?" attitude was just demented. When Blanche was trying to secure a date to escort her on an escapade of Mary's, involving a visiting German baron who planned to treat Mary and her friends to an evening of dinner and dancing, she invited a Green Lake neighbor. "He was reluctant to accept," Blanche remembered. "'The Bards are all screwy,' he said."[10]

During this period, the Bards were deeply in debt, as the public record bears out. Mary was sued by the Pacific Coast Coal Company for failing to pay for the coal that fueled the basement furnace. Later, an unpaid workman slapped a lien on the property. The family chipped away at bills, paying off a little here, a little there, like many other households during those grim years when simply not going under equaled success. They purchased everything they could on credit, shelling out payments to the most insistent creditors. Betty wrote of the stress induced by constant poverty, indebtedness, and relentless bill collectors: "A bill collector is a man with a loud voice who hates everybody. A collection agency is a collection of bill collectors with loud voices who hate everybody and always know where she works. . . . Each of my charge accounts had a collector, equipped apparently with second sight. They knew about my jobs before Mary found them for me and would often be milling around the door before I'd been properly hired."[11]

Using her daughters' earnings, Sydney alternately paid off and fended off debt collectors who arrived in person at her front door. Collections letters that came in the mail were easily ignored, but not so a collector on the doorstep, which is why in-person bill collection became a common tactic in the 1930s. It made the experience of indebtedness and of being dunned for payment extremely personal. The arrival of collections agents at Betty's workplaces compromised her efforts to appear professional. And it was humiliating.

Sydney, as ever, seems to have reacted to penury with sanguine acceptance. If she could not afford to serve lamb, she served oxtail, meatloaf, or vegetable soup. If the electricity was shut off, her family ate by candlelight. This quality of utterly accepting circumstance was framed as heroism in Betty's books. Perhaps it was, but for her daughters, it was also maddening. Sydney's impulse toward unquestioning acquiescence had served her well during her marriage but served less well without Darsie's well-reasoned leadership.

"When I was young if I'd wanted sixty dollars for stockings, and there was only sixty dollars in the house, Mother would have given it to me," Betty once told an interviewer.[12] Her mother was "a truly charming and most talented woman, [who] has no more financial sense than a hummingbird, arguing with her about money is like trying to catch minnows in your fingers."[13] Sydney was not a religious woman—by and large, nor were the other Bards. And yet, Betty wrote, she "emanates an aura of peace that is actually visible. Mother says this is merely long practice in the face of disaster. I think it is an inner serenity that follows in the wake of selflessness."[14] This mesmeric calm smothered whatever assertive qualities Sydney might once have possessed. Although the demands of caring for a family placed her in a de facto leadership role, Sydney was a follower.

Betty's children, Anne and Joan, were left mainly in their grandmother's care during these years. When the girls reached school age, Sydney enrolled them in Ravenna Elementary, a 1911 brick and concrete structure eight blocks east of the 15th Avenue house. Betty later acknowledged that she'd left the raising of Anne and Joan to her mother after her marriage to Bob ended. She plunged into the social life from which the Bards' move to Chimacum, her disastrous marriage, and her successive pregnancies had plucked her. Betty accompanied Mary, or was dispatched by her, to plays and parties and bad dates, leaving Sydney to tend to things domestic.

While their mother worked to put bread on the table, leaving them in their grandmother's care, Anne and Joan—living in a house whose occupants evidently changed frequently, and with perhaps more freedom to roam than was best for them—sometimes got lost in the shuffle. In a house full to the gills with adult family members and colorful, eccentric friends, perhaps Betty and Sydney trusted that the girls would just join the parade. In many ways, Anne and Joan may have raised themselves, making their own decisions and crafting their own safety nets. Unlike Sydney's own brood at those Montana campsites, Anne and Joan Heskett seem to have made their way through childhood without the precaution of a picket and a piece of string.

In this haphazard childhood, however, their mother's storytelling was a constant. In childhood, Betty had told her siblings stories to amuse them. Betty continued these stories for her own children, inventing a new character she called Mrs. Piggle-Wiggle. She also began telling her friends stories about life in Chimacum, with the dual result of entertaining listeners and turning those strange, hard years into a narrative she controlled. For their own enjoyment, Mary and Betty spun out the ongoing saga of a sorority girl who bucks propriety but still finds romance and the ultimate grail, a marriage proposal. They thought "Sandra Surrenders" was at least as good as the serial stories the radio drooled out, and they submitted it, unsuccessfully, for publication.

Determined to help Betty slam the door on her experiences in Chimacum, Mary launched her sister into projects that would shore up her battered self-esteem. Securing employment for Betty was the first priority, but Mary then applied herself to encouraging her sister's literary pursuits. In January 1933, the *Town Crier*—where Mary and Betty's friend Margaret Bundy Callahan was associate editor—published Betty's short story "Their Families," Betty's first appearance in print.[15] Although billed as fiction, "Their Families" strongly resembled the household Betty later described in her nonfiction book

Anybody Can Do Anything. A Mary-inspired character took the lead: Judith Ten Eyck, the clever, red-haired eldest of a poor but witty and artistic family.

At Mary's urging, Sydney too tried writing, plotting out scripts for a fifteen-minute daily radio serial, *Schuyler Square.* Busy running the household, Sydney squeezed this work into her day as best she could: "About ten or eleven or one or two o'clock, Mother would slide into the breakfast nook to drink coffee, to smoke millions of cigarettes, to cough and to write, in her absolutely unreadable handwriting, her twenty pages on both sides of radio continuity," Betty recalled.[16] For nearly a year, the program was broadcast live from the KOL radio station in Rhodes Department Store in downtown Seattle, featuring Rhodes employees as performers. It was a novelty for shoppers, who watched the broadcasts through a wall of glass.

Mary's ability to create scenarios and animate her family's participation in them was an asset. She encouraged Betty when life was grim. Mary's ferocity drove her through the family's loss of fortune and through the need to turn her back on college and find work. Even at the depth of the Depression, Mary was never without a job. She was engaged, so Betty tells us, several times, but when she married, it was to a man whose qualities were steadfast.

On June 27, 1934, with Betty as matron of honor and Anne and Joan as flower girls, Mary wed Dr. Clyde Reynolds Jensen in Thomsen Memorial Chapel at St. Mark's Episcopal Cathedral. Bridal showers and dinners honoring the couple preceded the wedding, with old family friends from the St. Nicholas days, Mary's business associates, and a new circle of the groom's medical colleagues rallying round. It was the closest to high society that the Bards had come in many years. Mary chose a dramatic wedding dress: sand beige with a cape trimmed in Russian wolf.[17]

Born in Waco, Texas, and raised in Douglas, Nebraska, in modest circumstances, Clyde Jensen—"Jens"—graduated from Dartmouth College, then from Rush Medical College. He came to Seattle in April 1930 to join the staff at Harborview Hospital when that facility opened in February 1931. Trained in internal medicine, Jensen was also board certified in pathology and directed Harborview's medical laboratories. He was steady, brave, and deeply dedicated to service, as the thousands of patients he went on to help during more than a half-century of medical practice, and his admiring medical colleagues, would eventually attest.

The social leap for Mary was significant. Once married, her foremost task was learning how to be a doctor's wife, as dictated by the requirements of that era. This role led, in time, to her serving on the Seattle Symphony and Repertory Theatre boards and as a Girl Scout leader. Her marriage shifted the balance between the sisters, and Mary turned from managing her natal family to building a family of her own. Fortunately, Betty respected Jens and was fond of him. If she was losing Mary's close company, at least it was to someone she approved of.

Betty's own life was not without romance. Some of her suitors during those years remained dear friends. One was Goddard Lieberson, a young composer who was part of the Bards' artistic circle. Betty met him in the early 1930s, when he was studying at the University of Washington. Lieberson later moved to New York and worked for Columbia Records, eventually becoming president of the company.[18] Another male friend was George "Mike" Gordon, whom Betty met at a luncheon in 1934. He was considerably shorter than Betty, and sixty-four to her twenty-seven. "It never occurred to me he would consider himself my suitor," she wrote, "and that he would endeavor during the next eight years to outsuit anyone else."[19]

Mike Gordon was generous to Betty's family. He owned a lumber mill in Peshastin, a small town near Wenatchee in one of Washington's prime apple- and pear-growing regions. He sent cases of fruit, vegetables, canned goods, and clothing to the Bard household during the family's leanest years. Blanche Hamilton—showing the moxie born of long friendship—once asked Betty if she felt obligated to Mike for all he did for her family, and if Mike expected anything in return. " 'All I have to do is reach down and pat him on the cheek and make him laugh a lot,' " Betty replied.[20]

After Mary's marriage, her earnings no longer supported the family, but nineteen-year-old Dede's income, combined with Betty's, kept the Bard household more or less afloat. Cleve, who worked as a car salesman, had married in 1933; it is not clear whether he was ever part of the 15th Avenue household. In August 1933, Betty began working for the National Recovery Administration (NRA), established by Congress to help revive labor and industry and stimulate America's crippled economy. Betty worked in Seattle's Exchange Building as an NRA labor adjustor—one of a very few women in the position—until the program shut down at the end of 1935. In January 1936, the U.S. Treasury Department hired her as a junior clerk in their procurement department. The office bought supplies and let contracts for the Works Progress/Projects Administration (WPA).

Betty's five years working at these government jobs brought a measure of financial stability, along with experiences of absurd regulatory bureaucracy that made good stories. By 1938, life at the Bards' was fairly stable: Alison was at Roosevelt High School, Anne and Joan in grade school. Dede was a secretary for the WPA. Mary and Jens were living in the Madrona neighborhood and had two daughters, Mari and Salli. But this stability was shattered when Betty was diagnosed with pulmonary tuberculosis at the age of thirty-one. On September 23, 1938, she entered Firland Sanatorium, Seattle's municipal tuberculosis hospital, twelve miles north of what was then the city line.[21] Anne and Joan remained with Sydney.

Tuberculosis is a highly contagious disease caused by the bacterium *Mycobacterium tuberculosis*, which can be inhaled or contracted through contaminated food or drink. The most common form is pulmonary tuberculosis (an infection of the lungs), but the bacteria can also infect the kidneys, bones, intestines, and lymph nodes. Miliary tuberculosis, known colloquially as galloping consumption, occurs when the infection is spread throughout the body in the bloodstream. Tuberculous meningitis, the most deadly form of the disease, is an infection of the tissue around the brain and spinal cord. When Betty was admitted to Firland, tuberculosis ranked sixth among causes of death in Seattle. People called it the white plague.

In the absence of any effective medication before the development of antibiotics, treatment focused on providing rest, wholesome food, and fresh air in dedicated sanatoria, where patients were isolated to prevent the spread of the disease. The sanatoria movement began in Germany in 1849. The first American facility, Dr. Edward L. Trudeau's Adirondack Cottage Sanatorium, opened in Saranac Lake, New York, in 1885.

Betty's X-rays revealed a tubercular cavity in her left lung and a shadow in her right lung. She traced her infection to one of her fellow Treasury Department employees: "For two years I had been very concerned about a co-worker of mine in the Government service, who looked like a cadaver and coughed constantly, with a dry little hacking cough, most of the time in my face. 'I think that man has tuberculosis,' I finally told my boss excitedly. 'Who don't?' was his laconic reply. When I entered the sanatorium and filed a compensation claim against the Government, naming the cadaverous co-worker as a possible source of infection, he was sent to a t.b. clinic and found to have had active, communicable tuberculosis for nineteen years."[22]

For Betty, hospitalization halted everything. "Getting tuberculosis in the middle of your life is like starting downtown to do a lot of urgent errands and being hit by a bus. When you regain consciousness you remember nothing about the urgent errands. You can't even remember where you were going," Betty later wrote.[23]

Having used up all of her accrued sick leave and annual leave, she wrote to her supervisor from her hospital bed, resigning her position. It seems likely that Mary and Jens helped Sydney and Dede cover the loss of Betty's income. Mary told Betty not to worry about money, but Betty could not help being overwhelmed when considering how to support her children, or, worse (as she would later write), imagining Anne and Joan laying flowers on her grave.

Admission to Firland was, in one sense, a lucky break for Betty. Hers was one of nearly two thousand diagnosed tuberculosis cases in Seattle in 1938.[24] Firland, where the cost of care was covered by Washington State and Seattle departments of health, had only a fraction of the number of beds required to hospitalize these individuals. The sanatorium's admissions policy favored patients whose disease had been diagnosed early: those whose disease was diagnosed at an advanced stage instead entered King County Hospital, which provided considerably less specialized care. For those with means, there were private sanatoria and nursing homes. Many tuberculosis patients remained at home under the care of family and visiting health department nurses, although this treatment was less effective and exposed family members to the risk of infection.

The stated goal of Firland's medical director, Robert Stith, was to ration available funds and limited beds by admitting those who were, in his words, "worth saving."[25] By this he meant the patients with the best chance of recovery, who might again contribute to society. Women with dependent children, like Betty, often jumped Firland's lengthy waiting list. Being Clyde Jensen's sister-in-law also helped.

At the time, the only treatment for pulmonary tuberculosis involved walling off the diseased portion of the lung from healthy tissue with fibrosis (scar tissue). Lungs were to be kept as close to immobile as possible to allow the delicate fibroid tissue to form. Patients had to endure inactivity, resting in a fully reclined position. Reading, writing, and talking were forbidden. Coughing, except to produce a morning sputum sample, was to be suppressed. Because patients in stuffy rooms were more likely to cough, spreading their germs and possibly rupturing their own fibroid tissues, fresh air was considered essential. Screened windows were kept wide open year-round. Nourishing food was plentiful, and patients were expected to eat well to build their strength.

Among American sanatoria, Firland's policies were quite rigid. All sanatoria prescribed bed rest, but patients' descriptions of the grim determination with which Firland's nurses enforced the rules make it sound almost like living in a penal colony. Anyone unwilling to fall in line was exhorted to leave and free up a bed for someone compliant. Visiting hours were twice weekly. For their own protection, children were permitted to see hospitalized parents for only fifteen minutes once a month. They had to stay at the door of the room and were not permitted to touch their parents.[26]

Some patients underwent surgical procedures to further immobilize the lungs. These involved injecting air into the space surrounding each lung (artificial pneumothorax) or removing ribs so that the chest wall sank in against the underlying lung (thoracoplasty). Because tuberculosis patients could not be subjected to general anesthesia, this thoracic surgery was performed under local anesthesia using Novocain or sodium pentothal.

Betty underwent artificial pneumothorax:

> I felt the prick of the hypodermic needle, just under my left breast, then an odd sensation as though he were trying to push me off the table, then a crunchy feeling and a stab of pain. "There now," the Medical Director said, as he attached the end of what looked like a steel knitting needle to a small rubber hose connected to two gallon fruit jars partially filled with a clear amber fluid. The nurse put one jar higher than the other and I waited frantically for my breathing to stop and suffocation to start. There was no sensation of any kind for a few minutes then I had a pulling, tight feeling up around my neck and shoulder. The doctor said, "I guess that's enough for today."[27]

The treatment was repeated periodically for months or (as in Betty's case) years.

At Firland, as at other sanatoria, patients from vastly varied walks of life were thrust together to live beneath the shadow of death. Some responded with courage, some with terror, some with humor, some by giving up. Their lives revolved around their symptoms and their treatment. Several of the women Betty met at Firland became close friends. Kazuko Itoi, nicknamed Kazi (later Monica Sone), had grown up in the hotel that her Japanese immigrant parents operated on the edge of the historic Japantown/Nihonmachi, in what is now Seattle's Pioneer Square. Kazi entered Firland at age eighteen, about a month before Betty arrived, and her droll humor was well matched with Betty's. They were discharged on the same day. Gwen Smith (later Croxford) was in the midst of a two-and-a-half year stay at Firland when she and Betty met. She was discharged around the same time Betty and Kazi left, but relapse forced her to return. Norah Olwell (later Flannery) was a young University of Washington graduate who captivated and comforted Betty with her kindness and bright intelligence. Betty's letters to these women, written after her discharge, are as intimate in tone as those she wrote to family members.

Betty was on complete bed rest for seven months. In her eighth month, she was allowed out of bed for eight hours each day. She was discharged in June 1939, nearly nine months after her admission. This was a remarkably short course of treatment: when she was admitted, the average stay for a Firland patient before being discharged alive was one year, eight months, and eighteen days.[28] Many Firland patients remained at the hospital for years or even decades, or were discharged only to experience relapse and readmission. Many died.

Patients who recovered from tuberculosis lived under the constant threat of relapse. Betty was encouraged to continue resting after being discharged and to have frequent checkups. She underwent outpatient intrapleural pneumolysis (the cauterization of adhesions between the chest wall and lung that, uncauterized, prevent a satisfactory collapse of the lung) and pneumothorax procedures for six years after her discharge, until the spring of 1945.

Betty's battle with tuberculosis did not crush her spirit, but it changed her. She emerged chastened that she had ever taken health for granted, grateful that fate and physicians had granted her a second chance. During the first weeks after her release, trying to regain her footing in the busy Bard household, Betty rose early and worked on transforming the simple journal she had kept during her hospitalization into a more complex description of her experiences. Unsure of how to make the jump from journal entries to full narrative, she kept the diary-style format, struggling to capture the vivid, varied personalities of her fellow patients and of the nurses—some gentle, some authoritarian—who had ruled her life for nine months. She submitted the manuscript to be considered for the Atlantic Prize, bestowed by Atlantic Monthly Press, but received a polite brush-off.[29]

Betty found work with the National Youth Administration (NYA), the Works Progress Administration (later Works Projects Administration) program charged with training and providing jobs for young people between the ages of sixteen and twenty-five. Hired as a secretary, Betty eventually rose to the position of the Seattle project's art supervisor and head of publicity, with ninety-five young artists and writers working for her. The work gave her plenty of opportunity to hone her writing skills. She wrote copy for brochures, drafted press releases, taught workers to produce newsletters for organizations such as the YWCA and the Boy Scouts, and critiqued manuscripts for young people enrolled in NYA writing programs. She also supervised young artists who created signs, murals, posters, book covers, and other artwork.

While she was working at the NYA, probably around late 1941, Betty met Donald Chauncy MacDonald. Bard family lore credits Cleve — whose fingers were apparently in every pie — with introducing Betty to Don, as he had introduced her to Robert Heskett.[30] When they met, Don was working for Boeing as part of the team that performed final quality checks before the company delivered airplanes to the military.

Born in Council Bluffs, Iowa, in 1910, Don spent his childhood in Omaha, Nebraska. He moved to Seattle at the age of sixteen with his parents, Beulah and Clinton.[31] Clinton MacDonald managed an apartment house near the University of Washington, and Don lived with his parents throughout most of the 1930s. From 1937 to 1939, Don was enrolled in Edison Technical School, a vocational program run by the Seattle Public Schools, studying dry cleaning. Don worked for the American District Telegraph Company as a signal timer and later for the American Alarm Company as a watchman.

Photographs of Don reveal a trim, attractive, impeccably groomed man. The camera rarely catches him smiling. He was, Betty drolly told friends and eventually wrote, a dour Scotsman. His hair was dark, like Darsie's and like Bob Heskett's. That Betty was divorced did not trouble Don; nor did the fact that she had daughters, who were by then twelve and fourteen.

Betty and Don were married by a justice of the peace on April 24, 1942, when she was thirty-five and he was thirty-one. Alison Bard and her fiancé, Frank Sugia, were witnesses. Betty and Don traveled thirty miles north of Seattle (in King County) to marry in Everett (in Snohomish County), perhaps to avoid having to apply for a marriage license where many people knew about Betty's treatment for tuberculosis: at the time, Washington law prohibited women under the age of forty-five who had advanced pulmonary tuberculosis from marrying.[32] Betty's disease was never advanced, but she opted for caution.

Betty and Don's courtship was apparently brief. Anne later remarked that she had never met or even heard of Don before the day she came into the kitchen and found Betty sitting with him in the breakfast nook, a celebratory orchid pinned to her lapel. "Meet your new Daddy," Anne remembered her mother saying by way of introduction.[33]

For a time—months or longer—the newlyweds lived alone in a little duplex on a steep hillside near the University of Washington, leaving Anne and Joan with Sydney.[34] With one marriage and at least a few other serious relationships behind her, Betty seems to have found in Don a man with whom she could be passionate. Dour though her husband may have been, Betty was happily and fully mated.

In fall 1942, Betty and Don purchased a home on Vashon Island. The modest cottage hugged the bluff overlooking Dolphin Point, near the ferry dock. They purchased the house and its custom-built pine furniture with no down payment. The house was clad in hand-split cedar shakes and used salvaged ship-decking materials—softer than velvet to the touch—for the wide plank flooring. When the MacDonalds bought the place, there was no road to the property, only a path along the beach and a primitive trail through the woods. Their new home had a view of Mount Rainier, one of Washington's towering volcanic peaks.

Anne and Joan were withdrawn from the Seattle public school system and certified for transfer to Vashon. The 15th Avenue house was rented out. Sydney moved in with Mary to help with Mari, Salli, and Heidi.[35] Jens was serving as a physician in the navy, leaving Mary to manage his pathology laboratory and run an officers' canteen with other naval wives.[36]

For the Bards, life in the 15th Avenue house was over. For all of them, and especially for Betty, a new chapter was about to begin.

PLATE 1. Cleve (far left), Betsy (center), and Mary Bard (far right) and friends, Placerville, Idaho, ca. 1910. Private collection.

PLATE 2. Betty Bard MacDonald's birthplace, 723 Spruce Street (formerly 725), Boulder, Colorado. Courtesy Boulder Public Library Carnegie Branch for Local History.

PLATE 3. Cleve (left) and Darsie Bard, ca. 1912.
Private collection.

PLATE 4. Montana School of Mines (top left), Big Butte (marked with letter M), and the Bards' Westside neighborhood, Butte, Montana. Courtesy Owen Smithers Collection (PH358), Butte–Silver Bow Public Archives.

Handwritten on photograph: F.1451 THE PALISADES. B-4, L-3. 5120-E-42 ST.

PLATE 5. Laurelhurst house, 5120 Northeast 42nd Street (formerly East), Seattle, where the Bards lived from 1918 to 1925, ca. 1937. Courtesy Puget Sound Regional Branch, Washington State Archives.

PLATE 6. St. Nicholas School students, Seattle, 1919. Betsy Bard, third row, farthest left; Mary Bard, top standing row, third from right. Courtesy Jane Carlson Williams '60 Archives, Lakeside School.

PLATE 7. Blanche Hamilton, ca. 1920. Blanche's friendship with Betsy was immediate, and her affection for the Bards was lifelong. Courtesy Katy von Brandenfels.

PLATE 8. Margaret Bundy Callahan, ca. 1924. With Margaret's friendship came her keen insight into character, and a journalist's eye. Courtesy Mikell Callahan.

PLATE 9. Betsy Bard (third from right) and friends in the Laurelhurst years immediately following her father's death, ca. 1923. Private collection.

PLATE 10. Betty Bard (left) and Margaret Bundy Callahan, Mount Rainier, ca. 1925. Courtesy Mikell Callahan.

PLATE 11. Betty and Bob Heskett's Chimacum house, 2021 Egg and I Road, Chimacum, no date. Their marriage was brief, but Betty's version of the tale resonated worldwide. Courtesy Jefferson County Historical Society, Photo No. 28.82.

PLATE 12. *Anybody* house, 6317 15th Avenue Northeast, Seattle, where the
Bard family battled the Great Depression with wit, grit, and one another, 1937.
Courtesy Puget Sound Regional Branch, Washington State Archives.

PLATE 13. Betty's younger sister, Dede Bard, ca. 1940. Private collection.

PLATE 14. Betty's daughters Anne and Joan Heskett, on the back steps of the *Anybody* house around the time their mother was hospitalized for tuberculosis, ca. 1938. Private collection.

PLATE 15. Firland Sanitorium, Richmond Highlands, Washington, where Betty Bard overcame tuberculosis. Courtesy Seattle Municipal Archives, Item No. 2655.

PLATE 16. Vashon Island house, 11814 Dolphin Point Trail, Vashon, 1938. Betty and her second husband, Donald MacDonald, moved here in 1942, with Betty's daughters, Anne and Joan. Courtesy Puget Sound Regional Branch, Washington State Archives.

CHAPTER FIVE

Egged On

THE little MacDonald house on Vashon clung to the bluff as if held there by incantation. Below the house was a beach, strewn by the sea with massive logs, littered with wet bark and bull kelp. Salt water and creosote-coated wood perfumed the beach, and in the house, the crackling woodstove and the ever-ready coffee pot scented the small kitchen, engendering a sense of calm, of home.

In 1944, with the whole world at war, a red-haired, thirty-seven-year-old woman sat in the house at the kitchen table, her fingers clacking across typewriter keys. The story she was writing would make her and her family and the house and all their houses famous. The words she wrote told a version of her life story, but they did more: when published one year later, they gave a world saturated with loss and destruction and death something to laugh about. They gave a world that had been holding its breath permission to exhale.

Vashon Island lies in Puget Sound, seventeen miles southwest of Seattle's waterfront. Over time, attempts to link the island to the mainland by bridge have failed: islanders do not want the casual contact such easy access would afford.[1] In Betty's day, Vashon's economy was agricultural, with a climate ideal for berry farms and commercial flower production. Vashon is where Betty MacDonald wrote *The Egg and I*, the book that catapulted her onto the public stage.

"Certainly when I was crouched in my kitchen on Vashon Island writing *The Egg* I didn't dream that I was oozing out a best seller," Betty reflected in an article for the *Washington Alumnus*. "The most I hoped for was to get the damn thing finished and published so that

I wouldn't have to move off the Island because I had told so many people on the ferry that I was writing a book and that every publisher in New York was fighting to get it."[2]

In interviews and at book signings, Betty was endlessly asked how *Egg* was hatched. The minutiae of the book's creation—the war in Europe and Japan still raging, rain lashing the windows of the little house, Don rising early to muddle down the muddy path from home to ferry dock bound for work, Anne and Joan coaxed out the door to school, another cup of coffee poured, another cigarette lit and gratefully inhaled, and finally, settling at the typewriter—eventually faded, smoothed into something honed and easily recounted. Betty unfailingly gave credit to Mary for needling, encouraging, and prodding the book into existence. "Are you going to spend all your life washing your sheets by hand, or are you going to make fifty thousand dollars a year writing?" Mary supposedly asked.[3] She had a friend, Henri Verstappen, who was the West Coast editor for Doubleday, Doran and Company, and was in Seattle looking for new authors. Mary told him that Betty was working on a book about the Pacific Northwest: she was refining stories she'd told about her years in Chimacum into a manuscript, using the working title *The Egg and I*. Betty had started this project before she met Don MacDonald, as an attempt to distract herself from the emotional aftermath of what she later described as a failed love affair.[4] When Betty's romance with Don blossomed, she set the writing project aside.

If Betty's attention had wandered from the book project, her sister's had not. Dispatched by Mary, Betty met with Verstappen, who gave her a day to pull an outline of the book together. Betty, in a panic, called in sick to work to do so. Verstappen liked it. He told her to send it to Doubleday, Doran, and to proceed with *The Egg and I*. Betty was fired for falsely calling in sick, and started working on the book in earnest.[5]

Betty sent Doubleday, Doran the outline, and then the opening chapters of *The Egg and I*, written in diary form. She also included one of the Mrs. Piggle-Wiggle stories she had told to Anne and Joan, a tale she called "Patsy, Who Would Not Take a Bath." Verstappen was encouraging, but since he was constantly on the road, months went by without Betty's hearing from him. Finances forced her to take a job, and work on *The Egg and I* lagged.

In late 1943, Verstappen left Doubleday, Doran and sent the *Egg* chapters and "Patsy" back. Betty stopped working on the book, but, as she later told the radio personality George Fisher, Mary "high-pressured me to go ahead and finish it." Asked if she'd written anything before *Egg*, Betty replied that she'd sent a couple of short stories to the New York literary agency Brandt & Brandt. "They were interested, but they sent back the stories asking me to make about 100 percent revision! So I put them away in a drawer too—but then when I finished *The Egg and I*, I remembered Brandt & Brandt and sent the manuscript to them. And after that everything happened so fast I'm still a little hazy on the details."[6]

Betty sent Brandt & Brandt her detailed outline of *The Egg and I* in February 1944, telling them that the manuscript was nearly finished, that she also had a draft of a book about her time at Firland, and that she'd completed eight Mrs. Piggle-Wiggle stories.[7] She later joked, "In my eagerness to prove that I wasn't a stinking old one book author I made it sound a little as though we had to wade through old manuscripts to go from room to room in our log house, and that I was a veritable artesian well of the written word."[8]

A Brandt & Brandt literary agent, Bernice Baumgarten, asked to see *The Egg and I* manuscript, which Betty quickly mailed to her. Baumgarten read and liked it and told Betty that she felt it "almost, but not quite, lives up to the promise of the outline."[9] She asked Betty to rework the material in narrative form rather than the diary format she'd used. She also told Betty that at fifty thousand words, the manuscript was too short: publishers wanted no fewer than eighty-five thousand words. Baumgarten suggested that Betty augment the manuscript with some biographical information to introduce readers to the narrator and her family. The details Betty added about her childhood in Butte and in Seattle, her grandmother Gammy's outspoken eccentricities, her boisterous siblings, and her adventurous parents accentuated her loneliness when—in the book's version of her life—her marriage separated her from her family. Betty's funny family stories gave her readers a sense of intimacy with her and made those readers feel as though she welcomed them as family friends.

Betty's original manuscript had one other problem: Baumgarten felt that it ended too bitterly. "I am truly sorry about the bitterness and the fact that you believed I almost hated my husband at one point," Betty replied. "Actually he was the most concentrate bastard that ever lived but I thought—I hoped it was not apparent. He was very handsome, very very attractive but I was definitely not the one to bring out the best in him. I tried, when writing about him, to keep my present husband, who is six feet two and very handsome and a lamb, before me but apparently I slipped. That I will fix because I am not writing a True Confession although I could and it would be a dilly."[10]

Betty's final draft was leached of bitterness, her portrait of Bob smudged until he was only demanding, not cruel. The character became a kind of two-dimensional golem, a composite of Bob and Don. Betty's contemporary readers did not balk at what now seems glaringly obvious about the book: there is no love or intimacy between the Betty and Bob characters.

At the end of *Egg*, Bob and Betty leave their rural ranch together, bound for a modern ranch nearer to Seattle with the benefits of electricity, linoleum floors, and indoor toilets. By slanting the truth of her first marriage, Betty reinvented herself as less vulnerable, less bruised, and more in control of her own narrative. It was this new Betty who beguiled readers, a Betty who was closer to the woman Betty Heskett had become by the time Betty MacDonald wrote *The Egg and I*.

Brandt & Brandt was New York's premier literary agency during the mid-twentieth century. Literary agent Bernice Baumgarten had begun working there in 1923, first as a secretary and from 1926 as head of the book department. Baumgarten's clients included many of the best known and most respected writers of the era, such as Raymond Chandler, e.e. cummings, John Dos Passos, Shirley Jackson, Thomas Mann, Ford Madox Ford, Mary McCarthy, Edna St. Vincent Millay, and Clifford Odets.

Bernice Baumgarten and Betty MacDonald were close in age and seemingly allied in temperament. Both had married in 1927: Baumgarten's husband was the writer James Gould Cozzens, one of her first clients at Brandt & Brandt. The Baumgarten-Cozzens's lives in Jazz Age Manhattan differed in every way from the Hesketts' Chimacum experiences, and Baumgarten's earnings as a successful literary agent, combined with Cozzens's royalties, ensured more comfort than chicken farming (or perhaps moonshine) ever could. In 1929, when Betty was struggling with chickens, the rain, and infant Anne, Baumgarten and Cozzens sailed to Europe, where they spent the spring touring the continent. In 1933, when Betty failed to earn commissions selling direct mail advertising, Baumgarten and Cozzens purchased and restored an 1818 stone farmhouse in Lambertsville, New Jersey, from which Baumgarten commuted by train to New York each day. She guarded her private life completely, creating with Cozzens an almost monastic existence in order to facilitate his work.[11] Bernice Baumgarten was formidable, but she found Betty MacDonald disarming. Their relationship warmed from strictly professional to cordial almost immediately.

In October 1944, while Betty was rewriting the manuscript, Baumgarten sold *The Egg and I* to the publisher J. B. Lippincott on the basis of Betty's detailed outline. Founded during George Washington's administration, Lippincott was a gentlemanly family business with headquarters in Philadelphia and an office in New York. Betty mailed her revised manuscript to Baumgarten in February 1945. Both literary agent and publisher were delighted with Betty's book, and Lippincott placed *The Egg and I* on their fall 1945 list.

Before the book appeared, however, the story was published in serial form in the *Atlantic Monthly*. Launching new books via serializations in periodicals was popular during the 1940s: prepublication serialization rights were lucrative, and feeding the work to magazine readers in installments built interest and provided word-of-mouth promotion. Betty's book appeared in the June, July, and August 1945 issues, meaning that the last issue was on the newsstand when the United States bombed Hiroshima and Nagasaki, bringing about Japan's surrender and the end of the war in the Pacific.[12]

At the last minute, Lippincott balked at the book's title. Their suggestion: *Fine Feathered Friends*. Betty was appalled. "I would like to call the book *The Yolk's on Me*," she shot back to Bernice Baumgarten, "but don't tell Lippincott, they'd probably use it."[13] Lippincott opted to keep the original title after seeing the *Atlantic Monthly*'s press release announcing the serialization as *The Egg and I*.

The dedication of *The Egg and I* reads: "To my sister Mary who has always believed that I can do anything she puts her mind to." Although the book's official publication date was October 3, Lippincott printed the first copies in July 1945. The book was produced under the War Production Board's austere standards, using lighter-weight paper to reduce bulk and smaller margins to yield more words per page. These measures saved paper, printing-plate metal, and labor. Because chlorine was rationed, the paper had a brown tinge. These standards began to be relaxed during *Egg*'s first months in print, and successive early printings show a marked improvement in paper quality.[14]

From the very beginning, reader response and bookseller enthusiasm were the firepower behind *Egg*. Buyers ordering for bookstores and department stores liked Lippincott's advance advertising to the trade and placed healthy orders. When advance copies arrived and they actually read the book, they increased their existing orders several fold before the book even went on sale. Lippincott increased their advertising in direct response to these buyers' increased orders.

The book's explosive popularity necessitated many reprintings. Because Lippincott had trouble securing materials such as paper and cloth for binding the book, print runs were insufficient to meet the demand. Lippincott was forced to let other titles on their fall 1945 list languish, wallflowers at the party.

Timing was crucial to *Egg*'s success. General nonfiction and technical books outsold fiction during the war years, when readers' attention was focused on themes of battle. In the years before *Egg*'s publication, the nonfiction best-seller list included Richard Tregaskis's *Guadalcanal Diary*, Gordon Seagrave's *Burma Surgeon*, and Ernie Pyle's *Here Is Your War* and *Brave Men*, among other titles. Some—

like Marion Hargrove's *See Here, Private Hargrove*, the *Publisher's Weekly* best seller for 1942—were humorous, but most ranged from serious to grim.

The Egg and I took the same themes of battle (with baby chicks), conflict (with uncouth rural neighbors), and endurance (Betty's lot as a young farm wife in a physically challenging locale) and made them domestic. In Betty's book, these wartime themes were spun into a tartly funny tale in which the true life-and-death stakes were low. *Egg's* bucolic setting reminded victorious Americans of what they'd fought for. *The Egg and I* hit the war-numbed public as a comforting tale of survival: one woman's successful effort to just keep getting up each morning in spite of challenges and discomfort.

When interviewers asked what inspired her to write *Egg*, Betty credited it to her own frustration with the genre exemplified by Louise Dickinson Rich's popular memoir *We Took to the Woods*, published by Lippincott in 1942, in which an enthusiastic wife follows an idealistic husband back to the land and loves it. Rich's rhapsodic account of life with her husband in rural Maine may well have set Betty's book in motion. "No, poor Riches, we don't have plays and music and contact with sophisticated minds, and a round of social engagements," Dickinson Rich warbled. "All we have are sun and wind and rain, and space in which to move and breathe. All we have are the forests, and the calm expanses of lakes, and time to call our own. All we have are the hunting and fishing and the swimming, and each other."[15] In her first query to Brandt & Brandt, Betty had noted that she called her manuscript *The Egg and I*, but it should probably be called *We Don't Take to the Woods*. "It still irritates me when women say they prefer to live without running water or electric lights. I know it's a damn lie," Betty said.[16]

In spite of this professed disregard for the rural life, Betty's lyrical descriptions of the Olympic Peninsula moved her readers. She wrote of mountains "so imminent they gave me a feeling of someone reading over my shoulder"; "giant virgin forests, black and remote against the sky"; the woods, "deep and cool and fragrant and treacherous with underbrush, sudden swamps and roots." In spring, the sun appeared "a bold-faced, full-blooded little wench, obviously no kin to the sallow creature who simpered in and out occasionally during the winter." It was country "describable only by superlatives. Most rugged, most westerly, greatest, deepest, largest, wildest, gamiest, richest, most fertile, loneliest, most desolate."[17]

The Egg and I revealed Betty's fundamental irreverence, a Bard family quality. For the Bards, it was fine to be mean as long as you were also funny. Exaggeration was encouraged and expected. Telling a good story outranked following the Golden Rule. They had an arsenal of family slang used to convey sharp jabs: a Black Future Charlie always foresaw gloom and doom, a Hootey-Poo was snooty, a Body Thinko was oversexed.

The Seattle painter William Cumming, who was Betty's assistant when she worked for the National Youth Administration, remembered, "We screamed in helpless mirth . . . as Betty recounted stories that would eventually reach the world as *The Egg and I*. . . . Betty's humor wasn't kindly, nor homey, nor gentle, nor friendly. It had the malicious edge of a scalpel, and it could cut. Betty saw the flaws of the race as vicious. The fact that these flaws generally ended in hilarious pratfalls didn't make them any less lethal in her eyes."[18]

This severe judgment of the personal flaws of others—what Margaret Bundy Callahan described as the Bard women's particular kind of snobbery—was part of being Bard. In *The Egg and I* and in real life, people's peculiarities were what Betty noticed first. They defined the person utterly, and she used them to whittle clever and easily understood portraits. If the whittling sometimes drew blood, so be it. When, with *The Egg and I*, she turned to "authing"—a Bard word encompassing everything that being an author entailed—Betty combined her family's particular snobbery with her highly developed storytelling muscle.

Describing a place where she felt she had no allies, Betty allied herself with her readers. Together, Betty and her readers explored the land and learned about (and judged) its colorful inhabitants, including the slovenly but good-natured Kettle family, her near neighbors. Betty's Kettles are earthy. They use a doorless outhouse clearly visible from their manure-speckled kitchen, in which animals run underfoot and countless children crowd around the table.

Betty rallies her readers against her adversaries: the often-dreary Pacific Northwest weather; the chicks, whose care requires Betty's round-the-clock attention; and Stove, the anthropomorphized wood-stove who takes Betty's desire to use him to prepare food as a personal insult and responds accordingly. Readers laugh with Betty at the foibles of others but also at Betty's wry descriptions of her own attempts to cope with the absurd demands of her situation.

Betty's snarkiness surprised and delighted her original readers, and it makes her tone seem contemporary today. One aspect of *The Egg and I*, however, feels decidedly dated, and that is the book's treatment of Northwest Coastal Native Americans. "The Pacific Coast Indians whom I saw were as unlike the pictures on the Great Northern Railroad calendars as slugs are unlike dragonflies," Betty wrote. "The coast Indian is squat, bowlegged, swarthy, flat-faced, broad-nosed, dirty, diseased, ignorant and tricky. . . . There were few exceptions among the many we knew."[19]

A modern reader flinches, but it is likely that few of her original readers even noticed these slurs. Theirs was an era rife with derogatory treatment of nearly everyone. Betty's eventual handling of racial issues in *The Plague and I* three years later was different from her treatment of the Native Americans in *Egg*.[20]

Descriptions of the Indians are not the only discordant notes for modern readers. Betty's account of leaving baby Anne alone in a parked car, held in place by a baby blanket pinned to the upholstery and covered with a mosquito net, while she visited the canning and fancywork exhibits at the Jefferson County Fair would bring down child protective services if recounted today. But in 1945, Betty MacDonald's book struck a cultural sweet spot, and readers rewarded her. Royalty checks soon brought in far more than the book's five-hundred-dollar advance. Her first splurge was to install a cesspool on the Vashon property. Her second was to purchase a beaver coat and hat. "I look simply exquisite in same but as it has been a long long time since I have bought myself anything and as I never expected to have anything in fur unless

I trapped and skinned it myself I am quite shaky," she wrote Bernice Baumgarten.[21]

Being suddenly flush with cash was a dizzying sensation. Immediately after the book was published, Lippincott told Betty that over six days, she had earned twenty-five-thousand dollars in royalties. "Imagine, $25,000 in six days," Betty wrote Norah Flannery, one of her Firland roommates. "Bests [a Seattle department store] who wouldn't even let me pay cash in their store last Christmas are imploring me to open an account and Frederick & Nelson instead of holding a conference of the entire store every time I charge a handkerchief, o.k. *anything*. I don't give a damn for the fame—it is the freedom from flinching when the phone rings—the ability to stare rudely at credit managers which thrills me."[22]

Lippincott threw its publicity budget behind the book, which continued to prosper.[23] *The Egg and I* reached the number 1 position on the *New York Times* nonfiction best-seller list on December 23, 1945, and remained there for forty-three weeks. It remained in the top five for seven more months. Although published late in the year, *The Egg and I* was eighth on the *Publisher's Weekly* nonfiction best-seller list for 1945. In 1946, it topped the list. The next year, Betty's book made the list again, this time at number 7. This three-year domination was as remarkable then as it would be today.[24]

In the original publication, the front of the dust jacket featured a woodcut of a farm scene by Richard Bennett, with Betty's smiling photograph on the back.[25] In all its advertising, however, Lippincott was using Betty's face to promote the book, a strategy MacMillan Publishing had implemented with its 1944 best-selling novel *Forever Amber*, which featured a glamorous head shot of its attractive author, Kathleen Winsor, on the back cover. "You must admit that you look like you're having fun," Lippincott's advertising director, J. A. "Mac" McKaughan, wrote to Betty about her expression in the photo. "Heavens knows these last few years have been bare enough of laughs, and it's about time someone like you came through with an antidote to the general depression of the war period."[26] *The Egg and I* used humor and nostalgia as tools for moving on; and like her book, something about Betty's photograph gave readers permission to laugh again.

After only a few months, Lippincott moved Betty's appealing head shot from the back cover to the front, ditching Bennett's art.[27] For her readers, the merry pinup-girl author and the yarn she spun were indivisible.[28] From this point on, *Egg* branded Betty, and Betty branded *Egg*.

On January 22, 1946, *The Egg and I* sold eight thousand copies in a single day. Noting this, *Life* magazine decided to send a photographer and reporter to visit the MacDonalds. "Good God, men, don't you realize that I haven't done any housework since the book came out?" Betty wrote to Lippincott when she heard about the plan. "That is alright for MacDonalds who are used to hoeing our way in and out but to have Life here taking pictures of us slogging around in this fox's den is something else again unless of course you got them to come out here by promising them the Washington Grapes of Wrath."[29]

The *Life* story brought national media attention to Anne, Joan, Don, and Vashon Island and gave Betty's readers a candid view of the vivacious author. The story, "Life Goes Calling On the Author of 'The Egg and I,'" appeared in the March 18, 1946, issue. The photographs gave readers more glimpses of the vivacious book-jacket Betty: reading fan mail with Anne and Joan, contemplating an egg balanced on end, visiting with friends, typing while surrounded by children, and buying eggs in a Vashon grocery.

Eastern reporters were clamoring to meet Betty, and Lippincott pressed her to plan a book tour. Bernice Baumgarten suggested she stay home and work on a sequel to *Egg*, but Lippincott's insistence and Betty's enthusiasm for the adventure won out. Other than her childhood train trip to Auburn, New York, to meet her maternal grandparents, Betty had never traveled east.

Betty, Don, and Sydney drove to Los Angeles and then to New York, promoting *The Egg and I* along the way.[30] The first stop was Portland, Oregon, where their enormous suite at the Multnomah Hotel had three bathrooms: she, Sydney, and Don all took baths at once "just to be rich," Betty wrote to her family.[31] In San Francisco they enjoyed a deluxe tourists' experience, staying at the Sir Francis Drake Hotel, sipping cocktails at the Top of the Mark on Nob Hill, and touring the San Francisco Zoo and Japanese Tea Garden. Betty had never been to California. "Oh, Joanie, you and Anne would just love San Francisco—everyone here is dressed so beautifully that I felt just like I was from Alaska," she gushed.[32] They had lunch with friends in Carmel en route to Los Angeles, where Betty was feted with a cocktail party at the Beverly Wilshire.

Just months before, Betty MacDonald had been unknown. Now, as her fame spread, every day brought her excitement. In the Southwest, she was thrilled that she and Don could stay in a real adobe house in Las Cruces and buy turquoise jewelry for Anne and Joan at an Apache trading post near El Paso. In Dallas, Betty wrote to her family, "they simply turned the city inside out for me. I had orchids to wear every minute—I had lunch and tea and in between drinks with the owners of every single store in Dallas."[33]

Stop by triumphant stop, signing *Egg* in bookstores as she went, Betty made her way to New York. Even sophisticated Manhattan had embraced *Egg*. A newspaper photograph of Betty at Brentano's at Fifth Avenue and 47th Street, at the time the city's largest bookstore, captured her wearing a perky hat and three strands of pearls, her manicured fingers cradling a real egg that she was carefully autographing. It was a far cry from gathering eggs in Chimacum.

Betty was the guest of honor at the *New York Herald Tribune's* book and author luncheon. Lippincott threw her a party at the Ritz-Carlton. Betty was reportedly the first woman ever asked to speak at the Dutch Treat Club, a private social club for New York literati, where she shared billing with Winston Churchill. In Washington, DC, Betty was guest speaker at the *Washington Post's* book and author luncheon. For the first time, she appeared on national radio broadcasts.

Lippincott took out a full-page advertisement in the *New York Times Book Review* to crow about the book's overwhelming success. The ad featured the familiar dust-jacket photo of Betty, surrounded by cartoon depictions of *Egg*-crazed readers unable to put their copies down: a dancing couple reading the book over one another's shoulders; a symphony conductor clutching his baton while his eyes stray down to *Egg* on the music stand; a bride at the altar, engrossed in her book, ignoring minister and groom; curvy female beauty contestants parading past male judges who ignore them completely to chuckle at *The Egg and I*. A banner across the ad read, "Everything Else Is a Substitute."[34]

The millionth copy of *The Egg and I* rolled off the press in Cornwall, New York, at 11 a.m. on August 15, 1946. *Publisher's Weekly* reported that Lippincott executives were there to watch. Lippincott issued statistics about the book to date: printing had required more than 207 tons of paper, which would cover 580 acres or make a one-inch tape that would reach twice around the world. If all existing copies were piled on top of one another, the tower would be more than sixteen miles high, or six times as high as Mount Rainier.[35] Betty's editor, Bertram Lippincott, told the *Seattle Times*, "Although *The Egg* is not the first book to reach the millionth mark, it is the first to have reached it in less than a year, and the first to have taken so firm a grip on the national imagination."[36] During its first year in print, *The Egg and I* was selling at the astonishing rate of one book every twenty-two seconds.[37]

Back in Seattle, Lippincott hosted a luncheon at the Washington Athletic Club to celebrate *Egg's* overwhelming success and also the intense public focus the book was bringing to Washington State and the Pacific Northwest. Betty's vivid descriptions of the region's physical grandeur intrigued people who had never been there and made them want to see it for themselves. The influx of *Egg* pilgrims jump-started the state's postwar tourism industry. In gratitude, the governor of Washington, Monrad Wallgren, presented Betty with the one-millionth copy of *The Egg and I*, which had been specially bound. Betty then presented Wallgren with his own commemorative copy, number 1,000,002. (The intervening copy had quietly gone to Betty's literary agent Bernice Baumgarten, at Baumgarten's request.) Betty and Wallgren were photographed grinning widely and balancing an egg on Wallgren's open copy of the book. When Wallgren handed her the book, Betty quipped, "Thanks a million."[38]

The Egg and I remains one of the most successful first books of all time. Betty's story touched something visceral in readers, whether because of timing or her writing style or fate. The book's success set a high standard for books that came after it, especially Betty's books. Having stumbled onto the magic formula for a best seller, Betty MacDonald would spend the rest of her life trying to re-create that alchemy.

CHAPTER SIX

Smelling Like Sugar Cookies

As sales of *The Egg and I* soared, Lippincott eagerly sought to capitalize on Betty's success. Accordingly, fifteen months after *Egg* made its debut, the publisher introduced *Mrs. Piggle-Wiggle*. The book was a collection of children's stories about a wise, kind, magical woman who gently but firmly assisted errant children and their beleaguered parents. Betty dedicated *Mrs. Piggle-Wiggle* to her daughters, nieces, and nephews, "who are perfect angels and couldn't possibly have been the inspiration for any of these stories."[1]

Lippincott nearly missed staking its claim in Mrs. Piggle-Wiggle's publishing empire. While Betty was revising *Egg*, she had sent the children's manuscript to her literary agent, Bernice Baumgarten, and Baumgarten had struggled without success to place it. The children's book editors who read the stories didn't understand Betty's mixture of naturalism and fantasy. The publishers Bobbs-Merrill, Farrar & Rinehart, McBride's, Messner, and Lippincott all turned the manuscript down. Once *Egg* began to rocket up the best-seller lists, Lippincott frantically reversed their rejection, and *Mrs. Piggle-Wiggle* was rushed into print.

As with *The Egg and I*, Mrs. Piggle-Wiggle's appearance was well timed. Children's book sales had risen sharply during World War II, partly because toys were unavailable or in short supply, their materials being needed for wartime production. The War Production Board restrictions that affected the publishing industry most severely had been lifted by the time *Mrs. Piggle-Wiggle* launched. Paper and cloth were in readier supply, and children still had a keen appetite for books.

Betty's youthful storytelling, begun at the insistent prompting of Mary's icy feet, continued when she was a teenager spinning tales to occupy Dede and Alison. When she had children of her own, making up stories was her natural reflex, and she invented Mrs. Piggle-Wiggle for Anne and Joan. "I have told Mrs. Piggle-Wiggle stories to children, hundreds of them, from two to twelve. Children like them because they think they are written about a sister, brother, friends, cousins, anyone but them," Betty wrote to Lippincott's Mac McKaughan. "I'm sure that one reason I have always loved to tell stories to children is because they are such enthusiastic audiences—they laugh loudly at anything the least bit witty, are terribly sad in the sad parts and grind their teeth with hatred for the wicked characters."[2]

Unlike book editors, children had no trouble whatsoever accepting Mrs. Piggle-Wiggle or her world. "Mrs. Piggle-Wiggle has brown sparkly eyes and brown hair which she keeps very long, almost to her knees, so the children can comb it. . . . [Her] skin is a goldy brown and she has a warm, spicy, sugar-cookie smell that is very comforting to children who are sad about something. . . . [S]he wears felt hats which the children poke and twist into witches' and pirates' hats and she does not mind at all. . . . [S]he wears very high heels all the time and is glad to let the little girls borrow her shoes," the book explained.[3] Among the many attractions of the book were the late Mr. Piggle-Wiggle's hidden pirate's treasure; the pets, Wag and Lightfoot (whose offspring were periodically divvied up among the neighborhood children); and Mrs. Piggle-Wiggle's willingness to allow little boys and girls to use her house as a cozy club while they baked cookies and enjoyed cambric tea.

Betty's newspaper interviews frequently mentioned the important role that children played in her busy life. She told the *Seattle Times* that *Mrs. Piggle-Wiggle*, like *The Egg and I*, was written while her house "crawled with children. . . . I had so much help that I almost never got it finished. Most of my best writing has been done to the accompaniment of heavy breathing, sniffing, and fat hands poking the wrong key of the typewriter. I hope this book sells. If it doesn't, it will prove that all these years I've been boring children instead of amusing them."[4] It did sell, and Mrs. Piggle-Wiggle was to become one of Betty MacDonald's most enduring creations, appearing in *Mrs. Piggle-Wiggle's Magic* (1949), *Mrs. Piggle-Wiggle's Farm* (1954), and *Hello, Mrs. Piggle-Wiggle* (1957).

Like Uncle Remus, Mary Poppins, and Nurse Matilda, Mrs. Piggle-Wiggle is an adult who helps children to learn the wisdom of good behavior.[5] She believes that misguided children truly want to behave well once their veil of ignorance is stripped away. Children liked the books' honestly depicted child characters and guileless acceptance of everyday magic. Parents appreciated Mrs. Piggle-Wiggle's breezy ways of presenting moral lessons and her effective solutions for behavior that was worrisome, trying, or just plain naughty. The Piggle-Wiggle books make both children and parents feel they are "in" on something. Children recognize behaviors that they themselves would never, ever exhibit (wink, wink), and feel superior, even as they identify with the child characters. Betty tosses inside jokes about parental behavior to the adults reading the books aloud. Unlike many books written in the same era, the Piggle-Wiggle books represent boys and girls equally: both are endowed with characteristics that worry or annoy their parents, and both are equally amenable to Mrs. Piggle-Wiggle's peculiar training methods.

Mrs. Piggle-Wiggle has Sydney's unflappability and Mary's confident, prescriptive authority, but her exciting sparkle mirrors that of her creator. Family members who spent time with Betty when they were young recall her gift for inspiring their intense, creative play. Like Betty, Mrs. Piggle-Wiggle is highly imaginative, and she encourages the children around her to use their own imaginations. Both promise and threat are present in the Piggle-Wiggle stories—as they were for the children in Betty's life, who recalled occasional erratic responses from her that could startle and dismay them. Child characters who alter their behavior are always rewarded, but those who hesitate to do so risk consequences ranging from missing a circus show to enraging an evil queen to literally drowning in their own tears.

Children's names in the Piggle-Wiggle books include both the commonplace (Anne, Joan, Mary) and the unusual: Hubert Egbert

Prentiss, Calliope Ragbag, Paraphernalia Grotto, Cormorant Broom-rack, and Pergola Wingsproggle, among many wonderful others. Adults answer to such names as Mrs. Moohead, Mrs. Grapple, and Mrs. Crankminor. In addition to helping parents overcome children's behavior problems like selfishness, sibling quarrels, and answering back, Mrs. Piggle-Wiggle offers solutions like the Radish Cure, which calls for radish seeds to be sprinkled by night over the grimy skin of a reluctant washer, resulting in a healthy but alarming crop of the vegetable. This and other rather extreme cures—such as the Slow-Eaters-Tiny-Bite-Taker cure, which involves gradually reducing the size of cups and plates on which a slowpoke eater is served until they hold only drops of milk and grains of toast—have their own logic.

Mrs. Piggle-Wiggle was instantly adopted by parents and teachers for reading aloud and devoured by children old enough to take up the book themselves. After its publication, Betty's mailbags bulged with fan letters from children. Blanche Hamilton, who'd heard Betty tell Mrs. Piggle-Wiggle stories to Anne and Joan on a few occasions and who later read the books aloud to students in her elementary school classroom, remembered, "I watched children smile knowingly when they heard about the 'Never-want-to-go-to-bed'ers and 'Don't-touch-it's-mine' kids."[6]

Mrs. Piggle-Wiggle's original illustrator was Richard Bennett, who had created the farm scene used for *The Egg and I*'s first dust jacket as well as the rooster silhouette on the book's cloth cover. When *Mrs. Piggle-Wiggle* was published, Bennett's illustrations were appearing regularly in *The Horn Book*, a magazine celebrating literature written for children. In his illustrations, Mrs. Piggle-Wiggle looks sincere and completely engaged in play. The feathered headdress and pirate hat she wears in various drawings are as believable on her as they would have been on the head of any child playing make-believe. Betty found Bennett's illustrations charming.

She felt otherwise about the work of Kurt Wiese, the German-born illustrator of *Mrs. Piggle-Wiggle's Magic*. Weise's career began in 1929, when he illustrated Felix Salten's *Bambi*, and he was prolific, writing and illustrating his own books and illustrating almost four hundred books by others. But Betty loathed Weise's illustrations, she wrote a friend, and suspected children would feel the same.[7]

For the illustrations for *Mrs. Wiggle-Wiggle's Farm*, Eunice Blake, the Lippincott children's book editor, tapped the young Maurice Sendak. Blake found Piggle-Wigglish humor in Sendak's illustrations for Ruth Krauss's 1952 picture book, *A Hole Is to Dig*. Betty told Blake that she would prefer Garth Williams, the illustrator of E. B. White's *Stuart Little* and *Charlotte's Web* and of Laura Ingalls Wilder's Little House series. Williams's animal illustrations were softer and more realistic than Sendak's, and at the time he was better known. Blake held firm against Betty's resistance, telling Betty that Lippincott had already given Sendak a contract. *Mrs. Piggle-Wiggle's Farm* was Sendak's thirteenth volume as an illustrator and his first project for Lippincott.

Lippincott liked Sendak's illustrations so much that they asked him to redo the first two Piggle-Wiggle books and agree to illustrate all future volumes. "Unfortunately he cannot do this for us," Eunice Blake wrote to Betty, "but we have been able to get Hilary Knight, the illustrator of *Eloise*, to agree to do the new book and redo the old ones except Sendak. I think he has very much the feeling of Sendak and the same kind of humor your stories have."[8]

Knight's first book-length effort, the illustrations for Kay Thompson's *Eloise*, was published in 1955, to immediate success. The impish-faced figures in Knight's illustrations seem to be in constant motion. Knight's work illustrated *Hello, Mrs. Piggle-Wiggle* and replaced the Bennett and Wiese illustrations in the first two books but did not replace Maurice Sendak's contribution to *Mrs. Piggle-Wiggle's Farm*. Sendak's reputation was growing, and Lippincott—mindful of possible future joint projects—would not have wanted to risk offending him. All three Knight-illustrated Piggle-Wiggle books came out in 1957.

Knight's daffy, charming illustrations suited Betty's prose perfectly. His brand of cleverness was Betty's brand, too. His Mrs. Piggle-Wiggle virtually twinkled as she cast a knowing glance from the cover directly at the reader, and his illustrations of child characters—cowlicks every which way, shirttails untucked, hair ribbons askew—matched Betty's descriptions hijink by hijink.

Betty adored Knight's illustrations, calling them "just like children but old fashioned too."[9] "I think the new Mrs. Piggle-Wiggle is the most adorable thing yet—especially Mrs. Piggle-Wiggle herself," Betty wrote Bernice Baumgarten. "All the other Piggle-Wiggle illustrations seem so wooden compared to his."[10] Betty wrote to Hilary Knight expressing her satisfaction with his work. Knight replied that he'd long been a fan of hers, and that working on the books had been great fun.[11]

Early print advertisements for the original edition of *Mrs. Piggle-Wiggle* featured Richard Bennett's illustration of the title character juxtaposed with a mirror image of the drawing in which Betty's laughing photo replaced Mrs. Piggle-Wiggle's head. "If you haven't met the most popular lady in town—you'd better get a wiggle on!" the copy read.[12]

As Betty's first follow-up to her still-best-selling *Egg, Mrs. Piggle-Wiggle* had the advantage of an eager audience. And, as with *Egg*, Betty never anticipated that this character would so thoroughly capture readers' hearts. She wrote the stories with little struggle. Their gentle absurdity and offbeat humor were another happy product of the way Betty MacDonald saw the world, another—and a less caustic—benefit of being Bard.

CHAPTER SEVEN

Betty in Hollywoodland

THE EGG AND I was a literary phenomenon, and Hollywood smelled a hit. In April 1946, just seven months after *Egg*'s publication and less than a year before *Mrs. Piggle-Wiggle* appeared, International Pictures (soon to become Universal-International Pictures) bought the film rights to *The Egg and I*.[1] Promoting the book from coast to coast had polished Betty's public persona and built her confidence. Back in Seattle after the book tour, Betty understood that she was popular. In Hollywood just weeks later, she would realize she was famous.

With the ink from Betty's signature on the contract for the movie rights practically still wet, the wacky independent press agent Jim Moran jump-started the film's prepublicity. Moran had made headlines in the past for stunts that included putting a bull in a china shop, finding a needle in a haystack, and changing horses in midstream. Just as *Egg*'s film rights sold, Moran learned that a bird at the Hollywood Ostrich Farm, a tourist attraction, had abandoned her egg. Moran volunteered to hatch the egg himself, starting on Father's Day. *Life, Liberty,* and other national magazines produced photo layouts of Moran reading *The Egg and I* while "incubating." Every major newspaper in the country ran stories.[2]

This stunt was a publicity bonanza. Hoping to keep the ball rolling, Universal-International Pictures summoned *The Egg and I*'s photogenic author to Hollywood. In response to an inquiry from the company about her preferences for "interviews, stunts, radio etc," Betty responded, "Have no objections as far as radio or interviews are concerned but shudder at the word stunts. Would suggest that you clear any radio or other commitments with Brandt and Brandt as I inhale and exhale according to their directions."[3]

The trip was a group adventure. In late June 1946, Betty, Don, Anne, Joan, and Mary drove south to Hollywood. Mary, loath to be left out of this glamorous escapade, was along to give Betty moral support. Newspapers reported that Anne and Joan were hoping for screen tests.

From Hollywood, Betty appeared on numerous nationally broadcast programs, her voice filling the radio airwaves. She was the guest of honor at a huge celebrity cocktail party held at Beverly Hills Club. Universal-International filled her Beverly Hills Hotel suite with fresh flowers and sent Betty a limousine to use during her stay. She and her family were whisked from sight to sight, trailed by reporters. If Anne and Joan had thus far taken their mother's literary success for granted, the Hollywood treatment the family received now dazzled them. They sat beside Betty at parties and night clubs, surrounded by movie stars, happily stunned.

Betty was interviewed constantly, charming the press with her clever answers to their rote questions. Her lifelong penchant for reading movie magazines had inadvertently prepared her for this moment. As Betty was feted, rumors flew. Shirley Temple, then seventeen, was said to be contending for the lead. Betty's daughter Anne—then eighteen, with no film experience—was also reportedly being considered to play the part of her own mother. Betty was said to have told a radio commentator that she, Don, and the girls planned to move permanently to Hollywood.

In a broad nod to the book's title, eggs were the overwhelming theme of Betty's Hollywood tour. At parties in her honor, buffet tables groaned with egg dishes in every shape and form. Claudette Colbert, Rosalind Russell, Joan Bennett, Mickey Rooney, Jack Benny, and other Hollywood elites grazed on the ovoid feast. Radio listeners heard that Betty never ate eggs, a half-truth that didn't stop hosts from surrounding her with them. Reporters loved the egg-hating angle. Multiple interviews pictured a grinning Betty with a pull quote along the lines of "I hope I never see another egg as long as I live."[4]

This fawning attention did not turn Betty's head. She was typically self-effacing on her return to Vashon when she saw photographs taken at these Hollywood events: "It was lucky that I had my strength when I got home and opened my mail and there were the pictures taken at the Press Club and that *old French prostitute* at the head of the table upon close observation turned out to be me."[5]

Soon after Betty's trip, Universal-International announced that Claudette Colbert had won the leading role in the film. In modern terms, this was the casting equivalent of Reese Witherspoon taking the part of Cheryl Strayed in the film *Wild*, or Julia Roberts playing Elizabeth Gilbert in *Eat, Pray, Love*. Glamorous, untouchable, her eyebrow arches plucked pencil thin, with skin so porcelain-perfect it appeared to have been airbrushed, Claudette Colbert was a major Hollywood star by the time she played Betty. She had been paired with Fred MacMurray, who was cast as Bob in *Egg*, for five previous pictures. MacMurray, too, was a star, with some fifty films already to his credit. *The Egg and I* would be by far the most popular of Colbert's and MacMurray's seven joint projects, and the only one to spawn sequels (albeit without the glamorous leading actors).

Claudette Colbert was forty-three when she appeared in *Egg*, more than twice Betty's age in the book. Colbert's china-doll frigidity and fresh-off-the-costume-rack perfection have more in common with the smiling Betty MacDonald book cover than with the book's contents. Colbert's Betty was as smooth and bland as well-stirred Cream of Wheat. One *Egg* fan weighed in on the casting decision in a letter to Betty: "I doubt Claudette's ability to portray your activities as you described them in the book. I doubt whether she can even make good coffee, let alone cook a geoduck!"[6]

Nearly as important as the casting of Betty and Bob were the choices for the leading character roles, Ma and Pa Kettle. The film gives the Kettles a more prominent role than the book does, a decision that helped inflame resentment among the Bishops, Betty and Bob Heskett's real-life Chimacum neighbors. The veteran character actress Marjorie Main was cast as Ma Kettle, and Percy Kilbride—then in his forty-seventh year in the theatrical profession—won the role of her shiftless but amiable spouse. Main and Kilbride brought these characters vividly to life. Ma's heart-of-gold sloppiness and well-used aprons and Pa's ever-present black derby hat became emblems for a pair of characters that filmgoers immediately understood. These parts would prove to be the defining roles of both these venerable actors' careers.

Before filming could start, the studio had regulatory matters to attend to. The screenplay, in draft form, was vetted by Universal-International's attorneys and by staffers in the office of the film-industry moral watchdog Joseph Breen at the Motion Picture Producers and Distributors of America (MPPDA). The Breen office read screenplays and then issued changes—some suggested, others demanded—that would help films conform to the restrictions of the Hays Code. Named for the MPPDA director Will Hays, the code was a set of moral guidelines for films. Films whose content violated the Hays Code were denied the Hays Office Purity Seal of Approval and could generally not be distributed or exhibited.

Universal-International paid lip service to the notes the Breen office sent after reading the final shooting script, omitting a few toilet gags and making sure Colbert wore a slip under her dress. The film's final cut still included a suggestively purred line delivered by Betty's romantic rival (invented for the film), the wealthy hobby farmer Harriet Putnam, about taking Bob into her barn to show him her Speckled Sussex.[7] The Hays Code enforcers had little to object to from Colbert and MacMurray, whose chaste portrayals of Betty and Bob were devoid of any suggestion of sensuality.

The Kettles were tidied up slightly to conform to the Hays Code. Pa's almost sinister shiftlessness in the book became lazy bemusement in the film, and his thick lisp was softened almost out of existence. Ma still scratched her itches, shifted her enormous bosom, and spoke with an earthiness born of raising fifteen children. She had a heart of gold, however, and was gratefully embraced by Betty (more so than in the book). And Tits Kettle, Ma and Pa's married daughter, whose baby in the book has "fits," fades into the sibling crowd in the film and is mercifully nameless.

The Humane Society weighed in too, demanding that the pig, Cleopatra (with whom Claudette Colbert would bravely tussle), be pushed or shoved rather than pulled; that the dead cougar called for in the film script be not a dead cougar but an anesthetized one, or better still a dummy; and that the tree scheduled to fall on and crush the chicken house not harm any chickens. So concerned was the Humane Society about this scene that they planned to have a representative present on the day it was scheduled to be shot.[8]

Studio lawyers were concerned that because *The Egg and I* was a work of nonfiction and the screenplay hewed closely to the book's depictions, making the picture could expose Universal-International to libel claims. Studio attorneys suggested obtaining releases from any living persons who could be identified as characters in the script, but only one person was apparently approached: Universal-International tracked down Robert Heskett and offered him a deal.

Betty's prolonged legal wrangling to try to force Bob to provide child support had petered out a year before *Egg's* publication, and she had no idea of his whereabouts. Studio personnel found him living in Oakland, California, aware of Betty's jollied-up literary version of their marriage and willing to sign over rights to the use of his name and story in the upcoming film. The document presented to Heskett stipulated that by signing, he would be released from the $5,500 judgment against him that King County Superior Court had awarded Betty in 1944.[9] Universal-International also paid him $1,000.

The cameras rolled. Claudette Colbert and Fred MacMurray's house was large enough to fit Betty and Bob Heskett's actual abode several times over.[10] The time period was changed to the present day, and Bob was portrayed as a freshly returned GI, a veteran of the Battle of Okinawa.[11] Colbert's wardrobe was glamorous—bridal outfit, satin negligee, gray wool traveling suits, checkered farm dresses in fresh green, blue, and white, and even a turquoise flannel robe, all created by the famous fashion designer Adrian.[12] How far from Chimacum the Betty character had journeyed![13] Marjorie Main's wardrobe was listed in the production budget as "Dirty House Dress." She had three of them, plus the new dress Betty sews for her.

Studio publicity and, later, reviewers made much of the fact that the perpetually pristine Colbert actually got dirty in the film, though the scene of her coaxing Cleopatra the pig and slipping in the mud was shot all in one day. "No one could have enacted Betty with more charm than Miss Colbert. She has to take quite a physical beating to project her role, but she faces everything with the superb sportsmanship of a true trooper," the *Hollywood Reporter* enthused.[14]

The movie's opening scene finds Colbert's neatly suited Betty in a dining car on a train, being served a breakfast egg by a smiling black waiter. The train sways, and the waiter drops the egg, then says soothingly to Betty, "It's only an egg." Betty's indignant response, "Only an egg! I suppose it never occurred to you that this egg was someone's child?" gives her an opening to shoehorn the book's title into her retort, "Well, so did I once. But that was before the egg and I!"

In early January 1947, Betty and Don departed Seattle's Boeing Field, bound once again for Hollywood. Betty was needed to shoot publicity photos with the cast and help gin up prerelease excitement.[15] Reporters noted that Betty was more polished, even sophisticated, on this visit—eager to sample fine cuisine and ready to dicker with antique dealers over their wares. Although Betty was not a movie star, her face had become instantly recognizable, and over the preceding six months she had grown secure in her celebrity. Making herself accessible to reporters, verbally deft, and easy to write about, she made good copy. Newspapers announcing Betty's Hollywood journey noted that Associated Press editors had just named her among the Women of the Year for 1946, an honor she shared with the actresses Helen Hayes and Ingrid Bergman, the singer Kate Smith, and the athlete Mildred "Babe" Didrikson.[16]

Being famous brought Betty offers for product endorsements, usually with a book plug thrown in. Betty's smiling portrait was used to advertise Loft Candy's chocolate eggs. "I thought I knew all about eggs," ran the ad copy, "but then our chickens never gave us eggs like Loft's."[17] Authors signing their books in Betty's day used fountain pens. Betty liked a broad, soft nib, and she signed so many books that keeping her pen in working order was a constant challenge. After much back-and-forth with first the Schaefer and then the Parker pen company, Betty endorsed the Parker, appearing in an advertisement. The Crosley appliance company ran Betty's picture under the headline "The Egg and I Are Ten Times Happier!" The ad copy, written in the first person, went on, "If you've read *The Egg and I*, you'll remember some of the troubles I had in the kitchen. But now things are different—because Egg and I have just treated ourselves to a wonderful new Crosley Shelvador Refrigerator! According to Egg, Crosley's new 'Care Free' Automatic Defrosting is the cleverest work-saver since women were invented!"[18] And in a tie-in that must have been too perfect to resist, Betty promoted Helene Curtis Shampoo plus Egg.

In Hollywood, everything Betty did was a potential photo op. Betty and Don visited the *Egg* set, accompanied by a studio photographer. Betty posed for photographs bending over Stove alongside Claudette Colbert. Betty's stylish hat (crowned with a plume of chicken feathers) and her smart suit both complemented and contrasted with Colbert's crisp, cheerful puff-sleeved gingham dress and spotless ruffled apron. The house set—so clean it sparkled—and Miss Colbert, that most glamorous doppelgänger—slopped yet another coat of whitewash onto the real Betty's history with Robert Heskett in the tiny cabin in the rain in Chimacum.

This photo op must have been mind-boggling for Betty. She had no doubt watched Colbert on Seattle movie screens, and to be played by her—controlled perfection in this flattened version of the expurgated recasting of her own story—must have been eerie. Whatever dresses the young Betty Heskett wore in Chimacum during her years raising chickens and fending off her husband's temper, it seems doubtful that they were perky or perfectly starched.

She had reclaimed those years and shaped what she'd experienced with Bob into a version she wanted to reveal, first to her family and friends, and then in print. Bob Heskett had known all about the book, acknowledged to his friends that he was *that* Bob, and never elaborated on the tale or contradicted his former wife. Then, for the film, Bob had released Betty, given (or sold) his name to her.[19] Now the Hesketts were represented by movie stars: MacMurray in his chipper plaid shirts, Colbert as sweet and crisp as the sugar crust on crème brûlée. With her messy actual history encased in Claudette Colbert's impervious interpretation, were Betty Heskett's demons finally exorcised? The film ensured once and for all that Betty's crafted version of her marriage to Bob became the truth of record.

Betty agreed to shoot an on-set promotional trailer for the film.[20] The trailer begins with a still photo of Betty's smiling portrait on the cover of *Egg*. Copies of the book multiply. The narrator announces: "Here is . . . the book that shook the world . . . with laughter. For two years . . . and still . . . a top best-seller (1,300,000 copies). [*Stacks of the book continue heaping up.*] A Book-of-the-Month smash (506,208 copies). A sensation to the twenty million readers of *Atlantic Monthly, Liberty, Reader's Digest.*"[21] The book-cover photo then comes alive, and Betty introduces herself, endorses the film, and lists the characters.

Betty's great strength in interviews was her spontaneity, her candid answers to even repetitive questions. *Egg*'s trailer gave her the chance for none of this. Her face is stiff with pancake makeup, her skin more matte than even Claudette Colbert's, and she looks ill at ease. The Rotogravure section of the *Seattle Times* accompanied a photo spread of Betty filming the trailer with the summation, "Betty was taut and nervous while a technician checked the light meter."[22]

As with movie stars of the era, Betty MacDonald's image was both magnified and flattened when she was scripted by Hollywood. Standing next to Colbert, she was projected, literally, into a higher stratosphere of public attention. Unlike her book, and unlike her candid sessions with reporters, Hollywood's version of Betty offered no surprises. Nevertheless, across the country, the trailer whipped up interest in the film and furthered Betty's fame.

Betty's several weeks interacting with studio bigwigs were draining, and she was relieved to return to Seattle. "We had a very good time in Hollywood," Betty wrote Bernice Baumgarten. "They are so tricky that Don and I got so we looked at both sides of our napkins before wiping our mouths for fear the napkin would really be a contract to write for Photoplay magazine and the gravy from my mouth would constitute a signature."[23]

CHAPTER SEVEN

After the film wrapped, the ballyhoo began. Universal-International press agent Ralph Ober took to the rails, roads, and sky with a Rhode Island Red hen he named Betty MacDonald, promoting the film. The fifteen-month-old hen's claws were varnished crimson, and lipstick was routinely applied to her beak. Ober and his feathered Betty logged over twenty-five thousand miles publicizing the film.

Publicity for the film, perhaps inevitably, featured quirky uses of eggs. Betty had long since become adept at autographing them. Fred MacMurray and Claudette Colbert quickly acquired the skill, which made for striking photo ops. Just signing eggs was not enough, however. The strangest publicity idea of all must be the one suggested by the studio's Boston flack, Bill Schulman. Messages could be inserted into real eggs, Schulman explained, by typing them onto thin strips of onionskin paper. The message could be tightly rolled and sealed into a small capsule, which could be placed in a hen's oviduct. Two days later, the hen would lay an egg with the message capsule contained in the yolk. Schulman proposed to serve such a message—signed by Claudette Colbert—to Massachusetts governor Robert Bradford in his breakfast egg. Bradford would see the film and—on his own onionskin strip inserted into some other unlucky fowl's oviduct—send return greetings to Colbert.

Another bizarre gimmick called for a four-foot papier-mâché egg to be placed atop a movie theater with a publicist inside, legs dangling and swinging while he or she called out to attract attention. Another, the lucky-number egg-hatching stunt, instructed theater owners to turn their lobbies into hen houses, complete with straw, live hens, and eggs. As the hens laid eggs, theater owners were to number them. Moviegoers could pick one of these numbers, and the number of the first egg to hatch won a prize.

Universal-International offered theater owners a three-minute cartoon by Walter Lantz that the studio's press kit claimed was the first animated cartoon trailer ever produced for a live-action film. The cartoon featured Romeo Rooster and Henrietta Hen, a fowl pair who visit Universal-International Studios together. During their visit, Henrietta—drawn sitting, knitting, in a hospital bed—lays an egg that, when it hatches, contains the ever-popular, green-dust-jacketed book.[24]

The studio even embedded a teaser for *The Egg and I* in another of their 1947 releases, *Brute Force*, a prison drama starring Burt Lancaster and Hume Cronyn. The film featured a brief scene in which male prisoners are treated to a viewing of *Egg*, with Colbert and MacMurray looming before them on a modest screen. Nestled in the rough drama, it was a Trojan egg, beckoning the book's many male fans.

Lippincott produced a special dust jacket featuring MacMurray and Colbert (and Stove) on the back cover. Rubber stamps of the stars' signatures were distributed to egg retailers around the country for stamping onto egg cartons. Families could enjoy a board game in a green box resembling the book cover and emblazoned with Fred's and Claudette's smiling faces. "The game is as egg-citing as the book and the movie!" promised the box copy. "Just like the story . . . with all the thrills of owning a chicken ranch!" All the publicity was—of course—billed as *eggsploitation*.

Despite the prerelease hoopla, critics saw *Egg* for what it was: a star-studded vehicle for a star literary property. "Material employed in the bid for laughs is good, standard prat-fall comedy, basically on the corny side, but streamlined and polished to a glitter. . . . Top laugh-getters of the piece are undisputedly Marjorie Main and Percy Kilbride in the main character roles of Ma and Pa Kettle. Both parts present constant temptation to burlesque and hamming. Miss Main and Kilbride resist the temptation and give an honest interpretation that simultaneously rouses the merriment and tugs at the heartstrings of the audience," *Daily Variety* opined.[25]

Egg was one of the top-earning films of 1947.[26] Marjorie Main was nominated for the Academy Award for best supporting actress (losing out to Celeste Holm in *Gentleman's Agreement*). At the time, films did not often have extended or open-ended runs. Film prints were expensive and moved from town to town after a week or two at the local movie house. The prints of *Egg* made their way across the country during the summer and fall of 1947.[27] And then the film retired to Universal-International's vaults.

Betty's tango with Hollywood completed her transition from private citizen to public personality. Betty was much too cynical and smart to swallow all of Hollywood's hype about herself, but feeling special and celebrated was still seductive and intoxicating. Having tasted celebrity, Betty noticed the lack of it. After her Hollywood treatment, feeling underappreciated became Betty's Achilles' heel, a source of recurrent conflict with her family, friends, and publishers.

CHAPTER EIGHT

Authing

B ETTY MacDonald was now a household name, known for her famous book and applauded for her personal vivacity. A *Cosmopolitan* magazine writer sought Betty out in late 1947:

> Mrs. MacDonald has green eyes, auburn hair and . . . an unquenchable energy. Her voice is quick with life, and it warms each sentence. She admires easily and often, without stiffness or self-consciousness. . . . She is an able mimic. In the space of a half hour, while I talked with her, she was a Swedish-American, a Japanese-American, a Hollywood writer giving his all to a vulgar joke, an uppity female expert on foreign affairs and a bubbling Texas girl. Her expression, never placid, shifts readily from amusement to anger. When she mentions someone she doesn't like, her eyes blaze. . . . "A lot of people are ready to crawl on their knees over broken glass in order to be introduced to me. Then they say, 'My, you're much fatter than you look in your pictures, aren't you?' or 'Whoever told you, dear, to wear bangs? They're hideous.' It bothered me at first, but now I realize that most of them are just disappointed authors. I've been that way myself, so I know how they feel."[1]

The Egg and I's success had brought Betty fame, but in the glare of the public spotlight, she tended to squint and blink rather than bask.

With fame came money, at least in the beginning. Betty's family members shared in her bounty, enjoying treats, trips, and good food. With Betty's help, Sydney finally paid off all the mortgages on the

15th Avenue house that the family had barely hung on to through the Great Depression.[2] Betty and Don settled their own mortgage and then undertook extensive home improvements, modernizing the existing bathroom and adding a second for Anne and Joan, creating a small suite for Sydney, moving the kitchen, and building a guest cottage. Betty hired Cleve to cut a road from Vashon's main highway to the house. The family later purchased adjoining land and built a barn, from which they briefly operated an egg business, casting Don—like Bob—as a chicken rancher.

The chicken project was public relations for *Egg* and make-work for Don, whose wartime employment at Boeing had evaporated right around the time the book was published. It gave reporters an angle for stories and brushed a gloss of truth onto *Egg*'s false happy ending. The monosyllabic husbands' names and the new egg operation perpetuated the light smokescreen obscuring Betty's divorce and second marriage, as did Anne and Joan's use of Don's surname and the names used in the film, in which Fred MacMurray's character was called Bob MacDonald. Betty had not yet announced in print that her *Egg* marriage was over. She brushed off those who did inquire with a quick "This is a different husband."

The years 1945–47, when copies of *Egg* were selling most strongly and the movie rights were sold, were almost certainly Betty's most lucrative. In 1947, Betty and Don purchased a house at 905 East Howe Street, in Seattle's North Capitol Hill neighborhood. The house overlooked Lake Union and had a view of the Olympic Mountains. After renovating the property and decorating it with antiques, Betty and Don began spending most of their time there, avoiding the ferry commute to Vashon.

The Egg and I was like a monetary geyser, but if Betty and Don had realized its tax consequences, they probably would not have sprung for the Howe Street house. Betty's royalty checks from Brandt & Brandt had no taxes withheld. After a blissful year or so of cashing checks, paying off mortgages, and splurging on family, the couple received their 1946 income-tax bill. As part of the struggle to pay this bill, they mortgaged the Howe Street house, then rented it out. For a while,

Betty and Don lived in its basement apartment. Lippincott advanced Betty money to cover her taxes, and Bernice Baumgarten and Betty's attorney, George Guttormsen, strategized to help Betty manage the income. Guttormsen kept Betty's financial woes out of the public eye, but the threat of disclosure worried Baumgarten and, to a lesser extent, Betty. Although royalties continued rolling in, Betty never felt financially secure again.

Mary blamed Don for her sister's ongoing money woes. Both Baumgarten and Mary noted that Betty was talented at mathematics and that she could easily look at a set of bookkeeping records and pick out the errors, but Betty deferred to Don on financial matters. That Don's money management only dug the couple deeper into debt despite Betty's success did not surprise Mary.[3]

When deciding to purchase the Howe Street house, the MacDonalds may have assumed that Betty's income would hold steady, enabling the couple to pay their 1946 taxes and all other expenses using 1947 royalties. But few books, even perennial favorites like *Egg*, sustain their highest sales for very long. Betty's financial situation made it imperative for her to write another hit.

Lippincott and Brandt & Brandt were eager for her to do so. Brandt & Brandt got a slice of every dollar she earned, and *Egg* was a cash cow for Lippincott, continuing to sell long after the firm's advertising dollars were allocated to other projects. About the same time *Mrs. Piggle-Wiggle* launched, both agent and publisher were encouraging Betty to begin a sequel to *Egg*.

If *Egg*'s readers had been asked what topic Betty MacDonald should tackle next, likely no one would have suggested tuberculosis. The fact that Lippincott agreed to a book on this subject is a testament to how impressed her publishers were by *Egg*'s sales.

For Betty, however, the topic was compelling. "My stay in Firland was certainly the most remarkable experience of my lifetime and I wouldn't have missed it for the world," Betty wrote to a fellow former Firland patient. "I was bitter when I entered, unhappy much of the time and longed to get out all the time, but I wouldn't have missed it for anything."[4] Being surrounded by death, and personally menaced by it, at Firland had taught Betty to appreciate her life. She'd made real friends in the sanatorium, and—like military combat veterans who share experiences no others can understand—in a large measure she credited these women with her survival. The journal version of her Firland experiences that Betty had worked on just after her release and had submitted, without success, for Atlantic Monthly Press's Atlantic Prize served as a strong foundation for her second volume of personal narrative, *The Plague and I*. Betty called this early draft *In Bed We Laughed*.[5]

The Plague and I was Betty's favorite among the books she wrote. Her self-portrait here seems to align more closely with the person she truly was during those years than does her self-depiction in *Egg*. *Plague* invites readers to enter into Betty's confrontation with mortality. Betty considered *Plague* a public service. She wanted the book to be a banner cry encouraging everyone, even those with no family history of tuberculosis, to get a diagnostic chest X-ray. "After all," she wrote, "there was no t.b. in my family, never had been, and yet I got it."[6] When she was penniless, Firland's medical director had admitted her to the facility without charge. With *Plague*, Betty repaid that debt.

As a personal gesture to Firland's staff and patients, Betty visited the sanatorium to attend a screening of *The Egg and I* for ambulatory patients. During the visit, Betty and Don dined with several of the doctors who had treated her. She gave an informal talk in the Josef House auditorium, where she recalled having watched Greta Garbo die of tuberculosis in the saddo film classic *Camille*. Betty signed copies of *Egg* for patients and told them that her next book would recount her Firland experiences.

As Betty was working on this book, American physicians began gaining access to newly invented antibiotic drugs, such as streptomycin, para-amino salicylic acid (PAS), and isoniazid, that (when used in combination) proved highly effective in treating tuberculosis. Mortality rates at Firland plummeted from 31 percent in 1948 to 6 percent in 1954. Identifying people who carried the disease—Betty's main reason for writing the book—was paramount because treatment carried more promise than ever before.

Using the same structure Bernice Baumgarten had suggested for *The Egg and I*, Betty began *The Plague and I* with childhood stories, then circled back to her main narrative. *Plague* begins with Betty's memories of Gammy's apocryphal belief that "childhood was a very hazardous time of life and if we children weren't bitten by rattlesnakes, eaten by wild animals, killed by robbers or struck by lightning, catarrh, consumption and leprosy were just around the corner."[7] In finally getting tuberculosis, Betty wrote, she was "achieving the goal Gammy had set for me so early in life."[8]

The Plague and I functions as a sort of exotic travel narrative: Betty leaves home and embarks on the experience of illness, meeting the natives (doctors and nurses) and fellow travelers (patients). As all trips do, the journey changes her. Betty is able to survive the fear and boredom of her ordeal only by turning her Bardish lens on those she encounters, noticing both annoying and endearing qualities. Tuberculosis, she finds, is an equalizer, but having a roommate who makes her laugh and appreciates her humor, instead of one who complains constantly or worse, plays the martyr, makes all the difference.

To differentiate characters who could so easily be seen as anonymous medical specimens, she focuses on the aspects of their behavior that make each person unique and interesting. With the exception of Betty's physicians, virtually all of the characters in the book are female: tuberculosis patients were strictly segregated by gender. At Firland, they were also usually segregated racially as far as was practical. Betty stands out in this environment because she has no problem rooming with women of varying ethnicities. Her favorite roommate is Kimi, a Japanese-American teenager who is hilarious and heroic.

The book is educational. Betty feeds this information about tuberculosis to readers through the device of patient dialogue. Her descriptions of her medical interventions are specific and graphic. She manages to convey the endless tedium of round-the-clock resting without making readers feel that they are enduring tedium themselves. She examines her own reactions to the situations she faces, drawing readers into her personal struggle. When she is discharged, they share her overwhelming awe at being privileged to reclaim ordinary life.

Lippincott stuck with a sure thing for *Plague's* cover: Betty Mac-Donald's smiling face, the photograph readers knew from the cover of *Egg,* this time inset into an oval on the book's lower right corner. The back cover photo featured Betty pruning a rose bush. "I wanted something out-doorsy and healthy looking to prove to my readers, or rather 'reader,' that I had not dictated the book from an oxygen tent," she wrote Mac McKaughan, Lippincott's director of advertising.[9]

Betty let Lippincott staffers know that she liked the roses picture — in which her bangs are cut straight across, bowl-like — better than the cover image. McKaughan shot back, "Lady, you are smart enough to know that the picture used on the wrapper of *The Egg and I* is one of the best-known trade-marks in the United States. You are as famous as the Smith Brothers and I think we would be 'nuts' to use any other illustration on the jacket of *The Plague and I,* or in our first advertising of the new book."[10]

Good Housekeeping published a three-part condensation of *Plague* in August, September, and October 1948. Betty was pleased with the result but told a friend, "As you can probably imagine, it was deleted, sweetened and cleaned up beyond recognition to meet the requirements of the Good Housekeeping advertisers. Son of a bitch has become 'rather unpleasant' and Jesus Christ is now 'dear, dear.'"[11]

Some health professionals were stung by how harshly Betty described her experiences at The Pines, her pseudonym for Firland. Dr. F. B. Trudeau, son of the legendary physician Edward Trudeau — who founded the most famous sanatorium in the nation at Saranac Lake, New York — refused a Lippincott publicity staffer's request to endorse *The Plague and I.* He feared, he explained, that the book's "grim picture of hospital life and the impersonal treatment received might frighten off some patients from going to a sanatorium."[12]

Plague was dark, and it was Betty: "There's one thing to be said in favor of life at The Pines," she reflected about her first night in the sanatorium. "It's going to make dying seem like a lot of fun."[13] Food at The Pines was good, she wrote, but the coffee "tasted as if it had been made out of burnt toast crumbs boiled well with ground-up rubber bands."[14] The patients at The Pines "differed in color, nationality, political beliefs, I.Q., age, religion, background and ambition. According to the standards of normal living, the only things that most of us had in common were being alive and speaking English, but as patients in the sanatorium we had everything in common and were firmly cemented together by our ungratefulness, stupidity, uncooperativeness, unworthiness, poverty, tuberculosis and longing for a discharge."[15] In facing disease, as with anything, being Bard required irreverence.

Jean South, a nurse who reviewed the book for the *American Journal of Nursing,* accepted Betty's tone: "It would hardly be expected that Mrs. MacDonald, who had such a successful response to *The Egg and I,* would change her style and treat this subject differently. Her book is written to sell, and much as we might regret that she did not write of the more positive phases of her experience, her book should be read by nurses with an open mind as to its purpose. While she has no doubt exaggerated the behavior of all about her, she has done so with great skill. . . . Her flippancy is refreshing."[16]

Reviewers from across the country agreed that only Betty MacDonald—who, several pointed out, was no Pollyanna—could have written this book. "You have to hold a hammer to t.b. patients' heads in order to get them to do anything about it," Betty told the *Seattle Times.* "I tried to have up-to-date information in this book and yet keep it bright so that people would read it."[17] The *Saturday Review* found Betty more than bright: "She is that even rarer human being—one who sees the funny side of everything that happens to her; that rare author—one who can make her experiences equally funny in writing."[18]

Plague's promotional campaign kicked off with book-signing parties at Seattle's University Book Store and in three local department stores: Rhodes, Frederick & Nelson, and the Bon Marché, which all had large book departments. Betty then undertook another cross-country promotional trip. In New York, she helped open the 1948 Christmas seals campaign for the National Tuberculosis Association and was photographed selling the New York chapter's first sheet of Christmas seals to Mayor William O'Dwyer.

Betty received a daunting—and humbling—amount of mail from patients in tuberculosis sanatoria around the world. These readers were grateful for and moved by *The Plague and I*. They saw Betty as a friend who understood their desperate quiet lives—and they had plenty of time to write. Institutional life had caused some of them to lose track of time: one letter was dated "I'm sure it's January." Their letters were detailed and extremely personal. Luckily for her, she had a new assistant who could practically read her mind: Gwen Smith Croxford, one of Betty's Firland roommates.[19] Gwen appeared in *The Plague and I* as Kate Harte. "[Gwen and I] had a wonderful time doing *The Plague and I* and deciding what we could put in and what we couldn't," Betty wrote to Norah Flannery, another Firland friend. "Miss Hermanson and Miss Rountree [Firland nurses] are both dead but even so my dopey publishers removed all of the sharp edges from my characterizations of them."[20] Gwen ghostwrote answers to many of the tuberculosis letters. "Write one of your best and most charming letters to this man," Betty scrawled across the top of a letter she received from a tuberculosis patient in Calcutta.

Not all of the fan mail from "lung-ers" was grim. Eleven tuberculosis patients who had contracted the disease while serving in World War II wrote from the men's ward at Stony Wold Sanatorium at Saranac Lake, New York, offering to swap stories with her. "You can come up and expectorate in our sputum cups anytime," they concluded enthusiastically. "Dear Boys," Betty replied, "If all of you kids behave and do just as you are told, no doubt you'll get big and fat and rich like me."[21]

Betty was at the pinnacle of her success when *Plague* was published, a household name around the country. As *Egg* began appearing in foreign editions, her international fame grew. In Seattle, she was homegrown royalty. The city was small enough that nearly everyone could boast of knowing her, or at least knowing someone who did.

After *The Plague and I*, Betty grew frustrated with the way Lippincott promoted her books. She may not have understood that Lippincott's *Egg* publicity expenditures were extraordinary because of that book's phenomenal early sales numbers and its unflagging performance. They never spent as much to advertise any of Betty's other books, in part because none of them, including *Plague*, caught fire before their public release the way *Egg* did. Lippincott waited fifteen years after *Egg* for its next huge best seller, Harper Lee's *To Kill a Mockingbird*.

Of all the fellow patients described in *Plague*, none resonated with readers more than Betty's teenaged Japanese American roommate, Kimi—modeled on Kazuko Monica Itoi (Kazi). Many fans wrote to ask Betty what had happened to Kimi after she left Firland, and even publishers were curious to know more. During World War II, Kazi and her family were interned at Minidoka War Relocation Camp in Hunt, Idaho, as a result of Executive Order 9066. Issued by President Franklin D. Roosevelt on February 19, 1942, the order set in motion the expulsion of Japanese immigrants (issei) and their American citizen children (nisei) from the West Coast and their internment in ten inland prison camps, solely on the basis of their ethnicity and heritage.

Kazi and Betty corresponded during Kazi's imprisonment in Minidoka and afterward, when Kazi was among the young nisei able to secure early release by showing evidence of a job offer or college acceptance outside the restricted West Coast area. Kazi (who also went by her middle name, Monica) found work in Chicago, went on to college, and then earned a master's degree in clinical psychology. She married Geary Tsuyuki, a nisei veteran from California, in 1947. The following year, the couple legally changed their last name to his mother's maiden name, Sone. They were expecting their first child, whom Geary refused to subject to a lifetime of hearing the name Tsuyuki mangled by Midwesterners.

Betty was able to interest Dudley Cloud of the Atlantic Monthly Press (an imprint of Little, Brown and Company) in reading the letters Kazi had sent her from Minidoka. "I raved about you so much while I was in the East and described you so exquisitely in The Plague and I that now all the publishers want you to write a book," Betty wrote Kazi. "I think you should write about the internment of the Japanese on this Coast, telling just how horrible it was but making it funny. . . . If I could be funny about tuberculosis, you could be killing about internment, now that it's over."[22]

Monica Sone sent Cloud a book outline in the summer of 1949. Cloud worked with Monica to shape a narrative drawn from her experiences growing up in prewar Seattle and during her internment. He sent Betty occasional reports on Monica's progress, telling her that Monica was following his advice to address a friendly, interested person as her reader, and that Monica was picturing Betty. Little, Brown published *Nisei Daughter* under the Atlantic Monthly imprint in 1953.

Monica's Firland experiences take up only a few pages of the book, but Betty is portrayed as Chris, one of her sanatorium roommates: "I was determined to be unobtrusive, not to intrude upon Chris's sense of privacy beyond routine conversation, but it was like trying to ignore a roomful of fireworks. I could not remain untouched by her brilliant humor and her irresistible zest for living. I felt as if I were being lured into bright sunlight, inch by inch, from the pit of self-pity into which I had sunk."[23]

Betty took steps to boost Monica's book: "I took the liberty of calling all the bookstores and the newspapers in Seattle—not one had received a review copy of course, but all were immensely interested—both papers promised to do a feature story on Monica," Betty wrote to Bernice Baumgarten, who had taken on Monica as a client.[24]

Betty endorsed *Nisei Daughter* on the book's back cover, beneath Monica Sone's photograph: "The internment of the American-born Japanese during the last war is handled with honesty and rare dispassion. It is certainly to Monica Sone's credit that she still sings 'God Bless America.'"[25] Critics hailed the book as an important addition to literature about Japanese Americans and discrimination.

Monica was not the only one who owed Betty a debt of thanks for publication. When, in *Egg*'s immediate wake, Lippincott determined that Betty was a gold mine, they were eager to uncover other Bard family writers. Sydney was not interested in writing a cookbook, Dede and Alison were busy with their own lives, and no one asked Cleve. But there was Mary.

"My success is killing Mary," Betty told Blanche Hamilton. Accustomed as Mary was to dominating and directing her sister, finding herself on the sideline as Betty soared bedeviled Mary. Perhaps in competition, or simply because she had her own story to tell, but certainly using the opportunity Betty's success provided, Mary made her literary debut in 1949. For the press, publication of *The Doctor Wears Three Faces* transformed Betty and Mary into the "writing Bard sisters." "To my sister Betty, who egged me on," read the book's dedication.

Mary's decision to write her own books may have been stimulated by the realization that Bernice Baumgarten, not Mary, now prodded Betty's literary production. It wasn't that Mary stopped giving Betty suggestions: she was a font of them, including writing schedules, ideas for places where Betty could write undisturbed, prescriptions for handling dry spells, solutions to problems concerning Anne and Joan, critiques of Don's character. She was, after all, still Mary. But Betty and Baumgarten had developed an excellent working relationship. Betty trusted and respected her agent and wanted to please her. Once Betty was authing, it was Baumgarten's guidance about her literary efforts that Betty followed, not Mary's.

Betty's published work was forged and polished by her warmly collaborative relationship with Baumgarten. Baumgarten was an editing agent (meaning that she edited her authors' manuscripts before sending them on to publishing houses), and she was considered by many to be the best literary agent in New York. She and Betty must have met in person only a handful of times—Baumgarten did not come west, and Betty was not in New York often—but author and agent were close. During some periods of Betty's career, they corresponded almost daily, their letters augmented by occasional long-distance phone calls. Betty mailed drafts of chapters to Baumgarten and reworked, added, or omitted material according to Baumgarten's suggestions. Only when Betty's manuscripts were up to Baumgarten's standard did Baumgarten submit them to Lippincott.[26]

Lippincott benefited greatly from Bernice Baumgarten's ministrations, but some people at the firm felt threatened. "Just how do you feel about Bernice?" Betty reported Joseph Lippincott having asked her. "'I think she's perfect. Why?' He said, 'Do you think it wise to always do exactly as she says?' and I said, 'It has certainly worked out so far.'"[27] "Joe's tactics amuse me very much," Baumgarten replied. "They can only mean that Lippincott live in terror that they will lose you."[28]

Betty's facility as a writer sprang partially from her skill as a correspondent. The Bards set the letter-writing bar high. "In our family when you write a dull letter everyone says, 'What's the matter with you, you poor thing? Have you lost your wits?' Next time you work harder and make it amusing. And not by faking. They'd despise you for that. You have to give them the details that make a situation funny or interesting. In this family you've got to talk and write fairly sharply or admit you're a dope," Betty told an interviewer.[29]

The mail system brought fans from around the world into Betty's rural Vashon Island mailbox. Many letters to Betty begin, "Dear Mrs. MacDonald, This is my first attempt at writing to an author," or, "Dear Betty MacDonald, May I call you Betty?" Betty felt familiar to her readers, like a friend. Throughout her career, Betty (or her proxy) responded to every letter. In response to a fan who asked about her writing process, Betty revealed that she tried to work from eight in the morning until five in the afternoon. Sometimes this was productive, she added wryly, and sometimes she passed the hours staring at her typewriter and drinking coffee.[30] She praised the practice of outlining a book before beginning to write and preached reading as the only shortcut for aspiring writers.

The volume of her mail forced Betty to give up on making each response unique. She hired secretaries she trusted and provided them with sample responses that could be lightly personalized. Delayed responses, for example, used the "Dear Fandelay" template, thanking the correspondent for writing and explaining that "life here is very hectic." Fans who sent praise and appreciation for her books received the "Dear Mrs. Fanilike": "One of the nicest things about my success has been the letters I have received from people like you who have been kind enough to take the time to tell me that you enjoyed my writing." "Dear Mrs. Comeandspeak" got a polite brush-off: Betty was too busy writing to accept engagements. *Mrs. Piggle-Wiggle* fans got the "Dear Little Buckaroo" letter, including the praise "You print (write) so well I could hardly believe you are only ___ years old." Children were thanked for their "darling letter," and for them, Betty closed her letters with "Love."[31]

Hundreds of the letters Betty received were from aspiring authors looking for the magic formula to literary success. Betty joked that she should answer these with the advice, "First have a big mortgage, then lots of coffee."[32] Instead, Betty's standard "Dear Mrs. Helpmepublishmybooks" response advised them to seek out the creative writing department at their local university and to work with a literary agent.

In addition, scores of people wanted to collaborate with her. Many sent her their manuscripts or asked permission to do so. Brandt & Brandt forbade her from collaborating and discouraged her from reading the manuscripts, because doing so might expose her to charges of plagiarism if she later wrote anything remotely like one of the suggested projects. Betty sent standard form responses politely turning down projects such as "Leukemia and I," outlined by a man in Tulsa who told Betty that if she could use his idea to fabricate a story, he'd split the money with her and spend his on pills; a query from a man in Springfield, Massachusetts, who wanted to write about tuberculosis but couldn't type and hoped he could visit Betty and get her help with that part; a retired pilot who wanted to tell her his life story and have her turn it into "That Bird and I"; and an Idaho woman who wanted Betty to rewrite her book, "From Sheep Camps to Hollywood and Back," so that it was funny. A woman in Long Beach, California, wrote to Betty for manuscript help because, she explained, her spiritual guides Moonlight and William Penn had directed her to do so.

Many people felt they had great experiences to recount but needed Betty's help adding wit, humor, and pathos. Some suggested that if she didn't want to collaborate with them, maybe she would buy their ideas outright. Many mentioned how easy it was to write to her because her warm, smiling book-jacket portraits put them at ease. Betty filed these letters under the heading "People Who Want Something."

All these people were drawn to Betty because she made her own foibles so central to the stories she told. Betty the character is vulnerable but sassy. Nothing ever goes too well for her, but whether the stakes are low or high, she fights on, buoyed by her family. Life never takes the Bards all the way down. And, most important, the writer who uses the first person gives herself to the reader. Betty gave herself to her readers—or at least a version of herself.

There was quicksilver magic in Betty's take on life that helped readers recast their own troubles and showed them a way of looking at life that drained some of the venom from adversity. Many of Betty's fan letters expressed deep gratitude. One reader wrote to Betty describing her own difficulties: a wayward daughter, an invalid husband, and the fact that she had to draw all the household water from a distant well and carry it up a hill to reach her home. She had been nearly despondent, the reader explained, but "then I read your book. I don't know. I just felt better. As if I'd had a bath, and the hell with carrying the water."[33] In her books, Betty's readers—strangers—divined a peerless recipe for rising above troubles, and sought this comfort through repeated rereadings. To them, Betty was an irreverent, illimitable guide. To people who actually knew Betty MacDonald, however, she absolutely had limits. And when those who knew Betty personally judged that she had violated society's accepted boundaries, had overstepped, Betty and everyone associated with her books discovered that there could be hell to pay.

CHAPTER NINE

The Name's Kettle

O N Betty's first trip to Hollywood, the radio personality George Fisher asked her on the air if she'd ever been back to Chimacum. No, she replied, and with luck she never would. Would her former neighbors be angry, Fisher probed? It wouldn't make any difference to them, Betty replied, because the characters in the book are largely composites. Only Pa Kettle would be immediately recognizable, and he wouldn't care.[1]

Betty was wrong. On March 25, 1947, her former Chimacum neighbors, Edward and Ilah Bishop, filed a lawsuit against Betty and Don, asking for one hundred thousand dollars in damages.[2] They alleged that they were the couple referred to as Mr. and Mrs. Hicks in *The Egg and I*; that the book was libelous and an invasion of their right to privacy; and that they had been exposed to ridicule, hatred, and contempt because of their alleged portrayal.[3]

The Bishops' suit validated the fears Lippincott's lawyers had expressed when the book was still in manuscript. At that stage Betty had given the characters she ultimately called the Kettles the name of Basket. Betty blithely told Lippincott that if basing a character on some characteristics of an actual person constituted libel, all of her characters were libelous. She ticked off characters one by one: the real Mrs. Basket was named Bishop, was deceased, and had been profane but also kind to her. Mr. Bishop lisped and borrowed from people. Maxwell Ford Jefferson was a man who'd made whiskey with Bob, but she'd made up that last name. Crowbar, Clamface, and Geoduck were Bob's good friends Skids, Pume, and Wesel, who were Indians. The

Indian picnic was an actual occurrence but had been more obscene. Since her name had been Heskett then, she concluded, the easiest way to dodge libel accusations would be to give *The Egg and I*'s author's name as B. B. MacDonald.[4]

Betty had been willing to make whatever changes Lippincott suggested, however. "I wanted to show how magnificent the country is in comparison [with] the unsavoriness of its inhabitants," she wrote to Bernice Baumgarten at the time.

> Now I wonder if perhaps my youth, inexperience, loneliness and upbringing didn't make me think the people were worse than they were—perhaps if I were able to move out there now I would be as discouraged, as lonely and as cold but would find the people less horrifying, more amusing. Perhaps the book would have a better flavor if I were to forget the truth and make the people less like the ignorant, immoral, amoral, unmoral, foul mouthed group they were, and more folksy and quaint. If depicting the people as they were is libelous, then by all means let's show them as they weren't.[5]

Lippincott made alterations, which Betty deemed "reasonable tho stuffy."[6] The only change she refused was "jackasses" to "folks." Asked to rename the Baskets, a name that Lippincott felt was too close to Bishop, Betty suggested the name Kettle.

When the *Atlantic Monthly* ran parts of *The Egg and I* as a serial before the book's release, they dealt with the libel issue by obscuring all of the place names, a move Lippincott followed right before the book went to print. Port Townsend became Town, Port Ludlow was Docktown, the Olympic Peninsula became the Pacific Coast or simply "the mountains," and Hood Canal became Canal. Betty responded to this cleansing of her manuscript with her usual acerbic wit: "I am sure that there is now no danger of libel from any source—our only risk now would be that someone might sue me personally for writing such a damn dull book."[7]

If Betty thought none of her former neighbors would read her book, she was mistaken. Residents of the Olympic Peninsula could purchase

Egg in at least three locations, to which—by the time Edward and Ilah Bishop filed suit—Lippincott had shipped more than eight hundred copies.[8]

Edward and Ilah Bishop and their son Bud had been the Hesketts' nearest neighbors. Edward worked as a logger and longshoreman until a work accident in 1930 in which he broke his back, necessitating multiple surgeries. Thereafter he and Ilah raised chickens, butchering and selling about thirty thousand each year. Ilah Bishop delivered birds and eggs to inns and resorts throughout the Olympic and Kitsap Peninsulas.

In the book, Betty and Bob's nearest neighbors are the Hickses and the Kettles. Edward and Ilah Bishop's suit alleged that they had been portrayed as Mr. and Mrs. Hicks, whom the book introduces as follows: "Mr. Hicks, a large ruddy dullard, walked gingerly through life, being very careful not to get dirt on anything or in any way to irritate Mrs. Hicks, whom he regarded as a cross between Mary Magdalene and the County Agent."[9] Edward and Ilah Bishop's complaint included every section of the book in which the Hickses were mentioned.

Had Betty felt as contemptuous of her neighbors when she lived in Chimacum? Her bitterness toward Bob had stewed, along with her other memories of that place, for fifteen years, during which she'd trotted out stories of Bob and her former neighbors for friends to laugh at. Whatever she had observed of these people's humanity had been stripped away by the time Betty wrote the book, leaving just caricature.

Betty sought the advice of her attorney, George Guttormsen. He was a former University of Washington football hero, a family friend who had been one of Clyde Jensen's groomsmen. "George is a very smart lawyer, an honest man and I've known him since I was fourteen but he has many even white teeth and he clenches them a lot and he has no sense of humor," Betty wrote Bernice Baumgarten.[10]

Through Guttormsen, Betty demurred the Bishops' charges on several grounds, including their legal capacity to sue, court jurisdiction, and the statute of limitations, but a King County Superior Court judge ordered the case to trial. "A publication will be held to be libelous if it tends to render a person odious, ridiculous, or contemptible in the estimation of the public," the judge's memorandum concluded, pretty well summing up every character in *The Egg and I* who was not directly related to Betty.[11]

Betty believed that a film company staffer had upset the Bishops when he was scouting filming locations in Jefferson County, a trip Betty had urged him not to take. The studio had asked Betty to accompany Chester Erskine, the director, and a small film crew to the area where her story took place. Betty wired back: "Think trip to Peninsula and attendant publicity very bad idea and likely to stir up trouble. I have never set foot on Peninsula since I left and do not intend to. . . . Am very serious in warning you not to arouse Peninsula people. Results not worth it."[12]

In May 1949, while Betty was working on her third autobiographical book, *Anybody Can Do Anything,* Edward and Ilah Bishop's case was moving toward a jury trial after two years of legal maneuvering. Just as the trial was about to start, the two sets of attorneys jointly filed a stipulation for dismissal, which was granted. They settled the case for $1,500. According to a copy of Edward and Ilah Bishop's signed release in MacDonald family archives, the settlement also stipulated that Edward and Ilah "forever refrain from mentioning or discussing" their claim.

Betty must have sighed with relief. But three months later, out from Chimacum trooped the patriarch Albert Bishop and ten others, looking for justice. On September 17, 1949, Albert Bishop and six of his sons, two daughters, and one daughter-in-law filed individual libel suits alleging their depiction as members of the Kettle family in *The Egg and I.*[13] Another Chimacum resident, Raymond Johnson, alleged his depiction as Crowbar, a Native American. All claimed that their depictions subjected them to shame and humiliation. Betty, Don, Lippincott, Pocket Books (which had issued a twenty-five-cent paperback edition of *Egg*), and the Bon Marché department store were named as codefendants in the suit. The suits were consolidated and tried together.[14]

As Betty's fan mail bore out, the Kettle characters had helped her book appeal to a tremendously wide audience, and Marjorie Main's and Percy Kilbride's well-crafted personifications did the same for the film and its sequels. The Kettles fall within the tradition of buffoon characters in Shakespeare or commedia dell'arte, roles designed to appeal to the groundlings, the masses. None of Betty's other books has such outrageous—or universal—characters. Kilbride and Main were now reprising their vivid interpretations of the slapdash couple in the wildly popular Ma and Pa Kettle film series. The Kettles were always good for a laugh, and their public popularity endured.

But who would want to be one? Betty described her 1920s neighbors using details that made them instantly recognizable to anyone who knew them. To most of Betty's readers, Chimacum residents were familiar comic types. To the neighbors, Betty's book was evidence of unconscionable hubris. She had believed that she could say whatever she wanted to about them and tell the world that her stories were true.

Albert Bishop was born on his Swiss immigrant father's farm in Provo, Utah. The family were converts to Mormonism, although Albert's father later recanted his faith and moved his family to Portland, Oregon, and then to Port Townsend. In 1891, Albert married Susanna Ammeter, who had been born in Switzerland and had immigrated to Jefferson County with her family. Albert and Susanna moved to Portland, where Albert worked in railroading and where Edward, the first of their thirteen children, was born. In 1895, the family moved to Port Townsend and then to Chimacum, where they lived on the Percy Wright property later mixed up in Sydney Bard's real-estate debacle. The Bishops eventually purchased a 160-acre farm and a fourteen-room farmhouse down the road from the Heskett property.[15]

"Here is how Betty collects without scratching a pen to paper," a front-page article in the *Seattle Times* reported. "Every time Universal-International puts Marjorie Main and Percy Kilbride into another rollicking 'Ma and Pa Kettle' adventure, a check wings its way to the writer. That's because she originated that fabulous couple with the 18 children. Two sequels to the original 'The Egg and I' have been made and with exhibitors reporting that they're one of the hottest bets at the box office today, it would appear Miss MacDonald is going to collect for a long time."[16] To those who felt caricatured and ridiculed by the book, Betty's windfall from the films must have rankled.

Marjorie Main's and Percy Kilbride's skillful use of physical comedy dovetailed with Betty's descriptions in *Egg*:

> Mrs. Kettle had pretty light brown hair, only faintly streaked with gray and skinned back into a tight knot, clear blue eyes, a creamy skin which flushed exquisitely with the heat, a straight delicate nose, fine even white teeth, and a small rounded chin. From this dainty pretty head cascaded a series of busts and stomachs which made her look like a cooky jar shaped like a woman. Her whole front was dirty and spotted and she wiped her hands continually on one or the other of her stomachs. She also had a disconcerting habit of reaching up under her dress and adjusting something in the vicinity of her navel and of reaching down the front of her dress and adjusting her large breasts. These adjustments were not, I learned later, confined to either the privacy of the house or a female gathering—they were made anywhere—any time. "I itch—so I scratch—so what!" was Mrs. Kettle's motto.[17]

Betty's description of Pa Kettle was just as vivid:

> He had a thick thatch of stiff gray hair quite obviously cut at home with a bowl, perched on top of which he wore a black derby hat. His eyebrows grew together over his large red nose and spurted out threateningly over his deepset bright blue eyes. He had a tremendous flowing mustache generously dotted with crumbs, a neckline featuring several layers of dirty underwear and sweaters, and bib overalls tucked into the black rubber hip boots. Drawing deeply on the cigar butt Mr. Kettle said, "Nithe little plathe you got here. Putty far up in the woodth though. Latht feller to live here went crazy and they put him away."[18]

Albert and Susanna's grandson Bud offered this physical description of his grandparents in a 1993 oral history interview: "My grandmother wasn't overly tall, but she was quite heavy. And my granddad was a little man. He was probably five-foot-seven, probably weighed about a hundred and forty or fifty pounds."[19] Bud Bishop told the interviewer that the strongest values his grandparents had taught him were to be honest and to treat other people as he would like to be treated. Family members remembered Susanna Bishop as an industrious and deeply religious woman of very clean habits. Susanna Bishop died in 1937, about a year and a half after the drowning death of her youngest child, Kenneth, an event from which her family felt she never recovered.

Almost from the moment *Egg* was published, carloads of tourists began arriving in Jefferson County via the Port Ludlow ferry. "Where is the farm Betty MacDonald wrote about in *The Egg and I?*" the tourists asked. The property was now owned by Anita and Alfred Larson, relatives of the Bishops by marriage, who used Betty and Bob's dwelling for a chicken house. Locals pointed the way to the Larson home, where Anita accommodated visitors' requests to see the house, the barn, the stove—anything Betty MacDonald had mentioned in the book. The Larson family posted a sign near the ferry dock pointing the way to the farm, and the Larson children showed tourists around. Anita Larson charged these curious fans a dollar a carload, a welcome windfall for the family, and kept a guest book that visitors could sign. This volume eventually documented signatures from residents of more than sixty countries.[20]

The Bishop family had claimed affinity with the Kettles since the book had first come out. Anita Larson's tours of the Heskett farm were covered in the *Pt. Townsend Leader*, as was the fact that the Bishops referred to the former Albert and Susanna Bishop home (by the time of the trial, occupied by their son Arthur) as the Kettle home.[21] But at some point, their excitement at being part of the *Egg* juggernaut turned to resentment.

Almost a year before the case came to trial, someone—most likely Guttormsen—met with Betty to discuss it.[22] According to the notes taken at this meeting, Betty—grasping at straws—acknowledged that there was a family on Vashon who were very like the Kettles, and that the father in that family was as close to being Pa Kettle as Albert Bishop was. She supposed, she said, that perhaps 90 percent of what she wrote about Pa Kettle stemmed from information she'd heard about Albert Bishop, whom she remembered as a principal topic of conversation on the Olympic Peninsula. It was true, she conceded, that Albert Bishop had a lisp and the same vocal tic (his voice rose at the end of his sentences) with which she'd endowed Pa Kettle.

Her description of the route Betty and Bob took to get from Seattle to their farm in *Egg*, she said, actually led to a community near Mount Walker in the heart of the Olympic Mountains.[23] She had deliberately avoided describing the route to Chimacum so that the people who lived in the Chimacum Valley would not think she was writing about them.

Betty told Guttormsen that Ed Bishop had turned Bob in to federal agents for making moonshine. When the agents searched Betty and Bob's property, she said, they found nothing because Bob—on the advice of another moonshiner—had built the still in the front yard, hidden in plain sight. Asked if she'd ever admitted that Albert Bishop was Pa Kettle, Betty said she'd been asked that question one billion times at least and had never admitted to anyone that a living person was being characterized, directly contradicting the earliest information on this point she'd given Lippincott. People she knew, she added, naturally crept into her writing.

The trial began on February 5, 1951. Albert Bishop, age eighty-seven, was too ill to appear in court. George Crandell and Frank Trunk represented the plaintiffs. Each Bishop asked for damages of one hundred thousand dollars. (Husband and wife Herbert and Janet Bishop asked for one hundred thousand dollars jointly.) Johnson sought seventy-five thousand. The case was tried in front of a civil jury in King County Superior Court, with Judge William Wilkins presiding. George Guttormsen again represented Betty.[24] J. Paul Coie represented Lippincott. Bon Marché, Inc., was dismissed as a defendant.[25] Pocket Books apparently was never served with legal papers and was not represented in court.

Newspaper accounts of the two-week trial mention that Judge Wilkins had a copy of *The Egg and I* in court so that he could follow passages during questioning, and that many spectators brought copies, With defendant Betty's smile plastered across the dust jackets, the scene in the courtroom recalled Lippincott's full-page advertisements depicting people in all walks of life unable to put the book down.

The question of whether *Egg* presented a libelous portrayal of the Bishops, an actual Jefferson County family, or merely offered a fictional account of a family of characters created by Betty MacDonald and nestled within an otherwise largely nonfictional autobiography seemed to rest on whether incidents that happened to the Kettles in the book had also happened to the Bishops in real life. Members of the Bishop family were questioned repeatedly along these lines.

The *Seattle Times* reported, "Under questioning by his own attorney, George H. Crandell, (Wilbur) Bishop . . . said the 'home place' of the Albert Bishop family between Chimacum and Port Ludlow, Jefferson County, was about a mile from the place where Mrs. MacDonald lived about 20 years ago. Crandell read a passage from the book describing an incident in which Pa Kettle set out to burn some trash in the backyard and burned down the barn. Crandell asked Bishop if his father, Albert Bishop, had done this. Bishop said he had."[26]

The courtroom was filled to capacity with witnesses and a curious public. Many more people waited in the corridor outside, hoping for a vacancy.[27] Seattle newspapers were giving the story copious daily coverage, and local residents wanted to see the circus.

Raymond Johnson, whom the *Seattle Post-Intelligencer* described as "a quarter-blood Indian," testified that he recognized himself as the character called Crowbar, and that the characters named Clamface and Geoduck were real people who went by the same names.[28] Johnson testified that he had gone on several cougar hunts with Robert Heskett, as Bob and Crowbar are described as doing in *The Egg and I*.

A number of other Jefferson County residents testified that the Kettle family was clearly recognizable as the Bishop clan. Annie McGuire, the seventy-five-year-old widow of a former Jefferson County sheriff, testified that on reading the book she not only immediately recognized the Kettles as the Bishops but thought she saw herself in the character of Mary McGregor, who worked her farm in such an inebriated state that she had to be tied to the plow. The *Seattle Post-Intelligencer* quoted McGuire's stated feelings about Betty MacDonald on reading *The Egg and I*: "If I could have got her at the time I'd have beat her up."[29]

Several male plaintiffs testified to being asked frequently if they were Kettle boys. One, Herbert Bishop, said he was ashamed of it. "They knew I was a Bishop—I had to be a Kettle."[30] But how ashamed? According to the *Seattle Times*, "Francis Risher, Port Orchard, said Walter Bishop approached him in July or August of 1949 to go in on the building of a dance hall at Port Townsend and a tour of 'the Kettles.' 'He said, Frank, there's a million bucks in it,' Risher testified."

The defense strategy seemed to be that if the Bishops had in the past acted proud of their resemblance to the Kettles, they could not now legitimately claim libel. The *Seattle Post-Intelligencer* reported the same day that the defense witness Dorothy Baird testified that at a 1947 barn dance, in front of five hundred people, the plaintiff Walter Bishop had introduced his father, Albert Bishop, as Pa Kettle. "'What if anything did he (Albert Bishop) have with him?' [defense attorney] Guttormsen inquired. 'A chicken,' Mrs. Baird answered. 'And what did he do with the chicken?' 'He jiggled it from one arm to another and sort of jumped up and down,' Mrs. Baird replied."[31]

Betty was in court every day, her lips set in a tight line. Newspaper photographs showed Don, his jaw clenched, by her side. Old friends offered Betty emotional aid. Blanche Hamilton, who was teaching school in Portland, Oregon, and following news of the suit in the Portland papers, wrote to Betty offering herself as a character witness: "I know the trial is in progress and am wondering if I could be of any help to you. I've known you a long time; enough to know you love people who do not fit into a set pattern and who are not seeking higher social strata. The very fact that they are unusual and uninhibited endears them to you. A little brown wren of a teacher from Portland might add the somber sober touch just needed."[32]

Testifying in her own defense, Betty told the court that she was not writing about the Albert Bishop farm when she described the Kettles' home; that she had not kept a diary, letters, or records of her years on the Olympic Peninsula; and that she hadn't visited the area for twenty years. She told the court that the only living people depicted in her book were herself and members of her family, and that her intention in writing the book was to make fun of her own incompetence as a farm wife. She said she had not known the Bishops well and had never seen some of the plaintiffs until they appeared in court.

When Guttormsen asked her to state whether she'd described the Albert Bishop family as the Kettles, Betty replied, "I did not." Asked if she'd been aware that there were real people named Crowbar, Geoduck, and Clamface when she assigned those names to characters in her book, Betty testified that she had not. The *Seattle Times* reported, "Mrs. MacDonald testified that she had lived on a farm with her mother near the Albert Bishop farm for more than a year before she married Robert Heskett and moved to the farm adjoining the Bishop place . . . under stiff cross-examination . . . Mrs. MacDonald broke into tears and fled the courtroom."[33]

Betty, calmer, took the stand again the following morning. She didn't remember her first meeting with Albert Bishop and did not have "the faintest recollection" of what he looked like. Under examination by the Bishops' attorney, Betty admitted that before her marriage to Bob, she had attended a dance with Walter Bishop.[34]

Port Ludlow, she continued, was not Docktown, Chimacum was not Crossroads, and Port Townsend was not Town. "In all my descriptions of towns I tried to picture a typical town," she testified, emphasizing that she'd done considerable research for the book at the Seattle Public Library. "I was writing about an imaginary place in an imaginary country."[35]

George Guttormsen's paramount act was a maneuver to block evidence of Betty's earlier settlement agreement with Edward and Ilah Bishop from being presented to the jury. "The prejudicial effect of allowing evidence of a compromise of a similar type of case to come in this case is obvious," Guttormsen argued in a memorandum.[36] In his closing arguments, Guttormsen mentioned the highway signs Anita Larson had posted on Swansonville Road to direct visitors to the farm, where Larson charged money to view the home, and the fact that Larson was a sister-in-law of one of the Bishop family. He told the courtroom, "There could not possibly have been a connection between the book and the Bishops if these people had not deliberately come out and made that connection themselves. . . . Is that Betty MacDonald's fault?"[37]

Judge Wilkins instructed the jury that a plaintiff could not recover damages solely on account of humiliation, chagrin, or mental suffering resulting from the alleged libelous statements themselves: to be libelous, statements needed to be published. "I have heretofore instructed you that the libelous statements were to be deemed published only to readers who understood the defamatory meaning thereof and understood them as being applicable to the plaintiff," Wilkins stated. In other words, libelous statements were only deemed published to readers who knew the plaintiffs personally and so could explicitly connect the Kettles to the Bishops. To the vast majority of worldwide readers, a Kettle was only a Kettle.[38]

The mere existence of *The Egg and I*, Wilkins went on, did not entitle plaintiffs to collect damages. The laws of Washington allowed neither punitive nor exemplary damages. Furthermore, damages, if any, had to have been sustained by the mental suffering or damaged reputation of the plaintiff himself, not a member of his family. In the eyes of the law, no family member could be compensated for empathic suffering.

"A great deal of evidence has been admitted solely for the purpose of permitting a plaintiff to establish his identification as one of the characters in the book. . . . [Y]ou are instructed to completely disregard such evidence in your deliberations concerning the amount, if any of damages which such plaintiff is entitled to recover," Wilkins stated. This covered nearly all of the testimony the jurors had heard during the trial. Further, any plaintiff who had in the past acknowledged or inferred that he or she was a character, or tried to profit from the possible Bishop/Kettle connection, was out of luck when it came to recovering damages. That knocked out anyone who had expressed the desire to take the Kettles on the road as paid entertainment.

In a spectacular gaffe by the plaintiffs' lawyers, the book that was entered into evidence was the Pocket Books edition of *The Egg and I*, not the hardcover Lippincott best seller or the Book of the Month Club best seller. Jurors were therefore instructed that damages, if any, could result only from the publication and sales of the Pocket Books edition. The potential golden egg shrank from ostrich- to quail-sized with this directive.[39]

Judge Wilkins also instructed the members of the jury to consider the book in its entirety. The jury accordingly read the entire book aloud as part of their deliberations. This took them twenty-four hours. They then took a vote, which was unanimously for the defendants. Betty, Don, and Lippincott were free and clear.

The *Seattle Post-Intelligencer* ran a banner headline: "BETTY MAC-DONALD WINS 'EGG' LIBEL SUIT." Betty was not in court to hear the verdict, but Don was present and thanked the jury. Betty told the *Seattle Post-Intelligencer* that she had spent the anxious day drinking cup after cup of coffee and "going crazy." She continued, "If the decision had been adverse, it might be possible for anyone to squeeze themselves into any book. . . . I have had letters from people from all over the world—from England to Bavaria—telling me that the Kettles lived next door to them. I even had a letter from a woman who said Mrs. Kettle was her mother-in-law. She lived in Florida."[40]

In his 1981 autobiography, Judge Wilkins wrote, "Betty, an attractive auburn-haired woman, was a very convincing witness. Throughout the two-weeks' trial the courtroom was crowded with people who were reading the book, following the exploits of the Kettles, and seeking Betty's autograph. It was really quite an ordeal for her."[41]

In the giddy, caffeine-fueled aftermath of the jury's decision, Betty told the *Seattle Post-Intelligencer* that she wished she'd been asked to testify as to why she wrote a book about the Olympic Peninsula. "It wasn't because I lived there. It was because it was the last untamed frontier." But, she added, if Lippincott had wanted a book about Alaska, "I'd have written about Alaska with nothing but Eskimos for characters."[42] Given that she'd never set foot in Alaska, that book would presumably have been marketed as fiction.

Betty wrote letters to every juror, thanking them from the bottom of her heart for returning the favorable verdict. "I certainly felt for you during those two weeks when you had to sit there on those very hard seats and hear those same bits of The Egg and I read over and over. Let's hope if I am ever sued again it will at least be on a different book."[43]

In reality, however, who else could Betty's Kettles be but the Bishops? Herself a Bard to the core, Betty had crafted an exaggerated version of her neighbors, not from a neutral perspective but from a merciless seat of judgment. Because she was a Bard telling a story, bending the truth was perfectly fine. And then, caught in the truth in court, Betty had lied. More than one relative of Betty's laughed at questions that tried to parse the distinction between fiction and nonfiction. "Nobody in this family ever let the truth get in the way of a good story!" they explained.

After enjoying years of public approval and increasing personal fame, having her book and its motives dissected in court and in the press was difficult for Betty. She felt a shift—real or imagined—in how Seattleites perceived her. But Betty's reading public didn't care. For those millions, liking the story she'd told was the same as liking Betty.

On March 16, 1951, Judge Wilkins issued an order denying the Albert Bishop case plaintiffs' motion for a new trial. For Betty, the Bishop lawsuit ended in victory. Unexpectedly, the Bishop family also saw it that way.

Bud Bishop's widow, Aldena Bishop, never knew Betty. When she first read The Egg and I, she thought it was funny and never guessed that Betty was describing her in-laws. She'd heard an earful from them when she praised the book. Aldena told the same story that Bud recounted in his oral history: no one did more for Betty and her family than Ed, Ilah, Albert, and Susanna Bishop. And the lawsuits—both lawsuits—were victories for them because Betty admitted she'd made up the mean things she said. Aldena also wondered why Betty made Mr. and Mrs. Hicks—whom she clearly identified as her mother- and father-in-law, Ed and Ilah—childless, when Ed and Ilah had one son, her Bud.[44]

"She got in trouble over it to start with," Bud Bishop said in his oral history, "because, see, her first edition was non-fiction. Well, then her second edition came out, and she stated it was fiction. So, she got in trouble over the first edition."

What was the difference between the first and second edition? the interviewer asked Bud. Were they called the same thing? "It was the same book, but, see, non-fiction is supposed to be the truth and fiction is just a story," Bud replied. "That's why she got in so much trouble because she belittled everybody. She wrote a good book—it was interesting to read—but the way she put people down it wasn't the truth at all. She just wrote a book that sounded good—and it did sound good."[45]

There was no second edition of *The Egg and I* and no evidence to suggest that it was ever marketed as fiction.[46] In Chimacum, however, this was the truth that brought the Bishop family peace.

PLATE 17. Betty MacDonald's literary agent Bernice Baumgarten, New York, no date. Betty trusted Baumgarten utterly. Courtesy Princeton University Library.

PLATE 18. Original cover of *The Egg and I,* featuring woodcut by Richard Bennett, 1945. Author's collection.

PLATE 19. Noting book buyers' positive response to Betty MacDonald's back-cover author photo, the publisher, Lippincott, moved it to the front cover just months after the book came out, 1945. Author's collection.

PLATE 20. Joan (left), Betty (center), and Anne MacDonald, Vashon, ca. 1946. Courtesy Museum of History and Industry, *Seattle Post-Intelligencer* Collection.

PLATE 21. Betty MacDonald riding the ferry *Illahee* between Seattle and Vashon Island, 1946. *The Egg and I*'s success brought global attention to Washington and the Pacific Northwest. Private collection.

PLATE 22. Betty MacDonald signs *Mrs. Piggle-Wiggle* with nieces Heidi (left with checkered bow), Mari, and Salli Jensen (center and right with bows), nephew Darsie Sugia (far right), and other children, Seattle, 1947. Courtesy Museum of History and Industry, *Seattle Post-Intelligencer* Collection.

PLATE 23. Howe Street house, 905 East Howe Street, Seattle, 1937. Betty and Don MacDonald purchased the house in 1947, to spare Betty the ferry commute to Vashon. Courtesy Puget Sound Regional Branch, Washington State Archives.

PLATE 24. Betty and Don MacDonald on steep stairs near their Howe Street house, Seattle, 1947. Courtesy Museum of History and Industry, *Seattle Post-Intelligencer* Collection.

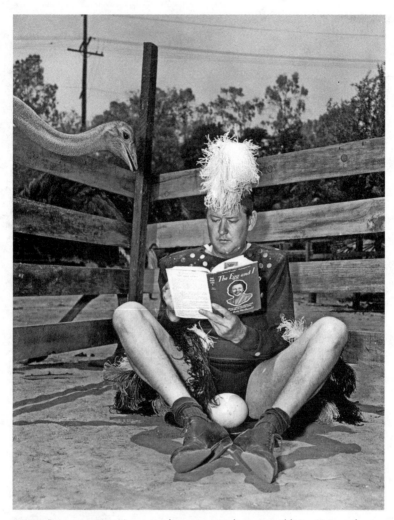

PLATE 25. Press agent Jim Moran incubates an ostrich egg to publicize Universal-International Pictures' acquisition of film rights to Betty's book, Hollywood, 1946. Author's collection.

PLATE 26. Betty MacDonald (left) and Claudette Colbert on set, Hollywood, 1946. Betty's photograph on the cover of her best-selling book made her as familiar to the public as Colbert, who portrayed Betty in the film version of *The Egg and I*. Copyright 1946, Universal-International Pictures. Author's collection.

PLATE 27. Fred MacMurray and Claudette Colbert as glamorous film versions of Bob and Betty, Hollywood, 1947. Copyright Universal-International Pictures, 1947. Private collection.

PLATE 28. Betty's family shared the excitement of her new-found fame. Joan MacDonald (front row center), Mary Bard Jensen (front row right), Betty, Don MacDonald (center), and Anne MacDonald (far left), the Trocadero, Hollywood, 1946. Private collection.

PLATE 29. Don and Betty MacDonald, Alison Bard Sugia, and Frank Sugia (left to right), New York, 1947. Born five months after their father's death, Alison had mother, grandmother, and four older siblings to raise her. Private collection.

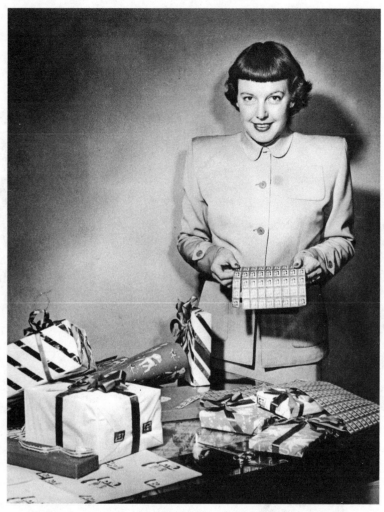

PLATE 30. Betty MacDonald publicizes the National Tuberculosis Association's Christmas Seals campaign, New York, 1948. Private collection.

PLATE 31. Betty MacDonald (seated, with corsage) signs *The Plague and I,* University Book Store, Seattle, 1948. Mary Bard Jensen, back row left. Don MacDonald, back row second from right. Courtesy University Book Store.

PLATE 32. Betty MacDonald, Mary Bard Jensen, and Sydney Bard (left to right), Seattle, ca. 1949. Betty credited her sister Mary with encouraging her literary efforts. Private collection.

PLATE 33. Susannah and Albert Bishop (second row, third and fourth from right) and family, Chimacum, Washington, ca. 1935. Believing they had been libelously depicted as the Kettle family, members of the Bishop family sued Betty and her publishers. Courtesy Aldena Bishop.

PLATE 34. Marjorie Main and Percy Kilbride (center) as Ma and Pa Kettle, with family. Copyright Universal-International Pictures, 1947. Private collection.

PLATE 35. Betty and Don MacDonald in King County Courthouse during the Bishop/Kettle lawsuit, Seattle, February 1951. Courtesy Museum of History and Industry, *Seattle Post-Intelligencer* Collection.

PLATE 36. Betty MacDonald posing for *Anybody Can Do Anything* publicity photo, Vashon, 1950. Private collection.

PLATE 37. Betty MacDonald, Anne MacDonald Evans, and Joan MacDonald Keil (left to right), 1955. As Betty published, her daughters rapidly grew up. Private collection.

PLATE 38. Betty MacDonald with grandchildren (from left) Darsie Evans, Tim Keil (wearing shorts), Johnny Evans, Betsy Evans, Heidi Keil, and Rebecca Keil, 1955. Private collection.

PLATE 39. Betty MacDonald autographing *Onions in the Stew,* Portland, Oregon, 1955. Private collection.

PLATE 40. Don and Betty MacDonald at their ranch, 907 Los Laureles Grade, Carmel Valley, California, ca. 1955. Purchased in 1952, the ranch was beautiful but quickly became a financial burden. Private collection.

CHAPTER TEN

Family Matters

As Betty battled with the Bishops and as her fame and literary output increased, her daughters grew up. In January 1949, Anne married Donald Strunk, a University of Washington student who aspired to a career in professional baseball. Don MacDonald walked his stepdaughter down the aisle of Blessed Sacrament Church, the sanctuary "fragrant and colorful with blue hyacinths, pink camellias and gladiolas and gardenias."[1] Anne wore a gown of imported ivory silk brocade, her bridesmaids varying shades of blue.

Almost exactly one year later, Joan married Girard Keil in a candlelight ceremony at the Church of the Epiphany. Joan's imported silk brocade gown was full-skirted with a court train; on her attendants, frocks of pink satin with copper or cinnamon overskirts added luminous warmth to the flickering glow.[2] Girard (Jerry) Keil had been one of a group of FBI agents who leased Don and Betty's Howe Street house in 1949. Betty had invited the agents to relax on Vashon at weekends, and Joan had met Jerry during these visits.

Joan and Jerry moved to Los Angeles immediately after their marriage. Joan was homesick, and Betty missed her daughter. Don and Betty drove down to visit the newlyweds, and during the trip they discussed purchasing property in California. The Keils' move to California did not turn out to be permanent—Joan and Jerry returned to the Seattle area within the year—but it planted a seed in the minds of Betty and Don.

In August 1949, Betty became a grandmother at the age of forty-two. She wrote gushing letters to family members describing Anne's baby,

127

Johnny, born when Anne was twenty-one. Joan's first child, Heidi, was born in January 1951, when Joan was twenty-one, and Anne's second, Betsy, arrived that October. Two months after that, Joan gave birth to Rebecca. Betty reveled in her role as grandmother, and Anne and Joan leaned heavily on their mother for help with childcare.

Coronet magazine ran Betty's picture in a feature about glamorous grandmothers, alongside those of the movie stars Joan Bennett, Gloria Swanson, and Marlene Dietrich. Betty had, the story said, "the vivacity of a teen-ager and the wit of a sage."[3] With grandchildren in the house, Betty often described her need to dodge swarming hordes of sticky (but adored) little people in order to write. "You really should come out here, Bernice, you'll never really know what bedlam is until you do," Betty wrote in a letter explaining that family duties had kept her from meeting a writing deadline.[4]

When Betty's family members became her material, she was less caustic and more careful and constrained than when describing friends, neighbors, or others. In Betty's books, the Bards and Mac-Donalds are idiosyncratic but crafted affectionately. Betty loved her family deeply, faults and frustrations and all. Although she sometimes feuded with her siblings, especially with Cleve and (despite their close friendship) Alison, she had no impulse to burn bridges or to hurt them by what she wrote about them. Even Mary, who still reflexively attempted to strong-arm Betty, was carefully and lovingly presented in Betty's books.

Beginning in at least 1947, Betty kept daily reminder books. These attest to the fact that during most of her writing career, she entertained almost constantly, sometimes cooking for company—eight guests here, seventeen there—three times a day. Many days, Betty's reminder book contained the admonition "Write."

The ongoing struggle to carve out writing time and cajole her family into acknowledging that need is evident in Betty's letters. Perhaps she exaggerated this problem or used her family's large and small needs as an excuse to procrastinate when inspiration lagged. She acquiesced in the expectation of her family and her era that she be a caregiver. This was a choice, but Betty does not seem to have seen it that way.

Betty exemplified the difficulty that the feminist writer Tillie Olsen described many—most—female writers battling from time immemorial: that the gendered demands placed on women effectively silence them as makers of literature. Nearly three decades after Betty struggled to carve out writing time, Olsen pointed out that the vast majority of published literature has historically been written by men, many of whom had what she called "wives, mothers, enablers" to meet their practical needs and safeguard space in which they had the freedom and focus to write.[5]

Betty could have used a "wife" who would ensure that she was happy in her work. Sydney played this role brilliantly for Darsie but doesn't appear to have facilitated Betty's writing, although she lived with Betty. Neither does Don, although he eschewed the mid-twentieth-century male gender role of family breadwinner. Margaret Bundy Callahan's son Tobey, who knew Betty and Don well when he was a child and a teenager, remembered Don as "Hollywood handsome" but noted that he had no paying job and that his many schemes often turned out poorly.[6]

Betty was smitten with Don from the beginning, but after years of complete responsibility for their financial support, her patience sometimes frayed. "Tomorrow I'm going to town to arrange to take swimming and driving lessons and then next time I get mad at Don I can either swim or drive away from here," she wrote to Joan and Jerry in 1950.[7] Despite her frustrations, Betty accepted the role of wife, placing Don's and her daughters' happiness above her own needs, while also shouldering the traditionally male role of the breadwinner. This double burden set her on a rocky path.

Betty addressed her lack of a literary helpmate in notes for an article that was apparently never published: "In my large family, being an author or 'authing' as we say, rates about the same as gilding cattails or pressing wildflowers. First comes wifing, viz. cooking, cleaning, washing, ironing, smiling when angry, and using a pretty voice when I want to shriek. Then comes mothering or complete sublimation of my hurts and slights and insomnia and highstrungness and delicate condition due to my former bout with t.b."[8] Ignoring her creative and financial compulsions to write, Betty continued, she dealt with Anne's and Joan's domestic crises, absorbed her grandchildren, nieces, and nephews into her household at her family's will, and steadily produced gourmet meals for everyone who made their way to her door.

Betty could have forced this point about writing time, perhaps, but doing so would have required that she upend her agreement—probably unspoken—with Don: he was the boss—the Laird, as she frequently referred to him in letters. Betty liked being married to Don: she relished the role of wife, the emotional security, and his company. Whatever private negotiations shaped the couple's relationship, Betty demonstrated repeatedly that she was willing to compromise her writing time in order to maintain this marriage. For most women of the era, such compromises were implicit in the marriage contract.

Because Bernice Baumgarten, more than anyone, pressed Betty to write, many of Betty's letters to her dwelt on the struggle for uninterrupted time. "I still cannot get them to mention the shameful word 'writing,'" Betty lamented to Baumgarten. "If someone calls and Don answers the phone, he holds the telephone two inches from his mouth and yells to ask if I want to speak to Mrs. Shannon. I tell him, in a very dignified way, to tell her I am writing and will be through at 2:00. Don turns back to the telephone and says, 'she's not home.'"[9]

After a weeklong disagreement with Don, Betty told Mary that she decided to apologize, but "before I got down on my knees I stood up very tall and called him every kind of a spoiled, disagreeable, disorganized, money spending but not earning, disloyal bastard that there is—I am hoping that, as he wipes my lipstick off his ear he will think of a few of those things—said in anger, of course, not really meant, but *said*."[10]

On the other side of the arrangement, being Mr. Betty MacDonald wasn't all cashmere sweaters and cashing checks. From the moment *The Egg and I* was published, Don had to endure the public confusion between himself and Bob Heskett. When Betty promoted *The Egg and I*, with Don at her side, many reporters and readers assumed that Betty had been married only once and that she and Don had experienced the *Egg* events together.

Betty was not publicly associated with the name Heskett; she had not used it since about 1930. Bob's first mention in the press (other than as a presence in *The Egg and I*) came when he signed releases before the making of the film of *Egg*. Robert Heskett next attracted public attention in July 1951, when he was murdered.

Heskett was living in Oakland, California, reportedly working as a carpenter. He was stabbed in the heart by Thomas Blake, a bulldozer operator and the estranged (some reports state divorced) husband of Thelma Blake, who, with her five- and seven-year-old daughters, had been living at Heskett's apartment, reportedly for about a week. "Blake appeared and demanded to see her and 'his babies,'" the *Chicago Daily Tribune* reported. "Heskett, fifty-five, admitted Blake but a quarrel ensued and he ordered Blake out. Blake pulled a knife and Heskett grabbed a hatchet. As the two struggled in the hallway, Heskett crumpled over a banister. Blake said he acted in self-defense."[11] Blake pleaded guilty to manslaughter and was sentenced to serve one to ten years in San Quentin prison. Heskett was buried at the Golden Gate National Cemetery in San Bruno, California.

Heskett's death freed Don to legally adopt Anne and Joan, who had used his surname since he and Betty married. On December 7, 1951, Judge William Long issued the decree of adoption.[12] Joan took the opportunity to change her middle name, Dorothy—honoring Bob Heskett's sister—to Sydney, becoming Joan Sydney MacDonald Keil. Anne added Campbell as a middle name, becoming Anne Elizabeth Campbell MacDonald Strunk, joining her mother and great-grandmother Gammy in the long family line of Anne Elizabeth Campbells.

With Don's adoption of Anne and Joan, the family's last legal connection with Robert Heskett was severed. Betty never commented publicly about her former husband's shocking demise, but with *The Egg and I*, she had given him immortality.

CHAPTER ELEVEN

Anybody Can Write Books

I N August 1950, after the Bishop family had filed their libel suits but before the case came to trial, Betty published her third auto-biographical book, *Anybody Can Do Anything*. *Egg* and *Plague* had been seasoned with family anecdotes from Betty's childhood. In *Anybody*, covering the Depression years, family members were the main dish. The book was a road map to being Bard, a dark valentine to Seattle, and a tongue-in-cheek thank-you to Mary. "The best thing about the depression was the way it reunited our family and gave my sister Mary a real opportunity to prove that anybody can do anything, especially Betty," the book began.[1] In *Anybody*, Betty is Mary's foil and sidekick, struggling half-heartedly to wrest her destiny from her sister's grasp even as she tumbles into Mary's escapades.

Betty and Mary initially wanted to write the book together, but Bernice Baumgarten discouraged them. She told Betty she felt the book would sell better under Betty's name and that it would be easier for Betty to write about Mary than for Mary to write freely about herself. As it turned out, writing about Mary, to whom she was so close but whose faults she had experienced so personally, exhausted Betty. Recalling her own experiences during the 1930s—a time when Betty's relief to be free of her troubled marriage was rippled through with economic stress—was also daunting. And Betty found it challenging to cover twelve years of experiences in a lively and engaging way. After *Anybody* came out, Betty told a fan that there were many times during the writing process when she felt like changing the title to *Oh, No, They Can't*.[2]

That Baumgarten could keep Betty from losing faith during the difficult gestation of *Anybody* is a testament to her skill and determination. "Frankly, Bernice, I'm not at all sure I have a book here at all," Betty wrote. "One chapter I think is amusing—but the point is who gives a Goddamn where I worked and why?"[3] And Baumgarten apparently agreed when she saw an early draft. Betty told a *Seattle Times* reporter that Baumgarten sent all but two chapters back, telling her, "This isn't you."[4] Betty rewrote it. She responded to Baumgarten's blend of intelligence, savvy, tact, prodding, and praise with steady trust and deep gratitude, relying on her guidance.

Anybody's first chapter invites readers into Betty's memories of Mary as a child: she is bossy, she likes feeling superior, and she has great enthusiasm for her own ideas. She is dramatic and theatrical. Her plans for Betty tend to end disastrously. Betty's acquiescence in Mary's outrageous schemes during their childhood sets the stage for the book's account of their experiences as young women. Once *Anybody* has established the childhood dynamic, grown-up Betty enters the story straight from her failed first marriage, bedraggled and destitute. *Anybody* depicts Mary as the family engine: confident, determined, willing her sister and all the family to survive hard times, sweeping obstacles away with her own unrelenting enthusiasm. Mary soon snaps Betty out of her rut, and Sydney steps in to take Anne and Joan off Betty's hands. *Anybody* then follows Betty from job to job in episodic style. She is the stooge, trustingly walking into situations Mary has orchestrated, which often end in pratfalls.

The *Anybody* years included Betty's sobering and transformative encounter with tuberculosis, which she had already described in *The Plague and I*. *Anybody* dispenses with her illness in a single sentence late in the book, set within a cascade of anecdotes about Betty's rumba with bureaucracy during her various government jobs. The book concludes with a brief chapter in which she recounts the genesis of *The Egg and I*. When Betty finds out her book is going to be published, she phones her sister. For the first time, Mary shows her hand: "You just feel successful," she tells Betty, "but imagine how I feel. All of a sudden my big lies have started coming true!"[5] Many fans wrote to Betty wishing they, too, had a Mary—someone to prod them or a family member to literary action.

A few of the incidents Betty describes in *Anybody* made it into the newspapers, and thus into the historical record: the massive Christmas party Mary ropes Betty into helping with, and the "Why I Like Old Gold" cigarette advertising contest in which Betty describes her mother winning a prize.[6] But did veracity matter? "How much is fiction, how much is fact—it is incredible that the natural impulse to retouch should have been resisted—has no bearing upon the constant flow of laughter," the *Saturday Review of Literature* commented.[7] The continuing adventures of the sisters Bard as they careened from one job to the next, battling poverty and championing their own eccentric flavor of family unity, were satisfying enough.

As Betty had come to expect when her work was serialized, the *Saturday Evening Post* editors toned down some of her colorful language. She carefully examined the galleys sent for her approval, ready to nix changes that sacrificed her tone. When a *Post* editor added the word *classy* to Betty's existing description of a department store into which Mary was unashamed to carry her home-packed lunch, Betty responded, "I would rather be dead than ever use the word 'classy.' Please change it to 'and went into an everything-imported-from-Paris shop swinging her big brown greasy paper bag.'" When the editor substituted *hash-slinging* for Betty's original *prostitution*, Betty wrote, "I would prefer 'shop-lifting' as 'hash-slinging' is not an expression I would ever use."[8]

Tay Hohoff, a Lippincott editor, wrote to tell Betty that she loved the book so much she wished she, not Bert Lippincott, was Betty's editor.[9] Bert Lippincott also praised the book, which he thought better than *Egg* or *Plague*. *Anybody* "is one of the few great books of humorous Americana ever written. It may take the public a while for this to sink in," he wrote. "While your method and style are different, your new book reminds me of Mark Twain's work in the way you capture the American scene. Sinclair Lewis got it in several early books but he was short on humor."[10]

Despite this praise, J. B. Lippincott publicized *Anybody* considerably less than they had Betty's previous books. And Betty, who'd taken her show on the road to promote *Egg* and *Plague*, had grown weary of crowded author events. For the first time, she chose not to appear at autograph parties, even in Seattle bookstores. She did no national promotion. She was weighed down by the Bishop lawsuit, worried about money, and tired of the grind of producing a book a year.

Lippincott's cover design featured boldly stylized typewriter keys spelling out the book's title. This time, the publisher chose to omit the familiar iconography of their cover girl: Betty's face, as much a part of her brand as Aunt Jemima or Betty Crocker, did not appear on *Anybody's* cover.

Betty's timing, impeccable for *Egg* and fine for *Plague*, faltered with *Anybody*. For the first time, American readers failed to fully embrace her effort. Perhaps a newly affluent nation did not warm to *Anybody's* recollections of hardship. Lippincott's Mac McKaughan blamed *Anybody's* slow sales on the fact that so many readers had already enjoyed nearly the entire book in its four-part *Saturday Evening Post* serialization. The magazine's circulation was four and a half million, and its cover price was ten cents. Readers who'd read it for forty cents were passing up the book and saving their $2.75.

Despite the hilarious details included in many of Betty's stories, this book's humor was thin ice over the abyss. *Anybody* was nostalgic, but it did not strike its original readers as hilarious (like *Egg*), informative (like *Plague*), or reaffirming of cultural norms, as *Onions in the Stew* would later be perceived to be. "It is a book to read for the enjoyment of the moment and forget," the *Saturday Review of Literature* concluded. "If one mulls it over, inevitably the bright, metallic threads of which its sparkling fabric is woven darken and tarnish with dismaying rapidity. Little tawdry and shabby spots eat into the surface shine. For if employers were cheap, licentious and phony, the Bard girls were habitually in the humiliating position of playing faker themselves. . . . Anybody can do anything, but is everyone willing to?"[11]

One underlying theme of *Anybody* was that the Bard women did not need men in order to survive, a dangerous flag to wave as gender roles constricted during the 1950s. In spite of Betty's ongoing negotiation between caring for her family and carving out writing time, neither Betty MacDonald the writer nor Betty the character conformed to postwar societal prescriptions for selfless female servitude. This attitude worked to her benefit early on, but not in the increasingly conservative climate of the early 1950s. The only male characters in *Anybody* play minor roles, and most of those are negative: doltish or bad bosses, bad or doltish dates. There are no cougar hunts like the one Bob went on in *Egg,* no Kettles, no husbands. Although *Plague* had featured female characters almost exclusively, it also featured a genderless disease, and its success resulted in part from *Egg's* popularity.

Current events may also have influenced *Anybody's* reception. The Korean War had begun, focusing attention, and again sending soldiers, far from home. Lippincott felt that the war made the book market volatile: readers' willingness to open their wallets depended on whether news reports were good or bad.

In addition, Betty's description of the Bards' lively household, bulging with artistic, eccentric friends, may have put some readers off. Senator Joseph McCarthy's witch hunt for suspected communists and communist sympathizers was well under way. McCarthy focused keenly on the 1930s activities of those he suspected. The kinds of people who had enlivened the Bards' house in those years— artists, writers, actors, directors, and musicians—were in McCarthy's line of fire. By 1950, nonconformity was suspect. *Anybody* taught Betty how thoroughly public taste could change the tune for even a successful author.

Lippincott urged Betty to keep on producing autobiographical books, but some reviewers wearied of them. The *New York Times* book reviewer Samuel Williamson began his ultimately positive review of *Anybody* with the observation, "When applied to Betty MacDonald, née Anne Elizabeth Campbell Bard, the cliché about one's life being an open book is a threefold understatement." Like other reviewers, Williamson noted the dark nature of the experiences Betty made light of. "Betty MacDonald is an alchemist," he concluded. "She transmutes some pretty grim experiences into rollicking reminiscence."[12]

Columbia Pictures wanted to turn *Anybody* into a film, and Bernice Baumgarten negotiated with them for months. The studio, spooked by the Bishop suit, demanded that everyone mentioned in the book sign a written release. Baumgarten could produce releases from family members, but beyond that, she felt that Columbia's demand was insurmountable. She told Betty she felt confident that she could sell the project to another studio, but it never happened.

Although its reception in the United States may have been disappointing, *Anybody* enjoyed an unexpected success in translation in Iron Curtain countries. Citizens of repressive regimes empathized with the book's emphasis on the power of family and the curative qualities humor brings to adversity, as well as its message that anybody could do anything and could—must—keep going. During the early 1950s, foreign-language editions of Betty's books provided a steady income stream. For Betty these editions required little more than signing contracts, finding space on her shelves as the exotic translations arrived in the mail, and depositing royalty checks.

Judging by fan mail, many *Anybody* readers lost their hearts to Betty's portrait of Mary and were eager to know more about this vivacious, domineering sister. Mary's own book, *The Doctor Wears Three Faces*, had been widely publicized when it came out the year before and had quickly leapt to the silver screen, with Dorothy McGuire—meltingly beautiful, but not of Claudette Colbert's star caliber—playing the leading role.

"Both Mary and I want you to treat her as though she were not my sister," Betty wrote to Bernice Baumgarten, who had become Mary's literary agent. "Mary is a very strong, very bright, very witty woman—she has a captivating personality and more friends than anyone in the world."[13] She felt too close to Mary to be a good critic, Betty explained. The sisters spoke on the phone nearly every day and read each other passages of their works in progress. Mary still tried to keep Betty on track, and Betty attempted to make the often-intense Mary laugh.

The Doctor Wears Three Faces recounts the early years of Mary's marriage to Clyde Jensen. Mary was twenty-nine years old when she married, leaving a career in advertising sales and subsequently staying home with her three daughters, born in quick succession. During this era, being a doctor entailed significant societal responsibilities as well as status, and social duties were also expected of a doctor's wife. In the book, Mary navigates her entry into this new arena with the commiserating support of other medical wives, whom she terms the Neglected Ones (because the needs of their husbands' patients always come first). In an era when physicians were deified, Mary's books demystified both doctor and doctor's wife.

Once Mary stepped onto the literary stage, she embraced the role of author. Like Betty, she traveled to New York and met the Eastern press. She was a guest on several national radio programs and a celebrity in Seattle. Betty, who said speaking in public made her nervous, watched her always self-assured sister swan into the limelight. Mary's vivacity and willingness to exaggerate if it better served her stories made her a natural public speaker. Even so, Mary's books made just a small splash compared with the tsunami of *The Egg and I*.

The sisters reveal themselves differently in their books. Mary seems unwilling to risk offending the friends and family members on whom she bases her characters. Perhaps it is because Betty, unlike Mary, did not hold a place in Seattle's social echelon, that her writing was less constrained. Betty was also willing to be sharper—meaner—which made her funnier and ultimately more modern.

Mary's second book, *Forty Odd*, is about perimenopause and her journey toward the understanding that (as she says in the book's dedication) age is a number, not a disease. The book was published in 1952, when Mary was forty-eight. In 1955, Mary published her first juvenile book, *Best Friends*. The title characters are Suzie and Co Co, who become best friends and then, when Suzie's mother marries Co Co's father, sisters. Their story continues in two sequels. These are gentle, realistic "girl books," reassuring rather than snappy like Betty's Piggle-Wiggle books.

In 1956, with her daughters nearly grown, Mary looked back at her late 1940s experiences as a Brownie leader following the Seattle Girl Scout Council's advice, which became the book's title: *Just Be Yourself*. Mary volunteered herself as a leader when her daughters pleaded to become Brownie scouts and the existing troop in their neighborhood was full. Mary's troop seems to have been surprisingly ethnically and economically diverse. Her portraits of her daughters are loving sketches of three very different personalities: Mari, "surgically clean" and authoritative; Salli, who "radiated the calm, unhurried serenity of her father" even as she dawdled; and Heidi, tender, animal loving, and a young iconoclast.[14]

While Mary wrote her books, Betty produced sequels to *Mrs. Piggle-Wiggle* and also wrote *Nancy and Plum*. A book about orphans, *Nancy and Plum* is itself an orphan among Betty's other works, four autobiographical books and four volumes of *Mrs. Piggle-Wiggle*. Betty said that the book evolved from stories she told Mary when they were young. Betty's daughters, Anne and Joan, felt that the Nancy and Plum characters were based on them.

Nancy and Plum uses a traditional fairytale format, laced with Betty's Bardish sense of humor. The sisters Nancy and Plum are residents in Mrs. Monday's Boarding Home for Children, an orphanage. They use their vivid imaginations and their pluck to triumph over difficulties. Hildegarde Hopkins, a commercial artist who lived in Seattle, illustrated the book. "I absolutely adore her illustrations and they are everything I dreamed of having," Betty wrote Lippincott children's book editor, Helen Dean Fish.[15]

Betty hoped to continue the sisters' adventures in further volumes, but Lippincott's enthusiasm for *Nancy and Plum* was lackluster. "Helen Fish suggested that I close Mrs. Monday's and dispense in some kind of way with the other inmates of the boarding home, which I do not want to do as there are hundreds more chapters of Nancy and Plum involving Mrs. Monday and the other orphans. Mrs. Monday finally died and her brother took over the house and Mrs. Campbell arranged for most of the other children to board with friends of hers," Betty explained to Bernice Baumgarten.[16] Lippincott promoted the book minimally, and neither Lippincott nor Baumgarten encouraged Betty to continue the series.

Although Seattle had celebrated her success in *Egg's* early days, by the time *Nancy and Plum* was published in 1952, Betty felt underappreciated. Local readers looked forward to her new books, but Betty was no longer news. Coupled with the lingering taint from the Bishop/Kettle trial and the long hours she was spending writing, this dimming of the spotlight left Betty feeling isolated and taken for granted.

She had phoned Mary, Betty wrote to her daughter Joan, to talk about how sad she felt. "[Mary] told me that people like Lucille MacDonald [sic] (reporter on the [Seattle] Times) write articles like 'Slip earwigs in your biscuit dough and watch your guests surprised faces' and everybody in Seattle says 'grrrrrreat wrrrrriting' but I write a book that sells a million copies and they all say 'Oh, her.'"[17]

In June 1952, partially because she felt underappreciated in Seattle, Betty and Don purchased a two-thousand-acre ranch property in Carmel Valley, California. The Corral de Tierra Ranch was sited at the top of the steep Los Laureles Grade, originally a stagecoach route and cattle-drive trail connecting Carmel Valley with Salinas. It offered views of the Sierra de Salinas Mountains and the Salinas Valley, the Santa Lucia range, Mount Toro, the Pacific Ocean, and the Corral de Tierra, a natural corral formed by landforms in the valley below.

The ranch possessed a small house and a larger barn and came with ranching equipment, horses, and livestock.[18] The seller agreed to carry the mortgage and to forgo a down payment. Betty and Don planned to run cattle, and Don was ready to cowboy. Their arrival was big news in Monterey County, both because of Betty's fame and because the property was so large. The Carmel Valley purchase provided Don with an alternative role to Mr. Betty MacDonald.

The ranch was not bought on impulse: Betty and Don wanted to leave Washington and had been looking at property for months by the time they found it. The way they bought it, however, was rash. They had no money saved. Betty and Don convinced themselves that they could dash back to Seattle and immediately unload the Howe Street town home and the Vashon house, along with the barn property, and use the proceeds to make their mortgage payments on the ranch. They listed the Vashon house nationally, making much of its provenance as Betty's home. Promotional brochures replete with photographs enticed potential buyers: smiling Betty fished, carried frosty glasses across the patio, and dug clams on the beach with Don. Some people looked, but no one purchased.

Don now spent most of his time in California. Betty, in Washington, chipped away at her writing, helped Anne and Joan with child care, and tried to sell the properties. Anne's marriage to Donald Strunk had ended in June 1952, and in the fall of 1953 she married Robert Evans. Betty added Anne's children Johnny and Betsy into her collection of resident children while Anne prepared for the wedding, honeymooned, and then was rushed to surgery to remove her ruptured appendix.

After the Howe Street house sold, Betty and Sydney made Vashon their home base, keeping the property ready for showings. Betty told Bernice Baumgarten that she was writing, cleaning house, painting furniture, and trying to keep twenty-seven acres mowed, weeded, and pruned. It had been raining continually, and there were no prospects for the house. Joan was nearing the end of her third pregnancy, and Betty was relieved to be available to help her, as she also helped out during Anne's pregnancies.

Although Betty missed Don fearfully at times, his absence eased some demands on her. "Don is leaving for the ranch tomorrow," she wrote Baumgarten during a time when she was struggling to meet a writing deadline. "Though I adore him I get a hell of a lot more done when he is not here. . . . Anne is swelling and swelling and so I am really writing against my usual deadline—another baby."[19]

Betty visited the ranch regularly, and Don traveled back to Vashon to see her, but it was not the same as living together. Because Betty didn't drive and the town of Vashon was beyond reasonable walking distance, she was stranded at the Vashon house. She began taking driving lessons and apparently passed her driving test in late 1953, but it would be years before she felt confident enough to drive at night.

Betty had children in the house almost constantly during this period. Caring for them energized her, Betty claimed. But when Sydney invited Dede's family over, refocusing Betty's attention on entertaining when she really needed to be writing, or Alison dropped her children off without warning, assuming Betty would stop her work to babysit,

Betty pictured Don relaxing in the California sunshine. The image rankled. "I sometimes wonder how you would feel if I really did stop writing, right this minute, which God knows is what I would like to do—how many people would suddenly have to take care of themselves. I honestly think, Don, that that ranch has ruined any chances we might have had for happiness because it showed me how you really feel about me—actions do speak louder than words, you know," she wrote darkly.[20]

With the Vashon house and farm properties still on the market, Betty and Don juggled renters, mortgages, and contracts, trying to find a way to afford the Carmel Valley property. By spring of 1954, Betty was feeling desperate. Don was in Carmel Valley but not living on the ranch. The calf crop was only 70 percent of what they had hoped for, curtailing their profits. Betty was on Vashon, struggling to sell the house, staying up at night to watch the McCarthy committee hearings on television, and feeling panicked about money.

Because the Piggle-Wiggle books were less taxing to write than the autobiographical books, Betty came to see them as a sort of piggy bank. "My problem always seems to be money," she wrote Bernice Baumgarten. "If I send you an outline of another Mrs. Piggle-Wiggle how much can I get on it—I want all I can get."[21] Inspiration, after all, was close at hand: caring for grandchildren, nieces, and nephews, taxing as it might be, stimulated ideas for new Piggle-Wiggle-worthy cures. While looking after all five of her grandchildren in June 1954, Betty wrote to Baumgarten, "If you could see me right now you would not believe it—I am in the living room with my typewriter on the top of the record player—the only safe place—and the beach party has returned—Becky is up from her nap—and they are all milling around my feet with enormous plastic alligators, ducks and boats and peanut butter sandwiches—I promised them they could help me set out zinnias and they are all ready."[22]

Children's books were steady work and relatively simple to write, but their immediate financial payoff paled in comparison with the potential earnings of another successful adult title. Betty's next autobiographical book was *Onions in the Stew*. It is different from her other books: sunnier, less prickly, more domestic, centered on her activities as wife and mother. As such, it is in keeping with many American women's experiences during the 1950s and with other autobiographical accounts by women during that era, such as Jean Kerr's *Please Don't Eat the Daisies* and Shirley Jackson's *Life among the Savages* and *Raising Demons*. Unlike her other autobiographical books, *Onions* contains almost no mention of Betty's mother and siblings, and it is the first book that mentions Don.

Egg was about catharsis and exorcising the demons of her first marriage. *Plague* was inspired by gratitude at surviving tuberculosis and by Betty's desire to raise public awareness about the disease. *Anybody* was born from Betty's love for her family, especially Mary. But what was finally published as *Onions in the Stew* sprang from one impulse only: the need to fulfill a contractual commitment Betty had made to Lippincott and earn out the advance payment she'd received, which was long spent.

She had originally wanted to write a novel, the kind of book she herself liked to read. In December 1951, Betty and Lippincott signed a contract for this venture, to be called *Onions in the Stew*. Writing fiction was one of her long-held dreams. She had been trying for years. Her first attempts at writing had been short stories: her debut in the *Town Crier* with "Their Families" and the stories Brandt & Brandt had rejected in the 1930s.[23] After three autobiographical books and her successful children's fiction, Betty wanted to try fiction again. She was tired of mining her own life for story. She wanted to tell a different tale, to create characters rather than be one.

Betty's novel featured wittily drawn characters marooned in a roadside motel in a remote coastal community during a fierce storm. Betty worked on the manuscript for two years while she struggled to sell the Vashon properties. Finally pleased with her efforts, she sent the completed manuscript to Bernice Baumgarten. Baumgarten liked Betty's heroine (a blowsy, gold-digging sweetheart named Blanche) but felt the book lacked dramatic action. She thought it needed more work, although she offered to show it to Lippincott if Betty wanted her to.

Betty trusted Baumgarten's opinion, but this was a painful blow. If she had been less pressed financially, she could have taken the time to revise the novel until Baumgarten deemed it ready for Lippincott. But Betty had no time for revisions: she needed money.

Baumgarten gently reminded Betty that if she chose not to revise the novel, she would need to substitute a project that was acceptable to Lippincott in order to make good on the ten-thousand-dollar advance, which she knew Betty couldn't afford to repay. "I don't know what to say about *Onions in the Stew*—I haven't looked at it yet," Betty told Baumgarten. "In case I find it too impossible how would you feel about a cook book and then a gardening book—I can be pretty funny about cooking . . . if necessary I could call it Onions in the Stew although I had thought of Stove and I—not that I like that, it makes me retch, but I think most people expect it. I will try to think of a killing name for a gardening book."[24]

Baumgarten discouraged Betty from trying gardening books or cookbooks, instead asking Lippincott to accept another autobiographical book. Lippincott readily agreed. Betty had made a devil's bargain. *The Egg and I* had proved she could spin her own story into gold. Now she was a captive, chained to the spinning wheel.

Betty retained her discarded novel's title for the autobiographical book. In outline, the autobiographical *Onions* included recipes, and if those had made it into the published book, the title would have made more literal sense. In the end, Betty included only two: clam chowder and clam fritters. In the book that finally bore the title, the stew was Betty's Vashon life. The onions were its savor.

For this book, Betty reached back to the last years before fame changed her circumstances. After three autobiographical books, Betty had written most of her story. Faced with a similar situation, a modern memoirist might drill down into one of the experiences success had brought. A book about her time in Hollywood could have been hilarious. But Lippincott would never have let Betty name names, and while she'd scraped her way out of a libel action by disavowing that the Bishops were the Kettles, nobody would have failed to recognized a renamed Claudette Colbert.

The events recounted in *Onions* occurred mainly between 1942 and 1945, immediately before *The Egg and I* propelled Betty into the public's consciousness. Betty spends the first chapters introducing readers to her Vashon Island world, taking them there and, with them, watching the ferry leave. She eases readers into the loose theme of living with teenagers on island time. It was, as one chapter title explained, "Life as usual in a very unusual setting."[25]

Onions presents a Betty with no real foe to battle, other than her daughters' adolescence, which she and her readers both understand is finite and has relatively low stakes. In keeping with the conservative decade in which it was published, *Onions* smoothed ruffled feathers and presented a traditional patriarchal household not glimpsed in Betty's other books.[26] Set during the period when in real life Betty's new marriage was fresh and passionate and she was creating the book that would remake her destiny, *Onions* presents Betty as a Claudette Colbert version of herself.

Homogenizing her life to fit the times, *Onions* embeds Betty in the tight family unit consisting of Anne, Joan, and Don. Her role as wife and mother is depicted as satisfying, if mildly frustrating. Her neighbors' foibles are minor, compared to those of the Kettles or her fellow patients at The Pines. Betty copes with mild household crises: not enough dry wood for the giant fireplace; plugged drains when guests are expected; a too-tall Christmas tree; a snowstorm that blocks the roads and forces Don to mush his way to town to buy nail polish and candy for Anne and Joan and restock the parental whiskey and cigarette supply. As her visitors rejoice in visiting her restful island paradise, she, as hostess, gets no rest. Her daughters fight with each other and refuse to go to school but unite when they are angling to do something Betty and Don would rather they didn't. The worst her Vashon neighbors dish out is a little surreptitious flirting with Don.

Only when Betty briefly describes her employment outside the house—the job she lost when she called in sick so that she could outline *Egg*—does she let her bitterness gleam through: "I was paid $47.50 a week which was never enough but was considered marvelous pay for a woman in those days in Seattle where it is still the prevailing idea that all female employees (bless their little hearts) would really rather be home baking Toll House cookies and any male not down on all fours (this does not include the government where you can be even farther down if political affiliations are okay) is automatically paid twice as much as the brightest female."[27] This protofeminist outburst is out of character for *Onions*, and that suited her publisher just fine.

The Lippincott editor George Stevens outlined his concerns about Betty's *Onions* manuscript in a letter to Baumgarten prior to revisions:

> Public taste has pretty radically changed in the nine years since
> *The Egg and I* was published. A sort of Puritanism has made great
> progress, and some things that would go without question in the
> late 1940s will now tend to alienate a large segment of the reading
> public. This situation is particularly important in the case of *Onions
> in the Stew*, because it is—as I have written Betty—in many ways
> her most attractive book. Funny as the book is—hilarious in many
> episodes—I think its main quality is the likeability of the family
> and the feeling of identification the reader will get with them. The
> more the identification, the more some readers will be put off by
> the Goddamns, the Jesuses and the passage towards the end about
> adolescent discovery of sex.[28]

Stevens was worried not just about readers' disapproval but also about legal liability. He included a list of every character in the book other than Betty's family members, asking for assurance that names had been changed and identifying features altered. Lippincott wanted no further libel lawsuits. How true to life Betty's nonfiction book really was seems to have mattered little. Betty responded that many of the characters were made up, and most of the others were composites. Of the character called Lesley Arnold, with whom Don in the book is described as having a flirtation, Betty wrote, "Pretty good description of summer with Irene Norwood—description of Lesley Arnold is not at all like Irene—she should be flattered." Of several other characters: "The alcoholic guest—the Madonna model—the woman from Arizona—I have had many alcoholic guests—All Anne's friends were models—most models are alike—there was no woman from Arizona—she was from New York—Montana—Texas and California."[29] Without complaint, she toned down all the language that had worried Stevens in the earlier draft.

Onions in the Stew was published in May 1955, returning Betty's smiling face to bookstore shelves. Clearly spooked by *Anybody's* lagging sales, Lippincott placed their photogenic author on both the front and the back of the book's bright orange dust jacket. Betty's head, so tightly cropped as to be disembodied, floated in the upper right-hand corner near her name. The *o*'s in *Onions* were whimsical renderings of the vegetable. The back cover featured a full-page shot of Betty pushing a lawnmower.

Reviewers noted that *Onions* skated into the category of housewife humor, its tone and subject matter more conventional than Betty's previous books. None of them minded. "Flip with a quip, as ever," reported the *Chicago Daily Tribune* reviewer Marge Lyon, "but with a new maturity that on her looks good. That is Betty MacDonald in 'Onions In The Stew.'"[30]

To Betty's immense relief, *Onions* sold twenty-six thousand copies during its first month in print. A *New York Times* book reviewer praised Betty as a humorist in "one of our lustiest traditions, that created by Mark Twain. . . . In person Betty MacDonald is a sophisticated individual. Indeed, I have met her a number of times and I would match her attractiveness against the girls she inevitably describes as her successful rivals. But this worldly and frequently city dwelling young woman has managed to capture some of those lusty and informal situations which have given both humor and a certain sadness to rural America." Despite Lippincott's categorizing *Onions in the Stew*—like all Betty's adult titles—as nonfiction, this reviewer advised, "The way to enjoy 'Onions in the Stew,' a dual Book-of-the-Month choice for June, is to regard it as predominantly fiction. This way, the reader's credulity will never be taxed."[31]

Anybody's disappointing sales had proved to Betty that she had to promote her books in person. Her Seattle autographing events drew crowds, and booksellers were thrilled that she agreed to travel to Seattle from Carmel Valley—where she was finally living full-time with Don when *Onions* came out—to sign books. The bookshop manager at Seattle's Frederick & Nelson department store told Betty that they'd sold 340 copies of *Onions* during her appearance—the most successful autograph party the store had ever hosted.

Thanks to her books, Betty and her family members, Vashon Island, and Puget Sound became household names in America and beyond. Betty was the Pacific Northwest's best ambassador since Paul Bunyan: darling, clever, tongue-in-cheek, and very Western.[32] It was work she wrung out of herself, as evidenced by a notation in her daily planner: "March 26, 1952: My birthday—wrote on books all day."

CHAPTER TWELVE

Goodbye, Goodbye
to Everything

T HE view from Betty and Don's Carmel Valley property was gorgeous: sagebrush, rolling rose and golden hills, a periwinkle sky dotted with fluffy clouds that shaded the valley floor like a diaphanous tent. In early 1955, Betty moved the last of their belongings from wet, green Vashon to this compellingly dry, burnished pocket of paradise. The place held energy, but in a way that felt somehow final. The Corral de Tierra ranch would hold the ends to many threads of her story.

Although it is only ten miles from quaint Carmel-by-the-Sea, with its fairytale cottages and breathtaking views, Carmel Valley feels like a completely different place. The Carmel River, for most of the year just a trickle, is its dominant aquatic feature: the Pacific Ocean—in truth so near—feels distant. Carmel Valley is much more business-like—drier in every way—than Carmel-by-the-Sea, Seattle, or Vashon.

The ranch was at the top of the Los Laureles grade, a winding, white-knuckle drive. "I am an excellent driver but Don still leaps four feet in the air whenever we encounter another car—is pure white and dripping sweat all the way down the Los Laureles grade and has almost poked holes through the floorboards of both cars," Betty complained to Mary.[1] It was a road she learned to drive alone, at night.

On Vashon, Betty's family both inspired her work and hindered it. Carmel Valley had fewer distractions, but Betty still felt stymied. Many writers made ends meet with work for periodicals: humorous articles in monthly magazines yielded quick cash and were less tax-ing than producing books. But despite Bernice Baumgarten's encour-agement, Betty never produced more than a handful of articles. Her money troubles persisted once she'd moved to Carmel Valley full time, but Don's presence meant that at least she was not wrestling them alone.

One impediment to Betty's writing, despite having more opportu-nity, was that she had developed a terrible skin condition, a persistent, exhausting, and nearly dementing itch. When it was at its most severe, Betty spent hours in the bath, hoping that the water would soothe her skin. She visited allergists and even tried self-hypnosis. Nothing helped for very long.

Some doctors told her the itching was psychosomatic. Betty re-garded this diagnosis as shameful, seldom mentioning the itching in letters to her family. Even Bernice Baumgarten knew nothing of her condition, although it drained Betty of the will and stamina to write. When the itching flared up, it made her a patient once more, this time a needy one.

The itching and the move to the isolated Carmel Valley property began Betty's subtle withdrawal, at age forty-eight, from the public stage. When *Egg* was published, her ordinary life had opened wide to admit the nation and then the world. After the move, Betty was largely silent in the public sphere, apart from the few weeks of publicity for *Onions in the Stew.*

As wrenching as it was to leave her daughters and grandchildren, Betty was relieved to finally settle on the property she'd come to love. During the three years she'd spent living on Vashon without Don, commuting to Carmel Valley only for brief visits, she'd felt the con-trast between the two places strongly. Vashon was beautiful, but gray and wet, and bleak without Don. She had come to long for the gold-en-brown Carmel Valley hills, the sweeping views from the top of the ranch, and her husband's company.

Betty and Don planned to build a large house at Corral de Tierra as soon as they sold their Washington properties. In 1955, in desper-ation, they finally rented out the Vashon house. Because the sale of the Howe Street house alone was not enough to finance construction on the ranch, Betty and Don made do with the small existing house on the property.[2]

A more pressing problem was that the ranch was short of water, which Betty and Don needed to support a commercial cattle business. Buying a cattle ranch without investigating its water sources was a rookie mistake. The property had two wells and two springs, but these were far from the house and often ran dry. In summer, providing drinking water for the cattle took precedence over bathing and watering the garden. Betty and Don hired a dowser and dug several wells following his instructions, but to no avail.

The Carmel Valley's natural beauty is legendary. John Steinbeck's first collection of short stories, *The Pastures of Heaven*, was set in a landscape that included Betty's large property. Even when she was itching or feeling guilty about not writing or worried about the lack of water and dwindling funds, she drew comfort from the overwhelming natural beauty around her.

Betty wrote of her love of the place to friends and family: "Don is happier than I have ever known him—he gets up at 6 or 6:30 every single morning no matter how late we have been out and he eats, breathes, and sleeps the ranch—he is very brown and very handsome and very sweet—I just absolutely adore it here and never want to live any place else," she wrote to Joan and Jerry. "Everybody is very proud of me down here and act like I'm terribly famous—already they have all my books in both bookstores.[3]

New friends kept Don and Betty busy. "Almost everybody down here is a good cook," Betty told Joan. "Almost everybody is poor and almost everybody is intellectual—everybody entertains very easily and [in] Margar [Sydney] fashion—lots of dust under the bed but beautiful flower arrangements, wonderful food and darling people."[4]

In Carmel Valley, Betty finally found neighbors who shared her literary and artistic interests. This was a relief, but it did not spare her new friends from sometimes being derided as phonies in Betty's letters. Betty and Don were invited to parties at the Del Monte Country Club, although Betty, a staunch Democrat, complained about fraternizing with so many Republicans. Don joined the Carmel Valley Horsemen's Association, participating in roundups throughout the valley and hosting barbecues, with Betty, for the members who helped with the MacDonalds' roundups at Corral de Tierra.

Once she was settled, Betty began working through the fan mail backlog the move had caused, using a form response: "Thank you for your friendly letter which I intended to answer long ago. However, when we moved to California, all my mail was lost and we finally found it among the 387,654,382 boxes in the barn."[5]

Betty was a prolific letter writer, and her missives to family members multiplied once she lived in Carmel Valley. She saved up correspondence and then spent a day tackling replies. When writing to her family, Betty frequently pitted one story against another, choosing sides to suit the relative she was writing to. She could be catty, even lacerating, when writing about one family member to another, and then she would reverse the skewering when writing to the family member the previous letter had skewered.

Betty had always insisted that her children and then grandchildren call her "Betty," never Mother, Grandmother, or any other nickname, but when she wrote to Anne and Joan from the ranch, she sometimes signed her letters "Maugham."[6] This was an inside joke, a reference to Somerset Maugham (a favorite writer), but it is interesting that finally, in her late forties, Betty was willing to use the maternal moniker, even if only as a pun. Betty occasionally signed letters to her grandchildren "BeNana MacDonald," appending a scrawled "Betty."[7]

Back in Seattle, Mary's domestic life was changing too. Her girls were still at home but nearly grown. The house in the Madrona neighborhood where Jens and Mary had raised their daughters was too large for just two people. Looking ahead, Mary and Jens purchased a piece of land on Vashon and, with Cleve's assistance, began building a year-round beach house. Real-estate agents ferried large families through the Jensens' Madrona home, which Mary and Jens needed to sell before they could move to Vashon.

In Carmel Valley, Betty struggled with her persistent itching problem, Sydney (who was becoming increasingly infirm), ranch hands, and Don. Despite her initial bliss at being back with Don full time, as time went by Betty became increasingly frustrated with him. He was "Bishopy," she wrote to several family members, by which (her opinion of the Chimacum family not having been improved by her courtroom confrontation with them) she meant ornery or lazy.

She also felt underappreciated by Sydney, who had lived with Betty and Don almost continuously since their marriage, visiting her other children for a week or a month, usually when child care was needed. Sydney's grandchildren—who called her either Grandmother or Margar—remember her as a quiet presence. She traveled light, carrying little more than a book, some clothes, her art supplies, and her ubiquitous Camel cigarettes. Once Betty was established at the ranch, Sydney was with her constantly.

An avid gardener, Sydney mourned the loss of the lush plantings she and Betty had created around the Vashon house. The hot and arid climate made the ranch a difficult place to cultivate plants. By the time she and Betty moved to the ranch, Sydney's health was poor, her heart weakened by decades of heavy smoking, and she could do little gardening work. Perhaps as a result, Sydney grew crotchety with Betty and Don.

Betty vented her frustrations to Mary, the only family member she felt would understand, in long, sad letters, apologizing for their dullness and thanking her sister for providing empathy. For her part, Mary was sometimes exasperated by the needs and demands of her three teenagers. "Every time anybody is mean to you, you come up here and every time anybody is mean to me I'll come down there and pretty soon we'll both be so mad we'll have a little house half way in between and never go home anymore," Mary suggested in a letter.[8]

Although Betty continued slowly to work at the stories that would become *Hello, Mrs. Piggle-Wiggle*, itching often rendered her unable to force herself to the typewriter. Her daily reminder book noted cattle roundups, visits from family members, and doctors' appointments. She could envision a book about the ranch, though: Betty decided that she was going to call it *Too Old to Ride* and that the theme would be her relationship with the beautiful sorrel horse she'd recently acquired.

His mane, she felt, was just the color of her hair. Bernice Baumgarten was pleased when she caught wind of this idea and encouraged Betty to get started.

Before she could outline the new book, Betty prepared a speech she'd agreed to deliver to a convention of insurance agents in Enumclaw, near Seattle. Betty disliked public speaking and rarely accepted such requests, but this engagement was too lucrative to turn down. Money was tight, as usual: she and Don relied on royalties to meet their living expenses, and this income fluctuated. Betty had used up her most recent advance from Lippincott and was hard pressed to make mortgage payments on both the ranch and the Vashon properties.[9]

During this Seattle visit, in late July 1955, Betty began hemorrhaging. Her physician feared that she might have uterine cancer. She was hospitalized and underwent curettage, but doctors found nothing of concern. She went home to Carmel Valley, returning to Seattle in autumn to stay with Anne during the final weeks of Anne's fourth pregnancy. Betty spent afternoons with her grandchildren, gathering windfall apples and reading books, giving Anne as much chance as possible to rest.

Whenever she was in Seattle, Betty saw her doctors. At one appointment during August 1956, Betty's doctor diagnosed probable endometriosis and scheduled surgery. This operation revealed ovarian cancer that had spread and was felt to be inoperable. Betty's doctors told her family that they thought Betty might die within just a few weeks. At Don's insistence, Betty was not given the news for ten days after the surgery.

Despite this grim prognosis, she recovered from the surgery and was discharged from the hospital. Betty recuperated at Mary's house and underwent eight weeks of radiation therapy. She then decided to return to the ranch.

Through Mary's staunch advocacy and Jens's connections, Betty seems to have received better medical care in Seattle than in Carmel Valley, where she frequently felt dismissed by doctors. "For five years I have been going from doctor to doctor because I itched and was tired and they all told me it was psychosomatic," Betty wrote to her dear friend Goddard Lieberson, now president of Columbia Broadcasting. "Creative people are all neurotic you know—of course now they say it was the cancer producing a foreign protein that made me itch."[10]

Resting in Carmel Valley, Betty wrote to Bernice Baumgarten that she was still very tired but feeling stronger. "Don is a saint—waits on me hand and foot and is so patient with my depressions which I must say I do have—try as hard as I can not to—I still can't see the good of telling a person they have cancer—I would have been so happy with endometriosis or whatever it was and I'm not sure I'm enough of a Pollyanna to go whistling through life with a huge axe on the back of my neck."[11]

As Betty struggled with the implications of her diagnosis, Sydney's health steadily declined. She suffered several heart attacks and by late 1956 was largely bedridden. Against all odds, Betty managed to fly her mother to Seattle in December 1956 to see family. Because Sydney required a wheelchair, she and Betty navigated the flights from Monterey to San Francisco to Seattle and back with much tipping of redcap porters.

Sydney's declining health made her increasingly physically dependent on her daughter. She also grew less tolerant and more critical when details such as Don's coffee-making skills or Betty's plans for the day failed to live up to her expectations. She needed ferrying to doctor appointments, and during her frequent hospitalizations it fell to Betty to manage her mother's care and keep her company. If she and Don and Sydney had still lived in Seattle, Betty's sisters would have helped with these details, but they were far away.

Betty and Sydney were both ill for much of early 1957, and Sydney was hospitalized several times. As she had promised her Seattle doctors, Betty saw doctors in California so that her health could be monitored. "I'll let you know what the cancer specialist says," she wrote Bernice Baumgarten. "I think they are all a little irked with me for not dying—[and] so upsetting their prognosis."[12] She owed Lippincott a fifth Piggle-Wiggle book and tried to summon the energy to get that project going.[13]

The beauty of the garden and the ranch gave Betty great pleasure, and going on walks helped her regain her strength. "My delphiniums are taller than the house and all in bloom—my cineraria are all in bloom also the gerbera, the camellias, rhododendrons, violas, freesias, lupines, daisies, roses, clematis, ranunculus, primroses, and orange and lemon trees," she wrote to Anne in April 1957.[14] Walking two miles down to the spring near the boundary of their property in the valley, she reported, "Both sides of the road are massed with California lilac—it ranges from pure white to almost navy blue—wild gooseberry which looks like fuchsia—blooming sage, chaparral which has pale pink blossoms and some kind of bush with bright yellow blossoms—the roadway [is] carpeted in wild forgetmenots white and blue. . . . All the hills are shades of olive green, from very pale to almost black—millions of birds were singing and the sky was pale blue without a single cloud."[15]

Mary visited the ranch for three weeks that spring. The sisters cooked and laughed together, and Mary observed that the marital tensions she had long perceived between Don and Betty seemed to have evaporated. Although no fan of Don, Mary forced herself to try to see him through Betty's eyes, which kept things pleasant. The sisters roamed through fields of wildflowers, remembering their childhood.[16] They concentrated on their love for one another and ignored anything disturbing: Sydney's illness, Betty's constant itching and need for medication, the knowledge that Don and Betty's financial troubles might prove insurmountable. But under all of this, Mary noted, Betty was trying to hide her fear.

All her life, Mary had directed and encouraged her sister, turning Betty away from worry and toward productive action. She did the same on this visit, which Mary must have suspected might be the last normal time they spent together, and encouraged Betty to get started on *Too Old to Ride*. "Mary thinks I should write my ranch book right away," Betty wrote Lippincott editor George Stevens. "It does seem to me that there is a tremendous need right now for a funny book so I'm going to try and do the outline next week—I am also started on my Piggle-Wiggle—Bernice will faint. Mary is really wonderful for me—she is so practical and doesn't hold with any temperament."[17]

Betty confided to Margaret Bundy Callahan that she was five thousand dollars in debt to Lippincott because of their advance on the fifth Piggle-Wiggle book, and she was struggling to finish the outline of the ranch memoir so that she could secure a twenty-five-thousand-dollar advance on that book. "Since I've had cancer Lippincott wants a doctor's guarantee that I won't die before completion of the book—loyal old pals that they are—I'm certainly going to have to type faster than I've been doing," she wrote darkly.[18]

Betty's itching continued, along with what she believed to be gallbladder attacks that left her depressed and exhausted. She was consuming no animal fat and taking atropine and Epsom salts before every meal in attempt to alleviate her symptoms. After suffering through a bad backache for over a month, Betty visited her gynecologist, who told her that the tumor they were keeping an eye on was very small and that judging by her general health, she was fine. "The doctors in Seattle are certainly one billion percent better than any I have seen down here," she wrote to Mary.[19] The Carmel doctor, although he knew she had cancer, barely examined her, she added.

Anne and her family visited in late June 1957. "Dinner in Loli's back yard—danced Calypso," Betty's reminder book noted. Loli Wilcox and her husband George, an architect, were among Betty's closest Carmel Valley friends. The weather was blisteringly hot. Betty and Anne shopped in Carmel Village and took the children to the beach.

On August 16, 1957, Sydney Bard died of heart disease in the hospital in Monterey. News of her death went out on the Associated Press wire service and was reported in Seattle and by the *Montana Standard*. As Betty MacDonald's mother, she had been famous.

"Sydney died Friday afternoon," Betty wrote Goddard Lieberson. "I went to see her five minutes before she died and she was sitting up in bed reading the Saturday Evening Post and complaining about the hideous maroon, peach and Kelly green décor of the room at the hospital—she had been in bed or in the hospital most of the past year and had grown frailer and frailer physically but sharper and sharper mentally—she wasn't at all deaf, still read a book a day and all magazines published but she had almost given up smoking."[20]

Except during Betty's first marriage, she and her mother had lived in the same house almost continually. Sydney was a gourmet cook, a dedicated reader, a gardener, provider of child care to her children's children, a source of love and frustration, and a link with the past—and with Darsie.

On August 21, 1957, Betty's engagement book noted an afternoon doctor's appointment. "The doctor said I was in fine condition—in fact he had never seen anyone look better—which info will make my trip to Seattle much pleasanter," Betty wrote Bernice Baumgarten.[21] This is the final entry in the volume. A few days later, Betty and Don left Carmel Valley and drove up the coast.

When Betty's Seattle doctors examined her, they found that her carcinoma had recurred. She underwent further radiation, and complications forced her to be in and out of Maynard Hospital, a private hospital in Seattle's First Hill neighborhood.

Her cancer and its treatment quickly narrowed Betty's world to a tight circuit between the hospital and Mary's house. Having faced death in Firland, Betty now slowly admitted to herself that she was facing death again.[22] Lying in Mary's guest-room bed, she redirected her terror toward the ranch, a huge expense, despite its loveliness—should she sell it at once and shrug off the terrible debt? Or should she go right back there, work hard, write anything she could to earn the funds to save it? She thought about Don, whom she loved to distraction but whose extravagance seemed ruinous. Perhaps they'd find oil on the ranch, and she would live to travel. And she thought about Sydney, whom she missed dreadfully.[23]

Bernice Baumgarten seems not to have known Betty's prognosis. As late as fall 1957, when Betty was receiving radiation and alternating between Maynard Hospital and Mary's house, Baumgarten was still encouraging Betty to continue writing. In December, she wrote to Betty that she was leaving regular employment with Brandt & Brandt, but that whatever happened, she would take care of Betty and Mary.

Women diagnosed with ovarian cancer in the 1950s generally had two options: surgery or radiation. Betty took both, and both failed her. Chemotherapy was in its infancy, and although researchers in Seattle were experimenting with using nitrogen mustard, Betty was apparently not a candidate for this treatment or was perhaps advised against it.[24]

Betty stayed with Mary and Jens as long as her care could be managed at home. Margaret Bundy Callahan visited and reflected that Betty's certain fate "haunts me to the point of nightmares. . . . The Bards are pretty thrown by it but keeping up in the same way, not allowing it to depress them. Betty herself is truly wonderful, and aside from wiping her eyes a few times, completely the same as usual. She is thin and showing the results of the surgery and the bad news."[25]

Betty's fans found her even in the hospital. Blanche Hamilton recalled that during one of her visits with Betty, a Chilean fan who had managed to locate Betty asked for and was granted permission for a bedside visit. Betty once phoned Blanche from the hospital and asked her friend to bring her a bologna sandwich, which Blanche happily did. But such light moments—a fan, a friend, a sated appetite—were the last glimmers of normalcy.

"I've had a really gruesome time these past few months—in fact the worst in my entire life," Betty wrote the Lippincott editor Tay Hohoff in early December. "I am as thin as a thread and expect to be much thinner as I am nauseated all the time—the only reason I am finally writing this letter is that I discovered yesterday that by taking two codeine, waiting 20 minutes for it to take effect and then hurrying like mad I can write 1½ letters before beginning to gag—this of course without any pause for thought, wit or clever phrasing."[26] A few weeks later, Betty's doctors decided she could tolerate no further radiation.

Just before Christmas, Betty reentered Maynard Hospital for the what would be the final time.[27] She had a private room and palliative care but no hope of recovery. With her world further narrowed to her creaking hospital bed, Betty's fear surged. Mary, who understood her so well and who had so many times during their fifty years of sisterhood been able to help, encourage, prod, or protect her, felt helpless.[28]

Don wrote to Bernice Baumgarten on February 3 that Betty was weaker, but he still thought improvement was possible, despite her doctors' attempt to extinguish his hope. He had asked Betty to hold on, he said, and she was trying. Betty, he added, was the bravest person that ever lived. With Don unable to release his wife, other family members—primarily Anne and Mary—had to step forward and accept the certainty of Betty's imminent demise, deal with the necessary wrenching details, and make difficult decisions. Her husband begged her to hold on, but Betty, in excruciating pain, could not.

Numbed by drugs, consumed by disease, and tended by nurses, Betty's spirit and her voice fell silent. On February 6, the *New York Times* carried a brief article drawn from the Associated Press wire service. Under the headline "Betty MacDonald Critically Ill," the story bore the news that Betty had lapsed into a coma. Since the publicity surrounding the launch of *Onions in the Stew* launch almost three years earlier, Betty had seldom been in the news. Because her cancer diagnosis was not public knowledge, this abrupt wire-service report shocked her readers.

Betty's fans around the world responded by mailing her letters expressing concern, gratitude, and prayers. Some of these missives were simply addressed, "Betty MacDonald, The Egg And I author, Seattle hospital." These people felt they knew her. "I wish you a speedy recovery," a woman from Johannesburg, South Africa wrote. "With all the courage you have shown in the past, you most certainly will be up and around soon and writing more of your delightful books. I have loved every one of them, and have read them over and over."

A fan from Sydney, Australia, offered, "I would like you to know how popular your books are in Aussie. I know you will be cheerful as you're that type. You may like to know that over here people think of you and wish you a speedy recovery and maybe another book soon."

From Dundee, Florida, came a postcard: "May God bless you and take you home to be with Him. I see in Tampa Tribune your picture—such a smile! So that I know you LOVE everyone. John 14: 1–6 is my favorite passage. What is yours? I'll meet you in Heaven later."

In the past, Betty had answered letters from such fans with special glee, touched and amused at the way their concern for her immortal soul revealed their own quirkiness. She'd spotted instantly the cracks where people's eccentricity showed through. But now it was far too late for Betty to notice the outpouring, to savor its Bardish twist. At eleven o'clock on the night of February 7, 1958, with her family gathered around her hospital bed, Betty died. She was fifty years old. She had requested that there be no funeral, and none was held.[29]

Someone—Mary or Anne—would have sent telegrams to Bernice Baumgarten and to Lippincott. Her agent and her publishers had been, like her family, intimates. They joined the Bards and friends— Blanche Hamilton, Margaret Bundy Callahan, and many more—and fans in mourning the loss of Betty.

For Don, Betty's death began a process of withdrawing from the world. He had been known publicly only as Betty's husband. After her death, he returned to a private obscurity. Betty's family maintained little contact with him, although Anne and Joan periodically prompted their growing children to send him drawings or thank-you notes for holiday gifts.

Anne and Joan grieved for Betty, but both of them were busy young mothers, their sadness crowded by the minutiae of family life. Anne, who was nearly thirty when Betty died, had four children under the age of nine. Joan, at twenty-eight, had three children under seven and would give birth to her fourth and final baby less than two years later. Anne and her family moved to California a few years after Betty's death. Joan and her husband, Jerry, and their children lived in Bellevue, across Lake Washington from Seattle.

Betty was gone, but her books lived on. And, though Baumgarten and Lippincott handled the matter gently in their communications with Betty's family, so did her contractual obligations. To prevent Betty's heirs from having to repay Lippincott for the advance she had received for the never-written fifth Piggle-Wiggle book, Tay Hohoff cobbled together a compilation of the episodes from Betty's books that were about her family.[30] The resulting volume, *Who, Me?* contained no new material and was marketed as Betty's autobiography.

Tay Hohoff was one of Lippincott's most gifted editors, as she was shortly to prove by her work with Harper Lee. But the task of dismantling and reconstructing Betty's books was daunting. Mary was supposed to have helped Hohoff with the project but could not bring herself to do so. Although Hohoff did her best, the result fell flat. *Who, Me?* lacked Betty's singularly witty way of weaving insight, insult, and recollection into a story.

Baumgarten and Hohoff toyed with a plan to lard *Who, Me?* with quotes from Betty's unpublished letters to Lippincott and Brandt & Brandt, but they gave it up. Betty's irreverent tone was unrestrained in her letters, and her professional correspondence characterizing people she'd worked with in the publishing industry was sometimes vitriolic. It seemed wrong to reveal this side of Betty. Hohoff told Baumgarten she thought Betty's character had been a collection of contradictory qualities and that Betty was the most complex person she'd ever met.[31] Baumgarten returned the heap of letters to Don's Carmel Valley post office box. He stashed them in the weathered barn at the ranch with all the rest of Betty's correspondence.

Shortly after Betty's death, Mary and Jens moved to Vashon, into their new, low-slung modern home hugging the edge of Colvos Passage. Vashon, which had been Betty's by virtue of her celebrity and its depiction in *Onions*, became Mary's place. It took nearly a year, but Mary gradually began to write again, and finally acquiesced to Lippincott's urging for another volume of *Best Friends*.

For the first time, Mary faced her work—and life—without her sister. The loss was huge. "Our relationship has always been such that Betty furnished our imaginative lives, and I provided the practical," Mary reflected to Bernice Baumgarten. "Together we were Mother's husband and managed her children. We had one fault in common— we actually required the praise and faith in one another that we funneled into each other at all times—other than that we were not in the least alike. We loved and admired each other and disagreed on almost everything. We verbalized easily and talked endlessly and at the end of the so-called discussion, we had convinced one another not at all."[32]

The world still took an interest in the Bards. In the absence of a Betty to satisfy it, Lippincott and Baumgarten pressed Mary to write a book about her mother. Betty had painted Sydney as stalwart but, for all her work to make a home in mining camps, mansions, humble houses, and amid her children's friends and offspring, ultimately passive. Lippincott wanted the bright, foot-stamping, pep-in-pepper Mary of Betty's childhood stories to yank this mother onto center stage, but Mary ultimately shelved the project. She just didn't know her mother well enough, she told Tay Hohoff apologetically.[33] Mary died in 1970 at sixty-six years old. News stories announcing her death noted that she had been teaching a weekly playwriting class to lower-income children, undaunted by the fact that she had never published a play herself.

Continued sales of Betty's books brought a steady flow of new readers. Not knowing she had died, many of these people wrote to Betty at Lippincott. Fan letters arrived for decades. The publishers forwarded the mail to Don, who stored it with her papers, unopened. Don lived on at the ranch, selling off bits of the property when funds grew low, becoming increasingly reclusive. He died in 1975. For years, the many boxes filled with Betty's correspondence lay undisturbed, wafted gently by the dry Carmel Valley winds. In time, before the ranch property was sold, Anne and Joan placed the boxes in storage.

Bernice Baumgarten handled Betty's literary estate until 1970, when she and her husband, James Gould Cozzens, retired to Florida. Baumgarten died of cancer in early 1978, Cozzens later that same year. Baumgarten's papers, donated to the Lilly Library in Bloomington, Indiana, included letters relating to Baumgarten's handling of Betty's literary estate.[34] The correspondence illuminated Lippincott and Brandt & Brandt's frustrations during the years of Don MacDonald's decline. Licensing Betty's work required Don, Anne, and Joan to sign documents, a process stymied by Don's reluctance to attend to correspondence or business matters. In the end, only gently firm directive letters from Baumgarten could coax Don into action, and those not always. One project whose option expired without Don's signature was a Ma and Pa Kettle television series.

Publishing houses were eager to find the next Betty MacDonald, and many writers aspired to the role. These hopefuls submitted manuscripts, a self-produced Lippincott history recounted, "in suffocating quantities. The more imitative, the less likely they were to make the grade. But there were a few which fell into the same category without being imitative—we began calling them 'funny women' books."[35]

Betty's humor had stemmed from her ability—her compulsion—to exaggerate. Following Betty's lead, exaggeration became a particular hallmark of domestic humor. Among the "funny women" who followed in Betty's footsteps were Jean Kerr, Erma Bombeck, Peg Bracken, Barbara Holland, and Judith Viorst.[36] Betty's brand of humor was unique, however, in hitting its mark without resorting to drollery or whining. Her work came from a deeper well.

Betty's friend and former National Youth Administration assistant William Cumming assessed her thus: "Like most people who laugh a lot, she wasn't a person warmed by humor. She was deadly serious, and her humor was a serious shield against the fears inspired in her by the world. Like Billie Holiday she laughed to keep from throwing up." Despite its origins, Cumming concluded, Betty's laughter "ended up joyous. The rasp of its sandpapered abrasiveness never obscured the pure joy that she derived from destruction of pomposity and ignorance."[37] It was that pure joy that Betty's readers recognized and loved.

Betty MacDonald was a woman deeply imprinted by her family's compulsion to create story, a member of a tribe—the Bards—who saw themselves as separate from their peers, superior regardless of fluctuating income or social status. She was the conduit for a particular female experience during the early and mid-twentieth century, crafting versions of the truth that both matched and challenged her era. She was quick to judge, quick to self-deprecate; gifted, flawed, sometimes tormented; instinctively and insistently turning her focus toward the unusual, as plant shoots turn toward the light. She never expected success and was amazed when it came. Like her father, she sensed the presence of buried treasure. Like her mother, she valued home. Betty MacDonald embraced the adventure that her first book miraculously enabled. She was that rare writer privileged to touch millions of readers. For those readers, what Mary had always claimed became true: Betty MacDonald could do anything.

Looking for Betty MacDonald

O VER the years I gazed at Betty's 15th Avenue Northeast house, and its decline was clear, even from the street. Paint peeled, and no one patched it. Grass sprouted in the rain gutters. Weeds filled the yard. Eventually the porch was enclosed by plywood. A cheerful mosaic address sign that had been propped against the front steps when Tanya lived there disappeared, as did the big steel mailbox where I'd left *The Plague and I* and *Anybody Can Do Anything* to thank Tanya for showing me through the house.

By late 2011, the house was clearly serving as a squat, sheltering souls more desperate than the Bards had ever been. The plywood covering the doors and windows was pried aside again and again. Neighbors repeatedly phoned police to report babies left crying in strollers on the battered back porch while who knows what illicit activity transpired inside. The house was past the limits of decline.

The news that Betty's house would be demolished, along with its neighbor to the north, came on a mid-May afternoon in 2012. Property redevelopment would follow.

The house was doomed, but I could not let it go. I e-mailed the developer and described Betty's fame and her tenure in the house. Acknowledging the property's derelict condition, I asked permission to salvage a few artifacts for Betty's legacy, and for eventual historical display. Fine, he replied. You should be ready to move quickly.

One night in late July, the developer e-mailed me to be at the house next morning. "There is nothing of significance left to salvage . . . don't get your hopes up," the e-mail warned, but I was hopeful, grateful again to Tanya for my brief glimpse inside the home years ago. I parked a block away amid peaceful bungalows, steeling myself. "I'll be the last person who ever goes through that house," I thought.

Wearing thick boots and gloves, carrying a face mask, headlamp, tools, and a camera, I checked in with the supervisor, Mike, as the backhoe idled. "Let me know when you come out," Mike said, briefly silencing his chainsaw. "We're demolishing that shed first, then the house, but we'll wait until you're through." I climbed the rickety back stairs. I stepped through the kitchen, pitch black and stripped of appliances, where Sydney had sat in the (long-gone) built-in nook and written her radio serial, *Schuyler Square*, smoking cigarettes through the night. My headlamp on, I started for the stairwell.

But for my tour with Tanya, I would surely have been lost. Walls were pulled apart, their debris blocking my path. Lath was exposed, paneling lay in heaps, wood was burned and scarred. The smell, strongest in the basement, physically repelled me. Flies buzzed. I hoped not to stumble on animal remains, or worse.

I climbed the stairs, relieved to find the second floor both brighter—no plywood covered the windows here—and slightly less damaged. Still the lath was exposed, still debris lay in heaps, still giant nails protruded at all angles from the walls. I asked myself what I could save.

I collected doorknobs, mostly, from the upstairs doors, encrusted with paint and certainly original. The bathroom medicine-cabinet door, which I'd hoped to salvage, was gone already. I found one picturesque double-hung window tossed on the floor in the middle of what had been Sydney's room and pried another from its frame. I marked each doorknob with its provenance, all the while thinking that the Bards had lived here. This place was respite, and it was battleground. All the good and bad parts of being a family, all of life's harrowing and triumphant moments, all of it happened to them here. This was a place where each Bard in her own way chose over and over again not to give up. Betty slept under this roof for more than four thousand nights and woke again each morning. By the time she left, it had become part of her, as houses do. And, as I felt strongly, she had become part of the house.

I looked out the west-facing bedroom window. The morning was warm and clear, the kind of Seattle weather that feels benign after so much chill rain. Below, Mike and his backhoe worked implacably, the steel arm swooping high and crashing through the flimsy old garage. He would be finished with that soon, I knew, anxious to turn the machine loose on the house I stood in.

Dragging my knobs and windows, I retraced my steps. The darkness downstairs was impenetrable even with a headlamp, but on my last pass through I found the brick fireplace, the hearth of Betty's home. It was intact, more whole than anything else in the entire house, and I wanted to salvage it—all of it or even just one brick—but it was much too solid. I snapped a picture, my flash briefly illuminating the dark, and then another. I tried to imagine the Bards' fires in that hearth, all of them gathered round. They had been present once, but I was here now, all alone. I let that truth sink in, allowed myself to fully feel what I was witnessing instead of straining to hear echoes of the Bards, or feel their ghosts. This place that had mattered to them, that still mattered to me, was vanishing.

The moment passed. I thanked Mike and left, unable to bear watching the backhoe. The house was whole in that last moment, still tangible. At dusk, I forced myself to drive by again. The house was a giant heap of kindling.

Being the last person in the *Anybody* house felt sad, important, and deeply disconcerting. This house had been my touchstone. All those years, driving past it had felt like glimpsing Betty. Her words and my brief peek with Tanya allowed me in my imagination to float through that sturdy oak door, into the living room, upstairs, downstairs, across the kitchen. The house had been a testament to Betty, a vector, somehow, to the life she lived there. Now Betty's words had become the only portal.

I let my thoughts shift to the Vashon house, where Betty had written almost all of her books. There she'd described Chimacum, Firland, the places she'd lived as a child, and—most important to me—this house, the *Anybody* house. The Vashon house was still standing strong, and the woman who owned it—Abby, a writer—invited me to visit.

When I saw it, I recognized much from Betty's descriptions in her books and from the photographs in *Life* and the *Saturday Evening Post*. I could smell wood smoke from the fireplace and the warm, round scent of rich coffee and buttery pancakes.

The dark wood floor entranced me. I pressed my palms against the highly polished surface. That floor was built from the same wood used for the decks of old sailing ships, Abby told me. Under my hands, it felt as solid as some magnificent, ancient tree. With this ship's deck beneath her feet, I thought, Betty MacDonald launched her story.

I had been looking for Betty MacDonald, off and on, for two decades. My children, who'd tried to spot Betty's houses from their car seats, were grown, or nearly. I had been looking for Betty for so long that, as each answered question made her brighter in my mind, for others her actual legacy was fading. Many of *Egg*'s first readers were gone. Their children, who knew Betty MacDonald better as the author of the Piggle-Wiggle books, knew little of her impact on Washington, on the publishing industry, on the genres of humor and autobiography. It was time to stop looking for Betty MacDonald: it was time to find her.

I knew that if I found her, I would write about her—tell her story, bring her back to readers, so they could know the stories she had told. I was convinced that Betty's places—like the *Anybody* house—were clues.

I started on the research trips—the pilgrimages—following the trail of breadcrumbs left by Betty's books and my own research. I spent a week in Butte, staying in an apartment near the top of the old bank building where Dr. Moore, who'd taken care of the Bards and signed Sylvia's and Darsie's death certificates, had had his office. Each day I walked a few blocks to the Butte–Silver Bow Public Archives, where I searched for every trace of the family in old newspapers, city directories, and public records. The archive building is next door to the site of the long-gone hospital where Darsie died. I visited the Mount Moriah Cemetery and found Sylvia's unmarked grave. I hiked up steep Montana Street, where the Bard children had gone sledding. I saw the old headframes and mine yards and the School of Mines building where Darsie taught. I found each house the Bards had lived in. I wandered repeatedly to the Granite Street house where they'd lived the longest, trying to picture the tiny, stubborn patch of grass where Betsy played with her dolls.

I went to Chimacum and walked the lonely land where Betty and Bob had lived and fought and raised their chickens. I met the Larson siblings who'd helped give tours of the place after *The Egg and I* made it famous. Aldena Bishop talked with me, and I thought about her late husband, Bud, whose kindness and pity impelled him to chop wood for Betty so she and her babies could stay warm. I found Bud's oral history at the Jefferson County Historical Society, along with the school census records mentioning Dede and Alison. I tried to untangle the knot of the Bards' property woes.

I spent a day in Placerville, Idaho, population twenty, flying into Boise early in the morning and out that night. I stood in the old general store (now a museum) where Betsy and Mary could have bought penny candy.

Admitted by workmen during its restoration, I wandered through the house Darsie and Sydney had rented during their first years in Seattle. Someone was polishing the brass push-button light switches, and I thought of Betsy's fingertips punching the button to light the dim electric bulb in her bedroom.

The current owners of the Bards' Laurelhurst house let me visit. They knew their house had once belonged to the Bards. "We think of Betty often," they told me. The parents read Betty's books to their sons—perhaps reading *Mrs. Piggle-Wiggle* in Betty's old bedroom. They'd found old shoeboxes inside an attic wall when they renovated, and we sifted through the contents, which included pamphlets about technical aspects of mineralogy: "Phosphate Rock in 1916" and "Salt, Bromine, and Calcium Chloride in 1916." Stamped across them was the name D. C. Bard. We looked at a small, 1910s leather shoe, perhaps Dede's, and a 1914 advertisement for an automobile, maybe treasured by little Cleve. There was an empty Chesterfield cigarette pack that could have been Sydney's.

In Boulder, sheer kismet and the homeowner's generosity gave me the chance to visit Betty's birthplace, to climb the stairs to what were once two small bedrooms facing Boulder's iconic Flatiron rock formations. In one of these rooms, more than a century ago, on a frigid night less than a week after a massive snowstorm, Sydney gave birth. The two small rooms are now one. I stood, absorbing the place where Betty entered the flow of time. I felt the quietude of that moment long past—the common miracle of any baby safely born and the power of being present where this particular infant drew her first breath, uttered her first cry. If all events mark the locations where they happen—and I think they do—Betty's birth is layered into 723 Spruce Street.

Near Grand Central Station in New York, I found 521 5th Avenue and stood in front of what was once Lippincott's Manhattan outpost. A few blocks south, I located 101 Park Avenue, home to Betty's literary agency, Brandt & Brandt. I drew an imaginary line connecting Betty's Vashon mailbox with Bernice Baumgarten's in-basket and thought of Betty's original manuscript of *Egg* making that journey.

I spent two days reading the Universal-International Pictures records covering the film version of *The Egg and I*, tucked into a tiny room at the University of Southern California Film and Television Library in Los Angeles. In the drought-stricken Carmel Valley, I drove the winding Los Laureles Grade looking for Betty and Don's property. The large barn and small house were barely visible from the road, and when I finally spotted them, I parked the car and picked my way along the edge of the narrow road, clutching my camera and hoping no one swerved. Betty's niece Alison had once told Betty MacDonald fans that all the letters ever sent to Betty had been stored in the barn from 1955 until sometime in the late 1970s or early '80s, when the place was sold.

I'd thought for years about those letters. I'd heard they'd ended up in several California storage facilities and that after decades some of Betty's grandchildren had recently transported them to Seattle. Not knowing what the letters might contain frustrated me. I'd looked in public archives for letters between Betty and Lippincott or Brandt & Brandt, but that sleuthing had uncovered nothing. Except for the handful of Bernice Baumgarten letters at the Lilly Library, the trail was cold.[1]

So finally, I did what I knew I had to do: intrude into Betty's family's privacy. I held my breath and e-mailed Betty's granddaughter Heidi, Joan's daughter, who lived on Vashon. I was working on a biography of Betty, I told her, and having no luck locating anything that explained her relationship with her literary agent or her publisher. Did she by any chance have those papers the family saved? Were they accessible? Could there be anything in there from Lippincott or Brandt & Brandt?

Come to my house and we can look through them together, Heidi replied.

The papers were stored in ancient banker's boxes in Heidi's immaculate garage. We carried them into her dining room, where huge clerestory windows bathed them in clear natural light. I pried open the first box, holding my breath. "Brandt & Brandt Correspondence, 1944–1946," I read.

Here's the thing about looking for Betty MacDonald: Betty herself helped me to find her. She was a former secretary, trained to save everything. Incoming mail was stapled or pinned to carbon copies of her replies: correspondence with Lippincott and with Brandt & Brandt; letters to and from fans, friends, and family; and her date books. And Betty's family saved it all after she died.

Engaging with this compelling treasure trove of Betty's life at Heidi's house was vastly different from using organized materials in an archive, where all those pieces of paper have been transformed from heaps of possibility and chaos into something finite. In archives, one reads a finding aid—a menu, basically, to the materials—then orders up whichever boxes of papers sound promising. The boxes are filled with numbered folders, and a researcher peruses one folder at a time, paging through it, keeping the sheets in order. There are surprises, but archival research is laboratory work. Heidi's materials were research in the wild. I touched and decided what to do with everything.

I opened each faded manila folder as if unwrapping a gift and tried to balance the need for haste—I was monopolizing Heidi's dining-room table—with the engulfing personal mandate to miss nothing.

Betty's letters were wonderful. If I had ever asked myself how much her books owed to Bernice Baumgarten's direct intervention, the letters testified to Betty's innate skill as a writer. She was there, unedited.

Betty's books describe a universe peopled with outrageous characters. I learned from tunneling through her letters that this was not an invention. She *saw* the world as outrageous, and so she wrote it that way. Exaggeration was as reflexive to Betty as breathing. I could never really have understood that trait without finding her letters, her extensive day books, her lists of worries and menus and obligations, her observations on family matters, what pressed on her, and how she responded to being pressed.

Heidi's support allowed me to absorb these materials. She nurtured me, prepared us lunches. I was moved to be fed by a woman who had herself been fed, many times, as a beloved grandchild, by Betty.

We worked for weeks, a day here, a day there. The ferry carried me to Vashon. I drove up the steep hill, past the house where Betty and Don and Anne and Joan and Sydney had lived. Most of the correspondence had originally been mailed to or from that house. After a summer of work, Heidi sent me to her brother Tim, who had just as many Betty materials. Tim was as encouraging as Heidi, and letter by letter, day book by day book, Betty appeared.

I also reached out to Betty's daughter Anne—Heidi and Tim's aunt—who was the last living witness to every chapter of Betty's story, from Chimacum to her final moments in Maynard Hospital. I did so with trepidation, knowing that the demands of Betty's readers over the years must have been a burden. But Anne was kind and gracious. We spoke repeatedly, and between our calls I kept a running list of questions only she could answer. Anne values Betty's legacy, which she has worked to further for more than half a century. I asked her if she had minded being turned into a character in her mother's books, something I'd long wondered. No, she replied, she didn't mind at all.

The children in Betty's life, now with children and grandchildren of their own, remember her as complex but often magical. One nephew recalled that Betty had him convinced that the clay hill behind the Vashon house was salted with diamonds. He and his brother spent happy hours digging to find them. Tim remembered combing the Vashon beach when the tide was out with a long line of his relatives—Betty, Alison, Joan—shoulder to shoulder, looking for agates. Heidi remembered Betty reading to her, curled on the bed in front of the crackling Franklin stove, while angry waves crashed outside.

Family gatherings ultimately swelled to forty or fifty people. The Bard sisters were all wonderful cooks, and they prepared elaborate potluck dishes. There was laughter and singing—Dede could play the piano by ear. There were beach parties, contests to see who could dig the most clams, huge pots of chowder, and, always, coffee. The Vashon house was redolent, Betty's family members recall, with the aromas of fresh coffee, frying bacon, wood fires, leather, cigarette smoke, Scotch. One of Betty's nephews told me that the way Betty wrote was the way the Bard family talked: sharp, fast, and breathtakingly funny.

But family feuds—what Betty often called little hurts and slights—could burn. Children are tender, and Betty sometimes was not. The quicksilver element in Betty that was her genius, inspiring her devilish wit, could jolt those she loved, intentionally or unintentionally. For the children in the family, Betty's company could be as thrilling as riding a fast carousel, more fun than anything, until the spinning made them too dizzy. Some of these nieces, nephews, and grandchildren best remember the colorful whirl. Some ruefully recall its queasy aftermath.

Talking with Betty's family members, touching the letters she'd signed with her fountain pen and the folders she had labeled in brown ink, was exhilarating and exhausting. It felt visceral. The letters brought her to life for me. I saw her typing in the pine-paneled house on Vashon and the Howe Street house overlooking Lake Union. I felt our proximity, unrestrained by temporal limits—Betty, Mary, me in my little house, all of us typing away, all of us authing. After each day of working with the letters, I felt the slap, the shock of Betty's death anew.

But Betty was there. She was in the letters and in Anne's answers to my questions. She was in the memories of the family members who'd known her as children. She was in the stories Blanche Hamilton Hutchings Caffiere told me as I perched on the edge of her single bed in the assisted living center, stories that made fourteen-year-old Betsy

Bard completely real to me. She was in Margaret Bundy Callahan's memoir. She was in the old newspapers and in all those boxes at Heidi's house, and at Tim's.

She was in her own books, lying so still in bed at The Pines in *The Plague and I*. She was scrambling onto the yellow-orange 15th Avenue streetcar on damply chill mornings in *Anybody Can Do Anything*. She was in *Onions in the Stew*, frying clam fritters and balancing her typewriter on the kitchen drain board. She was on the screen in the movie of *The Egg and I*, her desperate young mother's face hovering beside Claudette Colbert's perfectly arched eyebrows, a study in contrast.

She was in the houses in Boulder, Butte, Seattle, Vashon, Carmel Valley, and in the public records and city directories that led me to those homes. I had held fragments of Betty's story for so many years. Now I pasted them down in layers, overlapping, showing me—finally—Betty.

Why use Betty MacDonald as a portal to the past? Why did I fall so hard for someone else's family story? I had a grandmother who had tuberculosis in the 1920s, and who—like Betty—improved after treatment in a sanatorium. She married a much older man, as Betty married Robert Heskett. Like Bob, my grandmother's husband was an alcoholic. He died when my mother was eleven years old, a little younger than Betsy Bard was when Darsie died. My mother's grandmother helped raise her, like Betty's Gammy.

So there are echoes of my own family story in Betty MacDonald's life, places where certain lines intersect. On some level, I am looking for those points of connection, trying to touch those places in myself. Trying, as we all try, to dowse my past, to dip my fingers into stories that glisten just below the surface. Why do some moments in history, some people's stories, resonate for us more than others? Maybe because on some level, our own histories are deeply listening for them. Listening to the quiet voice saying, *Find me.*

THE BARD/MacDONALD FAMILY

Anne Elizabeth Campbell Bard [Gammy] (1850–1936): Betty's paternal grandmother.

James Bard(e) (1846–1921): Betty's paternal grandfather.

Mary Ten Eyck Cleveland Cox Sanderson (1851–1934): Betty's maternal grandmother.

Sydney A. Sanderson (1847–1924): Betty's maternal grandfather.

Elsie Thalimer Sanderson Bard [Sydney to friends and family, Margar or Grandmother to her grandchildren] (1878–1957): Betty's mother.

Darsie Cleveland Bard (1878–1920): Betty's father.

Mary Ten Eyck Bard Jensen (1904–70): Eldest child of Darsie and Sydney Bard. Married Clyde Reynolds Jensen [Jens] (1899–1988). Their daughters were Mari, Salli, and Heidi.

Anne Elizabeth Campbell Bard Heskett MacDonald [Betsy, Betty] (1907–58): Second child of Darsie and Sydney Bard. Married Robert Eugene Heskett [Bob] (1895–1951). Their daughters were Anne and Joan. Subsequently married Donald Chauncey MacDonald [Don] (1910–75), who adopted Anne and Joan.

Sidney Cleveland Bard [Cleve] (1908–80): Third child of Darsie and Sydney Bard. Married Margaret Tracy Howard Bard Gabbard (1909–99). Her son was Alvin Tracy Howard, who used the name Alvin Tracy Bard. Cleve subsequently married Mary Alice Miller Schoeppel Bard (1921–2004). Their sons were James and Sam.

Sylvia Remsen Bard (1912–13): Fourth child of Darsie and Sydney Bard.

Dorothea Darsie Bard Goldsmith [Dede] (1915–94): Fifth child of Darsie and Sydney Bard. Married Melvin Goldsmith [Goldy] (1915–76). Their sons were Steven, Christopher, and David.

Alison Cleveland Bard Sugia Beck Burnett [Alty] (1920–2009): Sixth child of Darsie and Sydney Bard. Married Frank Sugia (1920–94). Their sons were Darsie and Bard. Alison subsequently married Emil Bernard Beck [Bernard] (1919–97). She later married William Burnett (1924–78).

Anne Elizabeth Campbell MacDonald Strunk Evans Canham [Andy] (b. 1928): Betty's eldest daughter. Married Donald Strunk [Little Don] (1928–2002). Their children were Donald Jonathan Strunk [Johnny] and Anne Elizabeth Campbell Strunk [Betsy]. Subsequently married Robert Evans [Bob] (1924–2005). Their children were Robert Darsie Evans [Darsie] and Joan E. Evans [Joanie]. She later married Donald Ray Canham (b. 1934).

Joan Sydney MacDonald Keil [Joanie] (1929–2004): Betty's younger daughter. Married Girard Keil [Jerry] (1922–2000). Their children were Heidi Anne Keil, Rebecca Joan Keil [Becky], Timothy Girard Keil [Tim, Timmy], and Toby E. Keil.

BETTY'S HOUSES:
PLACE AS WITNESS

These are private residences, and visitors should respect the privacy of those who live there. Years listed reflect tenancy, not necessarily ownership. For archival and modern photographs of Betty and Mary's houses, visit HistoryLink.org and search for "Betty MacDonald Slideshow."

Bards in Portland, Oregon: 1241 Williams Avenue (1897–1901).
Sandersons in Boston: 131 Newbury Street (as lodgers) (1900).

BARDS IN BUTTE, MONTANA
415 West Granite Street (1903–5).
846 West Copper Street (1905).

BARDS IN ELKO COUNTY, NEVADA
Agee Ranch, Spruce Mountain (1905).

BARDS IN ELY, NEVADA
Mining camp (1906).

BARDS IN BOULDER, COLORADO
723 Spruce Street (formerly 725) (1906–7).

BARDS IN PLACERVILLE, IDAHO
Star Ranch Road (1908–10).

BARDS IN BUTTE, MONTANA
1039 West Granite Street (1910–16).

Bards in Seattle, Washington
Former Danish consulate: 2212 Everett Avenue East
  (formerly 2212 13th Avenue North) (1916–18).
Laurelhurst, 5120 Northeast 42nd Street (formerly East). The Bards' property
  comprised the lots on which 5114, 5120, and 5126 now sit (1918–25).

Bards and Hesketts in Jefferson County, Washington
Sydney: Large parcel near 5700 Beaver Valley Road, Chimacum (1925–27).
Betty and Robert Heskett: 2021 Egg and I Road, Chimacum
  (formerly 711 Swansonville Road, Center) (1927–30).
Sydney in Center/Chimacum: Exact location(s) unknown (1928–30).

Bards, Jensens, and MacDonalds in Seattle, Washington
Mary, 3519 Main Street (1928), 2700 4th Avenue, Apartment 69 (1930).
Bards, 15th Avenue house: 6317 15th Avenue Northeast (demolished) (1930–42).
Clyde and Mary Bard Jensen, 706 Bellevue Ave East (formerly North) (1934–35).
Clyde and Mary Bard Jensen, apartment across from Maynard Hospital,
  1222 Summit Avenue (1936). (Maynard Hospital has been demolished.)
Jensens, 623 37th Avenue (demolished) (1936–42).
Betty at Firland Sanatorium: 19303 Fremont Avenue North, Shoreline (1938–39).
Jensens, 1716 36th Avenue (1942–58).
MacDonald duplex, 5045 22nd Avenue Northeast
  (formerly 5041½ 22nd Avenue Northeast) (1942).
MacDonalds on Howe Street: 905 East Howe Street
  (1947–49, then intermittently until late 1952).

MacDonalds on Vashon Island, Washington
MacDonald Vashon house: 11814 Dolphin Point Trail (1942–1955).
MacDonald Vashon barn: 12000 99th Avenue Southwest (1948–1955).

MacDonalds in Carmel Valley, California
Corral de Tierra Ranch, 907 Los Laureles Grade (Marker 26)
  (Betty 1952–57; Don 1952–75).

Jensens on Vashon Island, Washington
13901 Southwest 220th Street, Vashon, Washington
  (Mary 1958–70; Jens 1958–88).

BARDISMS

Authing: being an author

Betty Jean: a spoiled little girl wearing frilly new clothes

Big Black Future, Black Future Charlie: predictor of doom and gloom

Body Thinko: someone who is primarily interested in sex

Bud and Polly's: public toilets

Choke cookies: bakery cookies, usually dry

Criminal girl: Bard name for Mary's maids

Get-happy: someone who exhibits false cheer

Get-in-good-with-the-company: someone who flatters others in order to get ahead

GooGoo: someone who talks in a baby voice or high voice to get their own way; someone who wants everything for themselves; someone who acts childishly

Hootey-Poo: a snooty person

Kick-Me-Charlie: a pessimistic defeatist

LeRoy: a person who is corny or common

My-husband-saider: a woman who quotes her husband constantly

Pee-pee talker: a person who uses barnyard talk and four-letter words

Saddo: a person consumed with self-pity

Smellbadall: an obnoxious person of either sex

Toecover: useless handmade item

NOTES

ABBREVIATIONS

Anybody	Betty MacDonald, *Anybody Can Do Anything* (Philadelphia: J. B. Lippincott Company, 1950)
Egg	Betty MacDonald, *The Egg and I* (Philadelphia: J. B. Lippincott Company, 1945)
Margaret Callahan	Brian Tobey Callahan, ed., *Margaret Callahan: Mother of Northwest Art* (Victoria, BC: Trafford, 2009)
Much Laughter	Blanche Caffiere, *Much Laughter, a Few Tears: Memoirs of a Woman's Friendship with Betty MacDonald and Her Family* (Vashon, WA: Blue Gables, 1992)
Onions	Betty MacDonald, *Onions in the Stew* (Philadelphia: J. B. Lippincott Company, 1955).
Plague	Betty MacDonald, *The Plague and I* (Philadelphia: J. B. Lippincott Company, 1948)
SP-I	*Seattle Post-Intelligencer*
ST	*Seattle Times*

PROLOGUE

1 MacDonald, *Anybody*, 42.
2 Betty MacDonald, *Mrs. Piggle-Wiggle* (Philadelphia: J. B. Lippincott Company, 1947), 11.
3 MacDonald, *Egg*, 138.
4 Paula Becker, "Time Traveling the Roosevelt District with Betty MacDonald," *Seattle Press*, February 14, 2002, 8.

CHAPTER ONE. THE RICHEST HILL ON EARTH

1 Biennial Report of the Inspector of Mines of the State of Montana for the Years 1905–6, Butte–Silver Bow Public Archives, Butte, Montana.

2 Thalimer is spelled Tholimer in *Anybody*, 95.

3 Darsie Bard stated on a Harvard questionnaire that he had lived in Lincoln, Illinois; Carthage, Missouri; Rollinsville, Colorado; Minneapolis, Minnesota; St. Paul, Minnesota; and Portland, Oregon.

4 "Portland Student Weds," *Oregonian*, March 25, 1903.

5 Information about Darsie's expenses and work activities is from the Class of 1903 survey, Harvard College, Class of 1903, Secretary's Files, Harvard University Archives. All other Harvard statistics are from "Harvard in 1900," Franklin Delano Roosevelt Suite website, www.fdrsuite .org/FDRcourseofstudy.html, accessed April 20, 2015. Roosevelt's time at Harvard (1900–1904) overlapped with Darsie's, although whether they were acquainted is unknown.

6 James Bard apparently went by both Bard and Barde, usually the latter. Darsie and subsequent family members used the form Bard. Historic newspapers and official documents often refer to James and Anne (or Ann) Barde.

7 MacDonald, *Egg*, 13.

8 James Bard died on November 20, 1921. He was staying with his sister in Carthage, Missouri, when his nightclothes caught fire from an open gas stove, and he burned to death, according to Missouri State Board of Health Certificate of Death #29626.

9 Class of 1903 survey, Harvard College.

10 Darsie worked for ACM until 1905, then as a field engineer for an exploration company. This work took him to Canada, Mexico, and throughout the Western United States.

11 Sydney's use of the name was never formalized, and she appears as Elsie Sanderson Bard on official documents. It is unclear why she opted for the slightly altered spelling.

12 Sydney's father was a bookkeeper, solidly middle class.

13 F. Sommer Schmidt to Betty MacDonald, May 8, 1947.

14 It is noteworthy that Mary Bard, who wrote of her life as a doctor's wife in an era when doctors were almost invariably male, was helped into the world by a woman doctor.

15 F. Sommer Schmidt to Betty MacDonald, May 8, 1947.

16 The Bards rented 725 Spruce Street. The house has since been renumbered and is now 723 Spruce Street. Built around 1872, it is among the oldest houses in Boulder and predates by a decade the Mapleton Hill Addition neighborhood in which it stands.

17 The Chautauqua movement began in 1874 and lasted until about 1930. Boulder's Chautauqua compound (now known as the Colorado Chautauqua) is one of the few that survive.

18 The veterinarian was William Fields, 603 Spruce Street.

19 The church is located at 1419 Pine Street, Boulder, Colorado.

20 Cathy Bredlau, a diligent Betty MacDonald researcher, thought to investigate baptismal records and made the find. Other official and unofficial documents, including Betty's high school and college transcripts and the U.S. Federal Censuses for 1910, 1920, and 1930, confirm that she was born in 1907.

21 MacDonald, *Egg*, 15.

22 Ibid., 16.

23 Placer mining involves using hydraulic hoses to wash gold out of stream beds and into inclined troughs called sluices.

24 Star Ranch Road no longer exists under that name, and the site of the Bards' cabin is not identifiable. Betty spells her brother's name Sydney in *The Egg and I*.

25 Betty states in *Egg* that she celebrated her fifth birthday in Auburn, but it was probably her fourth, since the family was well settled back in Butte by her fifth.

26 MacDonald, *Egg*, 17.

27 All six of Sydney's children were born at home, like almost all babies during this era. In *The Doctor Wears Three Faces*, Mary Bard states that her mother bore five children and that all were living at time of writing, erasing Sylvia from the family narrative. Betty also erases Sylvia, stating in the second paragraph of *Anybody* that her parents' marriage produced four daughters and one son.

28 Decades later, when Betty's youngest sister, Alison, had a stillborn daughter, several of Betty's letters mentioned Sydney's deep grief. Sydney, she said with some bitterness, was worshipping at the shrine of Alison.

29 In "The Most Unforgettable Character I've Ever Met" (*Reader's Digest*, July 1949, 15), Betty described her abhorrence of funerals, calling them "outmoded and barbaric rites."

30 Cleve was baptized November 12, 1911, at St. John's Episcopal Church, Butte.

31 Sylvia Remsen Bard, 1912–13, is buried at the Mount Moriah Cemetery, Butte, block A2, lot 171, grave 2. The only marked grave in lot 171 belongs to June Goodrich, 1899–1928.

32 The school is located at 915 W. Park Street.

33 MacDonald, *Plague*, 13.

34 Janet L. Finn, *Mining Childhood: Growing Up in Butte, Montana, 1900–1960* (Helena: Montana Historical Society Press, 2013), 143.

35 They stayed at the New Washington Hotel, now the Josephinum.

36 On June 8, 1917, less than a year after the Bards moved to Seattle, an explosion and subsequent fire in Butte's Granite Mountain mine killed 168 miners. It was the deadliest disaster in metal-mining history. The tragedy prompted a general strike demanding safer working conditions in the mines, which was followed by the retaliatory murder of an IWW organizer.

Chapter Two. Fate Alters the Plot

1 MacDonald, *Egg*, 28.

2 Bard & Johnson leased office 2105, on the building's north side, on the highest full floor. *L.C. Smith Building, Seattle* (Seattle: De Luxe, 1932).

3 Seattle also had (and has) a Women's University Club, founded in 1914.

4 The archival records of the Seattle public schools do not reflect the enrollment of any of the Bards at Lowell, for reasons unclear. Information regarding their enrollment is documented by Betty's application for employment with the National Recovery Administration around 1933. Cleve does not appear ever to have attended private school.

5 This building has been demolished. In 1926, the school built a new facility at 1501 10th Avenue East. In 1971, St. Nicholas merged with Lakeside School.

6 Untitled article, *ST*, October 17, 1917; "Fete Day for Nursery to Be Lively Affair Next Tuesday," *ST*, August 3, 1919.

7 MacDonald, *Anybody*, 32. The dancers Isadora Duncan and Anna Pavlova toured widely, and both performed in Seattle.

8 The legal description of the property is The Palisades, block 4, lots 3–4. Darsie purchased the property from University Investment Company.

9 King County Property Tax General Index, Puget Sound Regional Branch of Washington State Archives, Bellevue, Washington. The homesteaders were John and Bridget Hildebrand.

10 Darsie and Elsie purchased The Palisades, block 4, lots 1–2, from Daniel Lesh on May 3, 1919. E. C. Bard (Gammy) was paying property taxes on The Palisades, block 4, lots 5–6 in 1920, and on lot 5 only in 1925.

11 In 1922, city bus service finally extended to Laurelhurst. The neighborhood now abuts University Village, an upscale shopping center near Seattle's University District.

12 Margaret B. Callahan, "Story of a Full Life," *ST*, July 3, 1949.

13 Recounted in Betty MacDonald to Cynthia Waldrop, July 18, 1950.

14 Darsie was lodging at the Silver Bow Club, next door to the county courthouse, when he fell ill. "Body of Geologist Shipped to Seattle," *Butte Miner*, January 25, 1920.

15 Several newspaper articles state that Darsie died on January 23, but his death certificate gives the date as January 24. He probably died shortly after midnight.

16 Silver Bow County death certificate #26333, Butte–Silver Bow Public Archives, Butte, Montana.

17 *Anaconda Standard*, January 24, 1920. Darsie Bard's name was frequently misspelled as Darcy or Darcey.

18 King County Government Judicial Administration Superior Court Probate Case #26751, microfilm at Puget Sound Regional Branch of Washington State Archives, Bellevue, Washington (hereafter PSRA).

19 *ST*, May 24, 1920.

20 It is impossible to know whether Sydney ever purchased these bonds. If she purchased them in the month when the judge released funds for her to do so, they would have matured in June 1925.

21 This and the following details of the case are presented as Sydney stated them in King County Superior Court Case 203047, PSRA.

22 Callahan, "Story of a Full Life."

23 Caffiere, *Much Laughter*, 15.

24 Ibid., 23. If Alison was two at the time, Dede would have been seven.

25 MacDonald, *Plague*, 23. Gammy was referring to her grandchildren's refusal to consume her unappetizing homemade jam.

26 Folder "Texts related to the memoir," Box 1, Margaret Bundy Callahan papers, University of Washington Special Collections, Seattle.

27 Brian Tobey Callahan, ed., *Margaret Callahan: Mother of Northwest Art* (Victoria, BC: Trafford, 2009), 388.

28 Lincoln High School *Totem*, 1922, 32.

29 The Alaska-Yukon-Pacific Exposition, Washington's first world's fair, drew 3.7 million visitors.

30 Roosevelt High School *Strenuous Life*, 1924, 21.

31 "The Mandarin," *ST*, December 2, 1923.

32 "With Hot Days," *ST*, May 18, 1924.

33 This location is now the parking lot of the University Congregational Church.

34 This building was demolished shortly after the Mandarin's tenure. The retail building currently on the site was constructed in 1926 and as of 2015 was occupied by the Buffalo Exchange.

35 "Last Week I Had Luncheon at the Mandarin," *ST*, October 19, 1924.

36 This location is now the parking lot of the University Book Store.
37 "The Mandarin Has Moved," *ST*, April 19, 1925.
38 Caffiere, *Much Laughter*, 37.
39 King County Civil Court Case #187992, PSRA.
40 Sydney appears in these records as Elsie Bard.
41 Caffiere, *Much Laughter*, 37.
42 Callahan, *Margaret Callahan*, 386.
43 Mary may have initially moved to the farm, but she was back in Seattle working by 1927.

CHAPTER THREE. CHILD BRIDE

1   Ferry service connected Port Ludlow and Port Townsend to Seattle.
2   October 12, 1928.
3   Caffiere, *Much Laughter*, 38. Betty was twenty, not eighteen. Bob was thirty-one.
4   Mary described Heskett thus to Betty's attorney, George Guttormsen, in 1946, when Universal-International Pictures needed a physical description to aid the private investigator hired to secure Bob's signed release from liability.
5   MacDonald, *Egg*, 37.
6   King County Marriage Records, 1855–1990, Robert E. Haskett [*sic*]– Anne Elizabeth C. Bard (Reference Number kingcoarchmcvol16_873), Washington State Digital Archives, www.digitalarchive.wa.gov. Herbert Gowen was the father of Betty's friend Sylvia Gowen.
7   Date Books (1920–31), Box 4, Herbert H. Gowen Papers (Accession #1561–72–13), University of Washington Special Collections. The Gowens' address was 5005 22nd Avenue Northeast. This house still stands and as of 2015 was the site of the Chambered Nautilus Bed and Breakfast.
8   *ST*, July 17, 1927.
9   MacDonald, *Egg*, 204. In the book, Betty is seventeen.
10 Washington Department of Health Certificate of Live Birth, #146–1928–004792.
11 The initial complaint in this case (King County Superior Court Case 203047, PSRA) is not dated, but the answer to the complaint is date-stamped September 15, 1927.
12 H. K. Blonde was named in this Seattle litigation because of his real-estate wrangling with Sydney in Jefferson County. Percy M. Wright is also named, probably because at the time he was involved in his own suit against Blonde over a different piece of Jefferson County property.

13 It is possible that the Wrights and the Bards had traded houses, since the Wrights' Chimacum home was directly next to the Bards' dairy property. Purchasing lots 1 and 2 would have given Wright property on which to build his own residence.

14 The Jefferson County school census indicates that the family was receiving their mail at the Tarboo post office, southwest of Chimacum. Margaret Bundy Callahan recalled the Bards' moving to a smaller farm with a large flock of chickens after the dairy property was lost.

15 Affidavit of Robert E. Heskett, July 22, 1931, King County Superior Court Case #243838. In the book, Betty and Bob pay $450 cash and bring home the deed.

16 H. A. Norse, "Alderwood Manor Demonstration," *Poultry Herald*, February 1922.

17 Some modern maps still delineate the area where Betty and Bob lived as Center, but Jefferson County property tax files refer to it as Chimacum.

18 For more on Egg and I Road, see Paula Becker, "Jefferson County Resolution Officially Establishes Egg and I Road in Center on February 3, 1981," www.historylink.org, September 12, 2007.

19 Bud's full name was Edward Leroy Bishop (1917–97).

20 Washington State Department of Health Certificate of Live Birth #146–1929–003831.

21 No draft versions of *The Egg and I* appear to survive, but Betty MacDonald's correspondence with her literary agent, Bernice Baumgarten, and her publisher, J. B. Lippincott, mentions the need to reduce the discussion of illegal alcohol.

22 "Edward Leroy 'Bud' Bishop, Logger and Custom Farmer of Chimacum Valley," Jefferson County Historical Society Oral History Project, Volume 42, 1992, Jefferson County Historical Society Research Center, Port Townsend, Washington.

23 The Bards' ongoing presence in Jefferson County is attested by the annual School Census.

24 Sydney, Cleve, Dede, Alison, and Gammy were enumerated as renters, appearing on the April 1930 census form next to Edward, Ilah, and Bud Bishop. In 2014, Ed and Ilah Bishop's daughter-in-law, Aldena Bishop (Bud's widow), refuted the idea that the Bards rented from the Bishops. Sydney and her family might, however, have rented Betty and Bob's Pioneer House. The Seattle Public Schools records for fall 1930 show Dede attending Roosevelt High School and Alison at Ravenna Elementary.

25 Gammy died on December 14, 1936. Her ashes were interred at Green Mountain Cemetery in Boulder.

26 King County Civil Court Case 232270, PSRA.

27 Summons, filed June 27, 1930, King County Civil Court Case 232270, PSRA.

28 Jefferson County Deed Record Vol. 101, 300, #66276, Eastern Branch of Washington State Archives, Bellingham, Washington.

29 "Notes on Conference with Betty MacDonald, *The Egg and I*, Re: The Bishop Suits, Date: January 27, 1950," Betty MacDonald Collection, Vashon Heritage Museum Archive, Vashon Island, Washington.

30 MacDonald family archives.

31 King County Civil Court Case 243838, PSRA. Betty's attorney this time was George Walsteed.

32 Summons, July 16, 1931, King County Superior Court Case #243838, PSRA.

33 MacDonald, *Anybody*, 35.

34 "Vital Statistics: Divorces per 1,000 Marriages (National)," 106; and "Washington Divorces per 1,000 Marriages," Statistical Abstracts of the United States, 1933, 107. http://istmat.info/files/uploads/47672/statistical_abstracts_1933.pdf.

35 California instituted the nation's first no-fault divorce laws in 1969. In 1977, Washington's only grounds for divorce were the irretrievable breakdown of a marriage.

36 "Complaint," July 16, 1931, King County Civil Case 243838, PSRA.

37 "Affidavit of Robert E. Heskett," July 22, 1931, King County Civil Court Case 243838, PSRA.

38 "Order to pay support money and dismiss restraining order," July 28, 1931, King County Civil Court Case 243838, PSRA.

39 "Answer," July 31, 1931, King County Civil Court Case 243838, PSRA. "Reply," August 21, 1931, King County Civil Court Case 243838, PSRA.

40 "Ex-Husband Pays Family $10 under 'Added Stimulus,'" *ST*, January 17, 1936.

41 Betty could have finalized the divorce as early as November 1932. Her reason for waiting is unclear.

42 Joan was asked this question by a member of the audience during a Betty MacDonald Day celebration at the Vashon branch of King County Library, May 26, 2001. In summer 2014, I put the question to Anne MacDonald Canham. She too said she never saw her father after the divorce.

43 "Affidavit of Service," April 12, 1944, King County Civil Court Case 243838, PSRA.

44 Betty MacDonald calls this neighborhood the University District, but in the intervening years the neighborhood has developed a separate identity and is now considered the Roosevelt District. The University District lies south of the Roosevelt District.

Chapter Four. Especially Betty

1   MacDonald, *Anybody*, 44, 131.
2   Caffiere, *Much Laughter*, 42.
3   Callahan, ed., *Margaret Callahan*, 256.
4   Ibid., 384.
5   Betty Bard's National Industrial Recovery Administration personal history record, undated but probably from fall 1933, Official Personnel Folders, National Personnel Records Center, St. Louis, Missouri. This document states incorrectly that Betty was born on March 26, 1906 (not 1907). It may have been during an attempt to correct this inaccuracy that Betty veered in the opposite direction, giving 1908 as her birth year. The document states Betty's height to be 67 inches (5 feet 7 inches), her weight 125 pounds, her hair red, her eyes gray.
6   MacDonald, *Anybody*, 157.
7   *Town Crier*, October 8, 1932, December 8, 1932.
8   Folder "Texts related to the memoir," Box 1, Margaret Bundy Callahan papers, University of Washington Special Collections.
9   Caffiere, *Much Laughter*, 40.
10 Ibid., 44.
11 MacDonald, *Anybody*, 146, 162.
12 Robert van Gelder, "Interview with a Best-Selling Author: Betty MacDonald," *Cosmopolitan*, November 1947.
13 MacDonald, *Anybody*, 148.
14 Betty MacDonald, "An Unforgettable Character," *Reader's Digest*, February 1954, 91.
15 *Town Crier*, January 14 and 21, 1933. In 2015, the Book Club of Washington reissued "Their Families" as a chapbook.
16 MacDonald, *Anybody*, 180.
17 "Miss Mary Bard Becomes Bride of Dr. Clyde Jensen," *ST*, June 27, 1934.
18 "Goddard Lieberson, of Record Company, Dies," *ST*, May 30, 1977.
19 Betty MacDonald, "The Most Unforgettable Character I've Ever Met," *Reader's Digest*, July 1949, 11.
20 Caffiere, *Much Laughter*, 96. Gordon eventually held a mortgage on the 15th Avenue house. At Gordon's funeral in 1947, Betty delivered a eulogy, and Don MacDonald was an honorary pallbearer.
21 In 1943, King County assumed responsibility for Firland. In 1947, patients from Firland and the former King County tuberculosis sanatoria, Morningside and Meadows, were transferred to a decommissioned naval hospital at 15th Avenue Northeast and 150th Street in Seattle. The name Firland was retained for the new facility, which had 1,350 beds. It was closed in 1973.

22 MacDonald, *Plague*, 31.

23 Ibid., 11.

24 "Tuberculosis (All Forms) in Seattle," *Report of the Department of Health and Sanitation, Seattle, 1936, 1937, 1938*, table 21, submitted to Seattle City Council November 1, 1939. The chart shows rates per 100,000 residents. Seattle had 387,371 citizens in 1938. Tuberculosis killed 761 that year.

25 See Barron H. Lerner, *Contagion and Confinement: Controlling Tuberculosis along the Skid Road* (Baltimore: Johns Hopkins University Press, 1998), 28.

26 Dr. Stith would almost certainly have preferred to outlaw child visits completely. Faced with the prospect of never seeing their children, however, some patients might have refused to enter the sanatorium. Stith therefore compromised.

27 MacDonald, *Plague*, 152.

28 "Firland Sanatorium," *Report of the Department of Health and Sanitation, Seattle, 1936, 1937, 1938.*

29 Chester Kerr to Betty Bard, April 10, 1941.

30 In the final installment of the serialized version of *Plague* (*Good Housekeeping*, October 1948, 293), Betty is introduced to Donald MacDonald by a friend shortly after her release from Firland. This incident is omitted from the book.

31 Beulah was Clinton MacDonald's second wife, and they had four children, including Don. Don had five older half-siblings who were apparently out of the house when the family moved to Seattle.

32 This law was enacted in 1909, the year the Anti-tuberculosis League of King County was founded. It was still in force in 1970.

33 Telephone interview with Anne MacDonald Canham, May 21, 2014.

34 By an odd coincidence, this duplex was a stone's throw from the Gowen home, where Betty and Bob were married. Some family members report that Anne and Joan lived with the Jensen family for some period after Betty and Don's marriage.

35 Clyde and Mary Bard Jensen's daughters are Mari Hildegarde Jensen Clack, born May 28, 1936; Salli Dorothea Jensen Rogers, born November 16, 1937; and Heidi Elizabeth Jensen Rabel, born January 5, 1940.

36 It is unclear why Betty and Don did not simply remain in Sydney's 15th Avenue house.

CHAPTER FIVE. EGGED ON

1 Cleve Bard led one of the unsuccessful pushes to build a bridge linking Vashon with the mainland.

2 Betty MacDonald, "All That Glitters Isn't!" *Washington Alumnus*, Fall 1947, 6.

3 Variations were widely reported. Suzanne Martin, "Counterpoint," *SP-I*, n.d., Betty MacDonald Collection clippings file, Vashon-Maury Island Heritage Association.

4 Around 1940, Betty likely attended creative writing seminars at the University of Washington led by the English professor George Milton Savage. Savage taught personal narrative, and Betty later referred hopeful writers to him. In an October 18, 1945, letter to her friend Guy Williams, Betty recalled that Williams suggested that she write about her Chimacum experiences to try and get her mind off a failed romantic entanglement. This would have been around 1940–41.

5 The firm from which Betty was fired was the West Construction Company, where she had been employed as office manager. One of Betty's coworkers apparently let slip the real reason for Betty's absence.

6 Transcript of radio interview between Betty MacDonald and George Fisher, n.d., Folder "Promotion," Box 411, USC Cinematic Arts Library Universal-International Pictures Collection.

7 Betty's first letter to Brandt & Brandt is undated. Betty also submitted "Patsy, Who Would Not Take a Bath" to Simon and Schuster (March 1, 1944) and Reynal & Hitchcock, the publisher of P. L. Travers's *Mary Poppins* series (March 2, 1944).

8 MacDonald, *Anybody*, 253.

9 Bernice Baumgarten to Betty MacDonald, October 18, 1944. Unless otherwise noted, material relating to Betty's relationship with Brandt & Brandt and Lippincott is drawn from private family archives.

10 Betty MacDonald to Bernice Baumgarten, October 23, 1944.

11 Betty apparently breached this barrier: the only author dinner Baumgarten ever hosted at her home during her fifty-year career was for Betty and Don. Cozzens—whose tongue was as sharp as Betty's and whose opinions were often expressed as extremes—spoiled the event by making fun of *The Egg and I.*

12 *Egg* made a secondary serial appearance in *Liberty* magazine after the book was published, and was condensed for *Reader's Digest.*

13 Betty MacDonald to Bernice Baumgarten, May 4, 1945.

14 The denser format was used until new plates were struck in February 1946, for the book's twelfth impression.

15 Louise Dickinson Rich, *We Took to the Woods* (Philadelphia: J. B. Lippincott Company, 1942), 278.

16 Martin, "Counterpoint." Ironically, the back flap of the dust jacket on the

earliest impressions of *Egg* bore an advertisement for *We Took to the Woods*. By the fifth impression (one of three in October 1945), the ad had been replaced with glowing book-review blurbs under the heading "The Critics Are Cackling over *The Egg and I*."

17 MacDonald, *Egg*, 46, 111, 60, 106, 41.

18 William Cumming, *Sketchbook: A Memoir of the 1930s and the Northwest School* (Seattle: University of Washington Press, 1984), 179, 183.

19 MacDonald, *Egg*, 210.

20 Betty's daughters, Anne and Joan, addressed this issue in 1987, when they jointly issued an introduction to a new paperback edition of the book: "We are certain that if Betty were alive today, she would address the plight of the American Indian in a much different manner. We feel that she only meant to turn what was to her a frightening situation into a lighthearted encounter." Anne MacDonald Evans and Joan MacDonald Keil's introduction to Betty MacDonald, *The Egg and I* (New York: Harper and Row, 1987).

21 Betty MacDonald to Bernice Baumgarten, November 28, 1945.

22 Betty MacDonald to Norah Flannery, October 18, 1945. The median yearly household income in the United States in 1945 was less than three thousand dollars. "Family and Individual Money Income in the United States: 1945," Department of Commerce Current Population Reports Consumer Income, Series P-60, No. 2, March 2, 1948, www2.census.gov/prod2/popscan/p60–002.pdf.

23 For information on Betty MacDonald's interactions with Lippincott and Lippincott's promotion of the book (and Betty's subsequent eight books), I rely primarily on reports from *Publisher's Weekly* and Betty's correspondence with Lippincott and Bernice Baumgarten. After decades of sales and mergers, archival materials from J. B. Lippincott Company appear no longer to exist. Brandt & Brandt still exists as Brandt & Hochman, but the firm holds none of Betty's correspondence (Charles Schlessiger, longtime Brandt & Hochman literary agent, personal correspondence, September 26, 2014).

24 *The Plague and I, Anybody Can Do Anything,* and *Onions in the Stew* made the *New York Times* weekly best-seller list, but not the yearly. *Plague* was number 10 on the *Publisher's Weekly* nonfiction best-seller list for 1948.

25 Betty's head shot was taken by the Seattle photographer Leonid Fink in his studio in the White-Henry-Stuart Building, 1318 4th Avenue, in early January 1945. Fink was not credited. Betty MacDonald to Bernice Baumgarten, dated January 16, 1944, but contextually clearly written in 1945. Lippincott and Betty got lucky: among the formal portraits of Betty MacDonald, only this shot of Fink's reveals her merriness.

26 J. A. McKaughan to Betty MacDonald, October 19, 1945.

27 McKaughan alerted Bernice Baumgarten to Lippincott's plan to change the cover in a letter of December 17, 1945.

28 Betty never liked the photo, which she thought showed too much of her teeth, and tried early on to convince Lippincott to substitute another.

29 Betty MacDonald to Bertram Lippincott, January 15, 1946.

30 Sydney accompanied Betty and Don for the first leg of the trip, then traveled alone to visit her brother Jim, returning to Seattle by rail.

31 Betty MacDonald to Joan, Mary, Jens, Mari, Salli, and Heidi [Joan MacDonald, Mary Bard Jensen, Clyde Jensen, Mari Jensen, Salli Jensen, Heidi Jensen], dated "Monday night" [February 4, 1946?].

32 Betty MacDonald to Joan, Friday, February 8, 1946.

33 Betty MacDonald to Joan, Mary, Mari, Salli, Heidi, and Jens, February 16, 1946.

34 *New York Times Book Review*, July 21, 1946.

35 "Lippincott Celebrates Millionth Copy of 'The Egg and I,'" *Publisher's Weekly*, September 7, 1946, 1232.

36 "About People You Know," ST, September 1, 1946.

37 This figure is calculated as follows: 257 days elapsed between launch (October 3, 1945) and the millionth copy (August 15, 1946), yielding a rate of 3,891 books printed per day, 162.1 books per hour, 2.7 books per minute, or one book every 22 seconds.

38 "1,000,001 Egg and I," ST, September 13, 1946. The presentation copies were most likely bound in either green or gold leather; reports vary. Their current whereabouts is unclear.

CHAPTER SIX. SMELLING LIKE SUGAR COOKIES

1 MacDonald, *Mrs. Piggle-Wiggle*, frontispiece.

2 Betty MacDonald to J. A. McKaughan, November 18, 1946.

3 MacDonald, *Mrs. Piggle-Wiggle*, 10.

4 "New Betty MacDonald Book for Children Out This Week," ST, March 23, 1947.

5 Christianna Brand, *Nurse Matilda* (Leicester, UK: Brockhampton, 1964) was published after *Mrs. Piggle-Wiggle*. The two other characters predate Mrs. Piggle-Wiggle's first print appearance: Joel Chandler Harris's Uncle Remus first appeared in book form in 1881 and P. L. Travers' Mary Poppins in 1934.

6 Caffiere, *Much Laughter*, 28.

7 Betty MacDonald to Hildegarde Hopkins, December 7, 1949.

8   Eunice Blake to Betty MacDonald, March 22, 1956.
9   Betty MacDonald to Heidi, Becky, and Timmy [Heidi Keil, Rebecca Keil, Tim Keil], February 19, 1957.
10 Betty MacDonald to Bernice Baumgarten, April 27, 1957.
11 Betty's letter to Knight apparently has not survived. Knight's letter to Betty is in the MacDonald family archives. In 2007, HarperCollins brought out new editions of the Piggle-Wiggle books, replacing all the illustrations except Sendak's with new illustrations by Alexandra Boiger. Neither Boiger nor HarperCollins staff could explain why Sendak's work was again retained, and my query to a representative of Sendak's estate went unanswered.
12 *New York Times Book Review*, March 30, 1947, 29.

CHAPTER SEVEN. BETTY IN HOLLYWOODLAND

1   "'Egg and I' Bought for Colbert Film," *New York Times*, April 19, 1946. International Pictures merged with Universal in July 1946, becoming Universal-International Pictures, For the sake of clarity, it is hereafter referred to as Universal-International. Betty's contract guaranteed her one hundred thousand dollars in four installments, plus ten thousand for each remake or spin-off.
2   Bob Rains to Bud Ernst, June 22, 1946, Correspondence, Box 411, Universal-International Pictures Collection, University of Southern California (USC) Cinematic Arts Library.
3   Both wires June 10, 1946, MacDonald family archives.
4   Florabel Muir, "The Hen, The Egg, and Betty," *Chicago Daily Tribune*, March 2, 1947.
5   Betty MacDonald to Brownie Stewart, July 25, 1946, emphasis in original.
6   W. S. McClintic to Betty MacDonald, May 23, 1947. Geoducks are the world's largest burrowing clams, native to the Pacific Northwest.
7   Harriet Putnam was played by the Universal contract player Louise Allbritton.
8   Memo, William Gordon to Leonard Goldstein, September 13, 1946, Folder 21390 (Production Code), Box 669, Universal-International Pictures Collection, USC Cinematic Arts Library.
9   This figure is at variance with the judgment amount mentioned in 1944 court documents. The men who located Bob were the Universal-International employee John Beck and the former FBI agent H. Frank Angell.
10 Folder 25692, Box 817, Universal-International Pictures Collection, USC Cinematic Arts Library. The studio filmed the exterior shots in Southern

California, near Big Bear; at the Pasadena YMCA Meadow; at Shay Ranch; and on U.S. Forest Service land in the Mount Slattery Range. The rest of the movie was shot on Universal's stage number 12.

11 *The Egg and I* never specifies the years in which it is set. Betty makes several references that are anachronistic for the 1920s.

12 The film is in black and white, but wardrobe notes indicate the colors of the garments.

13 Claudette Colbert was not satisfied with Adrian's take on checkered farm dresses, rejecting four of them. The dresses that appeared in the film were manufactured in Universal's wardrobe department.

14 Jack D. Grant, "The Egg and I," *Hollywood Reporter*, March 24, 1947.

15 Sydney's presence in one on-set photograph indicates that she joined them at some point.

16 "Women of the Year," *Frederick Post* (Maryland), January 4, 1947.

17 *Trenton Evening News* (New Jersey), April 7, 1949.

18 "Crosley Sets the Pace Again," magazine advertisement, ca. November 1951, in the possession of the author.

19 Heskett's release specifically released use of his first name and story as it appeared in *The Egg and I* to Betty, Lippincott, and Universal-International.

20 Work Orders, Box 239, Universal-International Pictures Collection, USC Cinematic Arts Library.

21 Trailer Continuity and Dialogue, Folder 803, Box 109, Universal-International Pictures Collection, USC Cinematic Arts Library.

22 "Hollywood & I, or Betty in Screenland," *ST Rotogravure*, April 27, 1947.

23 Betty MacDonald to Bernice Baumgarten, February 11, 1947.

24 No prints of this trailer have apparently survived. These descriptions are extrapolated from animation cels reproduced in the press book for the movie, in the Press Book Collection, USC Cinematic Arts Library.

25 "The Egg and I," *Daily Variety*, March 24, 1947.

26 Clive Hirschhorn, *The Universal Story* (New York: Crown, 1983), 157.

27 Playdates, Folder 23010, Box 709, Universal-International Pictures Collection, USC Cinematic Arts Library.

Chapter Eight. Authing

1 Robert van Gelder, "Interview with a Best-Selling Author: Betty MacDonald," *Cosmopolitan*, November 1947, 11.

2 Sydney then sold the house, carrying the mortgage, which provided her with a modest monthly income.

3 Mary Bard Jensen to Bernice Baumgarten, February 15, 1958, Baumgarten

mss., Manuscripts Department, Lilly Library, Indiana University, Bloomington, Indiana.

4   Betty MacDonald to Mrs. DeGoojer, October 18, 1945.

5   This manuscript still exists in the MacDonald family archives. Although not dated, the byline reads "Betty Bard," indicating that the draft predated her marriage to Don MacDonald.

6   Betty MacDonald to Mrs. DeGoojer, October 18, 1945.

7   MacDonald, *Plague*, 15.

8   Ibid., 28.

9   Betty MacDonald to J. A. McKaughan, July 20, 1948.

10 J. A. McKaughan to Betty MacDonald, September 27, 1948. Since 1872, Smith Brothers cough drops have been marketed in boxes bearing their likenesses.

11 Betty MacDonald to J. Crissey, August 6, 1948.

12 Dr. F. B. Trudeau to Miss Suzanne G. Rhoads, October 8, 1948, copy in Betty MacDonald family archives.

13 MacDonald, *Plague*, 59.

14 Ibid., 121.

15 Ibid., 233.

16 Jean South, "Review: The Plague and I," *American Journal of Nursing* 49, no. 2 (February 1949): 42.

17 "Betty M'Donald's New Book Set for October," *ST Magazine*, June 27, 1948, 22.

18 Stephanie Benet, "TB Treat," *Saturday Review*, November 20, 1948, 17.

19 After Gwen Croxford, Betty's sister Dede Bard Goldsmith and then Elizabeth (Beth) McKimmons helped with correspondence and retyping manuscripts.

20 Betty MacDonald to Norah Flannery, August 13, 1948.

21 Stony Wold patients to Betty MacDonald, May 26, 1947; Betty MacDonald to Stony Wold patients, June 10, 1947.

22 Betty MacDonald to Kazi [Monica Sone], December 30, 1948.

23 Monica Sone, *Nisei Daughter* (Boston: Little, Brown, 1953), 139.

24 Betty MacDonald to Bernice Baumgarten, dated January 8, 1952, but contextually obviously from 1953.

25 *Nisei Daughter* was the only book Betty endorsed, despite requests from many other authors.

26 Betty outlined her projects, and Baumgarten sold them to Lippincott based on the outlines. Lippincott then issued Betty an advance, and Betty and Baumgarten began the writing and editorial process.

27 Betty MacDonald to Bernice Baumgarten, August 27, 1948.

28 Bernice Baumgarten to Betty MacDonald, September 8, 1948.

29 Van Gelder, "Interview with a Best-Selling Author."
30 Betty MacDonald to Carol V. Bird, November 22, 1950, Folder 1950, Accession 11708, Boxed with 11679, University of Virginia Special Collections, Charlottesville, Virginia. Betty was putting a positive spin on her writing process. Almost without exception, her letters to family, friends, and Bernice Baumgarten describe how little writing time she had and complain that the time she did carve out was fragmented.
31 Sample reply letters, Betty MacDonald collection, Vashon Heritage Museum Archives, Vashon Island, Washington.
32 Notes for a 1955 speech to insurance agents in Enumclaw, Washington, MacDonald family archives.
33 Maggie Spivey to Betty MacDonald, February 4, 1955.

Chapter Nine. The Name's Kettle

1 Paraphrased from Betty MacDonald and George Fisher radio transcript, n.d., Folder Promotion, Box 411, Universal-International Pictures Collection, USC Cinematic Arts Library.
2 The Superior Court of the State of Washington for King County, No. 382791, Memorandum filed September 27, 1947, PSRA. The damages they sought would amount to $932,000 in 2014 dollars.
3 The Superior Court of the State of Washington for King County, No. 382791, Complaint filed March 29, 1947, PSRA.
4 No date, but the context and use of Basket rather than Kettle as the family name indicates that Betty wrote this note in early 1945. A list of suggested changes for *The Egg and I*, also undated and written by either Bernice Baumgarten or a Lippincott staff member, includes the line, "Suggest changing name Basket to something else because it is too much like Bishop, the family's name."
5 Betty MacDonald to Bernice Baumgarten, March 12, 1945.
6 Betty MacDonald, draft for night letter telegram to Bernice Baumgarten, April 20, 1945.
7 Betty MacDonald to Bernice Baumgarten, May 12, 1945.
8 Stipulation, King County Civil Court Case 412157, PSRA. The stores were Eisenbeis Stationers and Harry Hirtzier's on Water Street in Port Townsend and Olympic Stationers in Port Angeles. Lippincott shipped 223 copies of the book to Olympic Stationers in the final months of 1945, 542 copies during 1946, 50 copies in 1947, 4 in 1948, and 3 in 1949.
9 MacDonald, *Egg*, 125.
10 Betty MacDonald to Bernice Baumgarten, June 20, 1946.

11 Judge Hugh Todd, Memorandum Opinion No. 382791, Superior Court of the State of Washington for King County, filed September 27, 1947, PSRA.

12 August 8, 1946, MacDonald family archives.

13 The other plaintiffs were Herbert, Wilbur, Eugene, Arthur, Charles, and Walter Bishop, Edith Bishop Stark, Madeline Bishop Holmes, and Herbert Bishop's wife, Janet Bishop.

14 The consolidated suit is King County Civil Court Case 412157, PSRA.

15 To clarify, two extensive families in Jefferson County are named Bishop. The patriarchs of the two families were William Bishop (a state senator) and Albert Bishop. In 1900, the marriage of William Bishop and Madeline Ammeter joined the two Bishop families, since Madeline Ammeter and Albert's wife, Susanna Ammeter Bishop, were sisters. William Bishop's first wife had been a Snohomish Native American woman known as Sally [Lagwah]. The couple divorced around 1895.

16 "Betty MacDonald Gets Movie Pay without Writing a Word," *ST*, October 15, 1949. In the book, the Kettle family is depicted as having fifteen children, not eighteen.

17 MacDonald, *Egg*, 114.

18 Ibid., 117.

19 "Edward Leroy 'Bud' Bishop, Logger and Custom Farmer of Chimacum Valley," Jefferson County Historical Society Oral History Project, Volume 42, p. 6, 1992, Jefferson County Historical Society Research Center, Port Townsend, Washington.

20 After Alfred Larson's death, Anita Larson kept a twenty-acre parcel where her house stood and where Betty and Bob's house had been, selling the other twenty acres. Dave Larson and Ilah Moody Larson told me that over time, the family lost track of the visitor's book.

21 The publisher of the *Pt. Townsend Leader*, Richard F. McCurdy, was deposed by Betty's attorney, George Guttormsen, on February 1, 1951. McCurdy told Guttormsen that Madeline Bishop Holmes visited the newspaper office to arrange for a story publicizing a Bishop family reunion at the Bishops' house which, she said, was known as the Kettle home.

22 "Notes on Conference with Betty MacDonald, *The Egg and I*, Re: the Bishop suits, Date: January 27, 1950," Betty MacDonald Collection, Vashon Heritage Museum Archive, Vashon Island, Washington.

23 Probably Quilcene or Brinnon.

24 DeWitt Williams appeared for the Bon Marché.

25 The Bon Marché, Inc., was dismissed as a defendant because Allied Stores, Inc., actually operated the Bon Marché store at the time.

26 "Betty M'Donald Is Sued," *ST*, February 7, 1951.

27 "Gold Bar Woman Never Denied Being a 'Kettle,'" *ST*, February 13, 1951.

28 Lucille Cohen, "Witness Says He's Crowbar in 'Egg' Trial," *SP-I*, February 14, 1951.

29 Lucille Cohen, "Witness Steals the Show at 'Egg' Trial," *SP-I*, February 8, 1951.

30 "'Crowbar,' 'Clamface,' 'Geoduck' References Highlight 'Egg' Suit," *ST*, February 8, 1951.

31 Lucille Cohen, "'Egg' Author Denies Depicting Bishop Family in Best-Seller," *SP-I*, February 16, 1951. Another witness, William Cundiff, contradicted Baird's testimony on this point the following day, testifying that he'd attended every one of the barn dances in question and had never seen Albert Bishop introduced from the stage as Pa Kettle.

32 Blanche Hamilton Hutchings to Betty MacDonald, n.d. [February 1951].

33 "Betty MacDonald Flees Courtroom While under Cross-Examination," *ST*, February 16, 1951.

34 "Resemblances 'Coincidence,' Author of 'Egg' Testifies," *ST*, February 16, 1951.

35 "Betty Tells Jurors 'The Egg' Imaginary," *SP-I*, February 17, 1951.

36 George Guttormsen, Memorandum of Authorities regarding admissibility of offers to compromise or executed compromise, King County Civil Court Case 412157, PSRA.

37 Lucile Cohen, "Betty MacDonald Winner in Suit by Unanimous Verdict," *SP-I*, February 21, 1951.

38 Instructions to Jurors, King County Civil Court Case 412517, PSRA.

39 Instruction 19, Instructions to Jurors, King County Civil Court Case 412517, PSRA.

40 "'Egg' Author Relaxes after Suit Verdict," *SP-I*, February 21, 1951.

41 William J. Wilkins, *The Sword and The Gavel: An Autobiography by the Last of the Nuremberg Judges* (Seattle: Writing Works, n.d. [ca. 1981]), 288. Wilkins served as a member of the U.S. military tribunal in Nuremberg, Germany, in the trial of the Krupp Munitions case after World War II.

42 "'Egg' Author Relaxes after Suit Verdict."

43 Betty MacDonald to jury foreman Frank Bishop, February 26, 1951. Frank Bishop was not related to the Bishops who brought suit.

44 Paula Becker interview with Aldena Bishop, Dave Larson, Ilah Larson Moody, and Katy McCoy, Chimacum, Washington, June 13, 2014.

45 "Edward Leroy 'Bud' Bishop, Logger and Custom Farmer."

46 The book has been redesigned and reset over the years. These versions are technically new editions, but, other than the correction of a few typographical errors in early printings, the text is unchanged.

CHAPTER TEN. FAMILY MATTERS

1 "Miss Anne MacDonald Takes Vows," *ST*, January 23, 1949.
2 "To a New Home in California," *ST*, January 22, 1950.
3 "Glamorous Grandmothers," *Coronet*, February 1951, 123.
4 Betty MacDonald to Bernice Baumgarten, August 26, 1949.
5 Tillie Olsen, "Wives, Mothers, Enablers," in *Silences* (New York: Delacorte Press, 1978).
6 Paula Becker telephone interview with Brian Tobey Callahan, November 9, 2012.
7 Betty MacDonald to Joanie and Jerry [Joan Keil and Jerry Keil], August 2, 1950.
8 MacDonald family archives.
9 Betty MacDonald to Bernice Baumgarten, September 12, 1947.
10 Betty MacDonald to Sissie [Mary Bard Jensen], May 19, 1957.
11 "Former Mate of 'Egg and I' Author Slain," *Chicago Daily Tribune*, July 24, 1951.
12 "In the matter of the adoption of Anne Elizabeth Strunk and Joan Dorothy Keil," King County Superior Court Decree of Adoption #122895, MacDonald family archives.

CHAPTER ELEVEN. ANYBODY CAN WRITE BOOKS

1 MacDonald, *Anybody*, 9.
2 Betty MacDonald to Joan Forrest, January 23, 1951.
3 Betty MacDonald to Bernice Baumgarten, August 26, 1949.
4 Lucile McDonald, "There's No More Privacy Once You're a Best-Seller," *ST*, August 20, 1950.
5 MacDonald, *Anybody*, 256.
6 Brown section, *Seattle Sunday Times*, January 1, 1933. The event was cosponsored by the American Legion and the Black Ball Ferry Lines, which was one of Mary Bard's major advertising clients. "The Winners," *Chicago Daily Tribune*, August 26, 1937.
7 Josephine Lawrence, "The Executives and I," *Saturday Review of Literature*, September 16, 1950.
8 Betty MacDonald to editors of the *Saturday Evening Post*, March 22, 1950.
9 Tay Hohoff to Betty MacDonald, December 2, 1949.
10 Bertram Lippincott to Betty MacDonald, December 23, 1949.
11 Lawrence, "The Executives and I."
12 Samuel T. Williamson, "Betty's Adventures (Con't.)," *New York Times*, August 27, 1950.

13 Betty MacDonald to Bernice Baumgarten, February 11, 1947.
14 Mary Bard, *Just Be Yourself* (Philadelphia: J. B. Lippincott, 1956), 11, 12.
    Salli's name is spelled Sally in Mary's books, as Salli herself spelled it
    during part of her youth.
15 Betty MacDonald to Helen Dean Fish, June 2, 1951.
16 Betty MacDonald to Bernice Baumgarten, June 2, 1951.
17 Betty MacDonald to Joanie and Jerry [Joan Keil and Jerry Keil], August 2,
    1950.
18 Julie Risdon, "Author Betty MacDonald Turns from Eggs to Cows at Los
    Laureles Ranch," *Monterey Peninsula Herald*, June 24, 1952, 6.
19 Betty MacDonald to Bernice Baumgarten, April 21, 1954.
20 Betty MacDonald to Don MacDonald, April 29, 1954.
21 Betty MacDonald to Bernice Baumgarten, March 9, 1953.
22 Betty MacDonald to Bernice Baumgarten, n.d., but marked by family as
    dating from June 1954.
23 The MacDonald family archives contain a draft of "Sandra Surrenders,"
    which Betty states in *Anybody* was one of the few things she'd written
    prior to *Egg*. The draft, dated February 10, 1931, carries Mary's byline.
    While she was revising *Egg*, Betty sent Bernice Baumgarten a short story
    called "The Red Satin Raincoat." Baumgarten thought it needed work,
    and with the excitement of *Egg*'s publication, Betty never returned to the
    project.
24 Betty MacDonald to Bernice Baumgarten, April 28, 1953.
25 MacDonald, *Onions*, 43.
26 Although *The Egg and I* depicts a marriage, Betty functions more as lackey
    than helpmate.
27 MacDonald, *Onions*, 16.
28 George Stevens to Bernice Baumgarten, July 7, 1954.
29 Betty MacDonald to George Stevens, n.d., but responding to a letter from
    Stevens, sent July 7, 1954.
30 Betty Lyon, "Meet Betty (Robinson Crusoe) MacDonald," *Chicago Daily
    Tribune*, May 15, 1955.
31 Richard L. Neuberger, "Delightful Discomfort," *New York Times Book
    Review*, May 15, 1955, 3.
32 The mythical lumberjack Paul Bunyan, while ostensibly "born" in Maine,
    was closely associated with the Western and Pacific Northwestern regions
    of the United States and Canada. The character was used extensively to
    promote the lumber industry. Widely depicted in popular culture and
    advertising, Bunyan captured the public's imagination.

1   Betty MacDonald to Sissy, Jensie, Mari, Salli, and Heidi and Irene [Mary Bard Jensen, Clyde Jensen, Mari Jensen, Salli Jensen, and Heidi Jensen. Irene may have been the Jensen's dog.], April 1, 1955.

2   I was told that the property's current owner has built a mansion near the peak, constructed so as not to be visible from the road and accessed by helicopter.

3   Betty MacDonald to Joanie, JerJer, Heidi and Beckie [Joan Keil, Jerry Keil, Heidi Keil, and Rebecca Keil], April 8, 1953.

4   Betty MacDonald to Joanie, JerJer, Heidi, and Timmy [Joan Keil, Jerry Keil, Heidi Keil, and Tim Keil], October 6, 1954.

5   Betty and her secretaries used this form response to catch up her back-logged fan mail sometime around spring 1956.

6   Betty's letters express her amusement at her young grandchildren's adenoi-dal rendering of Betty as Beddy.

7   Betty MacDonald to Heidi, Becky, and Timmy [Heidi Keil, Rebecca Keil, and Tim Keil], May 5, 1955.

8   Mary Bard Jensen to Dearest Ma Ma and Sissy and Donny and Mandy [Sydney Bard, Betty MacDonald, and Don MacDonald], n.d. Mandy was Betty's dog.

9   Although Don and Betty paid off their original mortgage on the Vashon property in the wake of *Egg*'s success, they remortgaged it in 1952.

10   Betty MacDonald to Goddard Lieberson, December 18, 1956.

11   Betty MacDonald to Bernice Baumgarten, December 4, 1956.

12   Betty MacDonald to Bernice Baumgarten, March 21, 1957.

13   Betty ultimately left only one story for this volume. In 2007, Betty's daughter Anne Canham added an updated version of this story, "The Just-One-More-TV-Programmers," to stories she'd written herself to create a new collection, *Happy Birthday Mrs. Piggle-Wiggle.*

14   Betty MacDonald to Andy, Bobby, Johnny, Betsy, Darsie and Joanie and Margaret [Anne Evans, Bob Evans, Johnny Evans, Betsy Evans, Darsie Evans, Joanie Evans, and ?], April 8, 1957.

15   Betty MacDonald to Joanie, JerJer, Heidi, Becky and Timmy [Joan Keil, Jerry Keil, Heidi Keil, Rebecca Keil, and Tim Keil], April 9, 1957.

16   Mary Bard Jensen to Bernice Baumgarten, February 15, 1958, Baumgarten mss., Manuscripts Department, Lilly Library, Indiana University, Blooming-ton, Indiana.

17   Betty MacDonald to George Stevens, April 27, 1957.

18   Betty MacDonald to Margaret, Kenneth, "Princess Margaret," and Dave Beck [Margaret Bundy Callahan, Kenneth Callahan, ?, and ? It is highly

unlikely that Betty was actually addressing the Seattle resident and West Coast Teamsters Union leader Dave Beck. She was almost certainly making a joke, although the meaning is now unclear. It is also possible that Princess Margaret and Dave Beck were pets], May 18, 1957.

19 Betty MacDonald to Mary Bard Jensen, May 18, 1957.

20 Betty MacDonald to Goddard Lieberson, August 22, 1957.

21 Betty MacDonald to Bernice Baumgarten, August 22, 1957.

22 Mary Bard Jensen to Bernice Baumgarten, February 15, 1958, Baumgarten mss., Manuscripts Department, Lilly Library, Indiana University, Bloomington, Indiana.

23 Don did not stay with Betty at Mary's house but possibly with Anne and Bob Evans. Mary Bard Jensen to Bernice Baumgarten, February 15, 1958.

24 M. Stephen Piver, "Treatment of Ovarian Cancer at the Crossroads: 50 Years after Single-Agent Melphalan Chemotherapy," *Oncology* 20, no. 10 (September 2006): 1156–58.

25 Callahan, *Margaret Callahan*, 400.

26 Betty MacDonald to Tay Hohoff and Lynn [Carrick?], December 11, 1957.

27 Hospitalization dates are from the Maynard Hospital's creditor's claim submitted to Betty MacDonald's estate during probate, King County Superior Court Case #149165, PSRA.

28 Mary Bard Jensen to Bernice Baumgarten, February 15, 1958.

29 Newspapers reported that no funeral was held, but the Bonney-Watson Funeral Company's bill to Betty MacDonald's estate contains a line item for "professional services and supplies for funeral of Betty MacDonald as ordered by Donald C. MacDonald, husband of deceased," as well as a charge for cremation. King County Superior Court Case #149165, PSRA.

30 Royalties from Betty's other books actually paid back the money owed before *Who, Me?* was published. The title is a reference to the title of chapter 3 of *Egg*: "Who, Me?" or "Look 'Peasant,' Please!"

31 Tay Hohoff to Bernice Baumgarten, January 16, 1959, Baumgarten mss., Manuscripts Department, Lilly Library, Indiana University, Bloomington, Indiana.

32 Mary Bard Jensen to Bernice Baumgarten, February 15, 1958.

33 Tay Hohoff to Bernice Baumgarten [Mrs. James Gould Cozzens], October 14, 1959, Baumgarten mss., Manuscripts Department, Lilly Library, Indiana University, Bloomington, Indiana.

34 After Bernice Baumgarten retired, she continued to work with a few clients, including Betty. Lilly Library materials document this period of Baumgarten's work. Matthew Bruccoli, Cozzens' biographer, was the author of numerous other biographies and had earlier been frustrated by

his inability to access Baumgarten's Brandt & Brandt correspondence with Raymond Chandler. Presented with the opportunity to safeguard Baumgarten materials, Bruccoli made sure it happened.

35 J. B. Lippincott Company, *The Author and His Audience* (Philadelphia: J. B. Lippincott, 1967), 19.

36 Shirley Jackson's nonfiction work on domestic themes might be included under the "funny women" rubric, but as her publications were roughly contemporary with Betty's, Jackson cannot be said to have followed in her footsteps. If anything, Betty's domestic focus in *Onions* could have been influenced stylistically by Jackson's work. Beginning in about 1950, Jackson and Betty were both clients of Bernice Baumgarten.

37 William Cumming, *Sketchbook: A Memoir of the 1930s and the Northwest School* (Seattle: University of Washington Press, 1984), 183.

Epilogue

1 The Vashon Heritage Museum also houses a small collection of photocopies of Betty's letters.

FURTHER READING

BOOKS BY BETTY MACDONALD

The Egg and I (Philadelphia: J. B. Lippincott, 1945)
Mrs. Piggle-Wiggle (Philadelphia: J. B. Lippincott, 1947)
The Plague and I (Philadelphia: J. B. Lippincott, 1948)
Mrs. Piggle-Wiggle's Magic (Philadelphia: J. B. Lippincott, 1949)
Anybody Can Do Anything (Philadelphia: J. B. Lippincott, 1950)
Nancy and Plum (Philadelphia: J. B. Lippincott, 1952)
Mrs. Piggle-Wiggle's Farm (Philadelphia: J. B. Lippincott, 1954)
Onions in the Stew (Philadelphia: J. B. Lippincott, 1955)
Hello, Mrs. Piggle-Wiggle (Philadelphia: J. B. Lippincott, 1957)
Who, Me? (Philadelphia: J. B. Lippincott, 1959)
Betty MacDonald and Anne MacDonald Canham, *Happy Birthday, Mrs. Piggle-Wiggle* (New York: HarperCollins, 2007)

BOOKS BY MARY BARD

The Doctor Wears Three Faces (Philadelphia: J. B. Lippincott, 1949)
Forty Odd (Philadelphia: J. B. Lippincott, 1953)
Best Friends (Philadelphia: J. B. Lippincott, 1955)
Just Be Yourself (Philadelphia: J. B. Lippincott, 1956)
Best Friends in Summer (Philadelphia: J. B. Lippincott, 1960)
Best Friends at School (Philadelphia: J. B. Lippincott, 1961)

BOOKS BY OTHER MEMBERS OF THE BARD FAMILY

Darsie Beck, with Mari Jensen Clack, Salli Jensen Rogers, Heidi Jensen Rabel, Chris Goldsmith, Dottie Goldsmith, and Alison Beck, *E. S. Bard: Drawings and Paintings* (n.d. [ca. 2009]), private publication

Darsie Beck, *Your Essential Nature: A Practical Guide to Greater Creativity and Spiritual Harmony*, 2nd ed. (Vashon Island, WA: Waterworks Studio, 2011)

Heidi Rabel, *The What to Fix for Dinner Cookbook* (Seattle: Hara, 1995)

Memoirs by Betty's Friends

Blanche Caffiere, *Much Laughter, a Few Tears: Memoirs of a Woman's Friendship with Betty MacDonald and Her Family* (Vashon, WA: Blue Gables, 1992)

Brian Tobey Callahan, ed., *Margaret Callahan: Mother of Northwest Art* (Victoria, BC: Trafford, 2009)

William Cumming, *Sketchbook: A Memoir of the 1930s and the Northwest School* (Seattle: University of Washington Press, 1984)

Monica Sone, *Nisei Daughter* (Boston: Little, Brown, 1953)

History of Portland, Oregon

Polk's Portland, Oregon city directories (multiple years)

History of Butte, Montana

John Astle, *Only in Butte: Stories off the Hill* (Butte, MT: Holt, 2004)

Ellen Crain and Lee Whitney, *Images of America: Butte* (Mt. Pleasant, SC: Arcadia Publishing, 2009)

Patty Dean, ed., *Drumlummon Views: Coming Home, a Special Issue Devoted to the Historic Built Environment and Landscapes of Butte and Anaconda, Montana* (Helena, MT: Drumlummon Institute, 2009)

George Everett, *Butte Trivia* (Helena, MT: Riverbend, 2007)

Janet L. Finn, *Mining Childhood: Growing Up in Butte, Montana, 1900–1960* (Helena: Montana Historical Society Press, 2012)

Richard I. Gibson, *Lost Butte, Montana* (Charleston, SC: History Press, 2012)

Adolf H. Heilbronner, *Sights and Scenes and a Brief History of Columbia Gardens, Butte's Only Pleasure Resort* (Butte, MT: Butte Miner, 1902)

Don James, *Butte's Memory Book* (Caldwell, ID: Caxton, 1980)

John H. McIntosh, ed., *Butte: Metropolis of Montana* (Butte, MT: Chamber of Commerce, Merchants Association, Rotary Club of Butte, 1915)

Mary Murphy, *Mining Cultures: Men, Women, and Leisure in Butte, 1914–1941* (Chicago: University of Illinois Press, 1997)

Polk's Butte, Montana, city directories (multiple years)

S. H. Soule, *The Rand-McNally Guide to the Great Northwest* (Chicago: Rand, McNally, 1903)

Ruth Kedzie Woods, *The Tourist's Northwest* (New York: Dodd, Mead, 1917)

Workers of the Writers' Program of the Works Progress Administration in the State of Montana, *Copper Camp* (New York: Hastings House, 1943)

History of Boulder, Colorado

Boulder telephone directories, 1906–8

Polk's Boulder, Colorado, city directories (multiple years)

History of Washington State

Christine Barrett, *A History of Laurelhurst*, rev. ed. (Seattle: Laurelhurst Community Club, 1981)

Thomas W. Camfield, *Port Townsend: The City That Whiskey Built*, vol. 2 (Port Townsend, WA: Ah Tom, 2002)

Roland Carey, *Van Olinda's History of Vashon-Maury Island* (Seattle: Alderbrook, 1985)

Hector Escobosa, *Here's Seattle* (Seattle: Frank McCaffrey, 1948)

Elisabeth Webb Herrick, *Native Northwest Novelties: What to Look for besides Scenery* (Seattle: Ivy, 1937)

HistoryLink.org, free online encyclopedia of Washington State history, www.HistoryLink.org

Lincoln High School *Totem* yearbook, 1921, 1922

Polk's Seattle, Washington, city directories (multiple years)

Roosevelt High School *Strenuous Life* yearbook, 1923, 1924, 1932

Peter Simpson and James Hermanson, *Port Townsend: Years That Are Gone* (Port Townsend, WA: Quimper Press, 1979)

Nile Thompson and Carolyn J. Marr, *Building for Learning: Seattle Public Schools Histories, 1862–2000* (Seattle: Seattle Public Schools, 2002)

Pat Thompson, ed., *In and around Port Ludlow* (Port Ludlow, WA: Olympic, 1987)

University of Washington *Tyee* yearbook, 1923, 1924, 1925

History of Carmel Valley, California

Daisy Bostic, *Carmel Today and Yesterday* (Carmel, CA: Seven Valley Arts, 1945)

James Ladd Delkin, *Monterey Peninsula*, 2nd ed. (San Francisco: Northern California Writers' Project, 1946)

Sharon Lee Hale, *A Tribute to Yesterday: The History of Carmel, Carmel Valley, Big Sur, Point Lobos, Carmelite Monastery, and Los Burros* (Santa Cruz, CA: Valley Publishers, 1980)

FAMILY HISTORIES OF PROFESSIONAL MINING ENGINEERS

Anne Beiser Allen, *An Independent Woman: The Life of Lou Henry Hoover* (Greenwood, CT: Westport, 2000)

Christiane Fischer, ed. *Let Them Speak for Themselves: Women in the American West, 1849–1900* (Hamden, CT: Shoe String, 1977)

Alice Gommersall Scott, "Westward Ho! With a Mining Engineer," *Journal of Arizona History* 39, no. 2 (July 1998): 176–90

Josephine Hoeppner Woods, *High Spots in the Andes Peruvian: Letters of a Mining Engineer's Wife* (New York: G. P. Putnam's Sons, 1935)

SOCIAL HISTORY

Isabel Drummond, *Getting a Divorce* (New York: Alfred A. Knopf, 1931)

Judith Lorber and Lisa Jean Moore, *Gender and the Social Construction of Illness*, 2nd ed. (Walnut Creek, CA: AltaMira Press, 2002)

Tillie Olsen, *Silences* (New York: Delacorte, 1978)

Glenda Riley, *Divorce: An American Tradition* (New York: Oxford University Press, 1991)

Jan Whitaker, *Tea at the Blue Lantern Inn: A Social History of the Tea Room Craze in America* (New York: St. Martin's, 2002)

TUBERCULOSIS

Barbara Bates, *Bargaining for Life: A Social History of Tuberculosis, 1876–1938* (Philadelphia: University of Pennsylvania Press, 1992)

Frederick G. Hamley, *Firland* (Seattle: Firland Occupational Therapy Department, n.d. [ca. 1937])

Barron H. Lerner, *Contagion and Confinement: Controlling Tuberculosis along the Skid Road* (Baltimore: Johns Hopkins University Press, 1998)

Frank Ryan, *The Forgotten Plague: How the Battle against Tuberculosis Was Won—and Lost* (Boston: Little, Brown, 1992)

Isabel Smith, *Wish I Might* (New York: Harper & Brothers, 1955)

Marian Spitzer, *I Took It Lying Down* (New York: Random House, 1951)

Books about the Publishing Industry

John Bear, *The #1 New York Times Best Seller* (Berkeley: Ten Speed, 1992)

Matthew J. Bruccoli, *James Gould Cozzens: A Life Apart* (San Diego, CA: Harcourt, Brace, Jovanovich, 1983)

Jason Epstein, *Book Business: Publishing Past Present and Future* (New York: W. W. Norton, 2001)

J. Stuart Freeman Jr., *Toward a Third Century of Excellence* (Philadelphia: J. B. Lippincott, 1992)

Alice Payne Hackett, *70 Years of Best Sellers, 1895–1965* (New York: R. R. Bowker, 1967)

Tay Hohoff, *Cats and Other People* (Garden City, NY: Doubleday, 1973)

Michael Korda, *Making the List: A Cultural History of the American Bestseller, 1900–1999* (New York: Barnes & Noble, 2001)

J. B. Lippincott, *The Author and His Audience* (Philadelphia: J. B. Lippincott, 1967)

Charles A. Madison, *Book Publishing in America* (New York: McGraw-Hill, 1966)

Molly Guptill Manning, *When Books Went to War* (New York: Houghton Mifflin Harcourt, 2014)

John Tebbel, *A History of Book Publishing in the United States*, vol. 4, *The Great Change, 1940–1980* (New York: R. R. Bowker, 1981)

Books Relating to the Filming of *The Egg and I*

Bernard F. Dick, *Claudette Colbert: She Walked in Beauty* (Jackson: University Press of Mississippi, 2008)

Clive Hirschhorn, *The International Story* (New York: Crown, 1983)

Richard Koszarski, *Universal Pictures: 65 Years* (New York: Museum of Modern Art, 1977)

Lawrence J. Quirk, *Claudette Colbert: An Illustrated Biography* (New York: Crown, 1985)

Charles Tranberg, *Fred MacMurray: A Biography* (Albany, GA: BearManor Media, 2007)

Michelle Vogel, *Marjorie Main* (Jefferson, NC: McFarland, 2006)

Books Discussing the Illustrators of Betty's Books

Dilys Evans, *Show and Tell: Exploring the Fine Art of Children's Book Illustration* (San Francisco: Chronicle, 2008)

Joyce Y. Hanrahan, *Works of Maurice Sendak, Revised and Expanded to 2001* (New York: Custom Communications, 2001)

David F. Martin, *The Art of Richard Bennett* (Seattle: Museum of History and Industry, 2010)

Domestic Humor and Betty's Contemporaries

Martha Bensley Bruere and Mary Ritter Beard, *Laughing Their Way: Women's Humor in America* (New York: MacMillan, 1934)

Penelope Fritzer and Bartholomew Bland, *Merry Wives and Others: A History of Domestic Humor Writing* (Jefferson, NC: McFarland, 1949)

Barbara Levy, *Ladies Laughing: Wit as Control in Contemporary American Women Writers* (Amsterdam, The Netherlands: Gordon and Breach, 1997)

Judy Oppenheimer, *Private Demons: The Life of Shirley Jackson* (New York: G. P. Putnam's Sons, 1988)

Nancy A. Walker, *A Very Serious Thing: Women's Humor and American Culture* (Minneapolis: University of Minnesota Press, 1988)

Rural Humor

Tim Hollis, *Ain't That A Knee-Slapper: Rural Humor in the Twentieth Century* (Jackson: University of Mississippi Press, 2008)

Periodicals

Anaconda Standard
Boulder Daily Camera
Butte Miner
Carmel Pine Cone
Carmel Valley News
New York Times
Port Townsend Weekly Ledger
Publisher's Weekly
Seattle Post-Intelligencer
Seattle Times
Town Crier (Seattle)
Digital newspaper collection, www.Ancestry.com

Archival Collections

Bernice Baumgarten Papers, Lilly Library, Indiana University, Bloomington, Indiana

Richard Bennett collection, Museum of History and Industry, Seattle

Butte–Silver Bow Public Archives, Butte, Montana

Margaret Bundy Callahan Papers, University of Washington Special Collections, Seattle, Washington

Carmel Valley Historical Society, Periodicals Collection, Carmel Valley

Department of Institutions, Firland Hospital, Washington State Archives, Olympia, Washington

Herbert Gowen Papers, University of Washington Special Collections, Seattle, Washington

Jefferson County Historical Society Oral History Project, Jefferson County Historical Society Research Center, Port Townsend, Washington

Jefferson County Superior Court Records and Jefferson County Civil Case Files, Eastern Branch of Washington State Archives, Bellingham, Washington

King County Superior Court Records and King County Civil Case Files, Puget Sound Branch of Washington State Archives, Bellevue, Washington

Betty MacDonald Archives, Vashon-Maury Island Heritage Association Museum, Vashon

Betty MacDonald's family archives, accessed summer–fall 2014

Monterey Public Library California History Room Collection, Monterey

National Personnel Records Center and Military Personnel Records, St. Louis, Missouri

Zola Helen Ross Papers, University of Washington Special Collections, Seattle, Washington

George Milton Savage Family Papers, University of Washington Special Collections, Seattle, Washington

Seattle Public Schools Archives, Seattle, Washington

Albert H. Small Special Collections Library, University of Virginia, Charlottesville, Virginia (Betty MacDonald letter, 1950, accession no. 11708)

Universal-International Pictures Collection, University of Southern California, Los Angeles

University of Washington Registrar's Records, unofficial transcripts

U.S. Federal Census Collection, multiple years, accessed via Ancestry.com

Films

The Egg and I (Universal 100th Anniversary Collection, 2012)
Ma and Pa Kettle Complete Comedy Collection (Universal Studios Home
    Entertainment 2011)
Mother Didn't Tell Me (20th Century Fox Cinema Archives, 2012)

IMAGE CREDITS

Note: credit name, where provided, refers to the image's copyright holder

PLATE 1. Cleve, Betsy, and Mary Bard. Private collection.

PLATE 2. Betty Bard Macdonald's birthplace. Boulder Public Library Carnegie Branch for Local History, Image 5–475 (207–15–7 #1).

PLATE 3. Cleve and Darsie Bard. Private collection.

PLATE 4. Montana School of Mines. Owen Smithers Collection (PH358), Butte–Silver Bow Public Archives.

PLATE 5. Laurelhurst house. Puget Sound Regional Branch, Washington State Archives.

PLATE 6. St. Nicholas School students. Jane Carlson Williams '60 Archives, Lakeside School.

PLATE 7. Blanche Hamilton. Katy von Brandenfels.

PLATE 8. Margaret Bundy Callahan. Mikell Callahan.

PLATE 9. Betsy Bard and friends. Private collection.

PLATE 10. Betty Bard and Margaret Bundy Callahan. Mikell Callahan.

PLATE 11. Betty and Bob Heskett's Chimacum house. Jefferson County Historical Society, Photo No. 28.82.

PLATE 12. *Anybody* house. Puget Sound Regional Branch, Washington State Archives.

PLATE 13. Betty's younger sister, Dede Bard. Private collection.

PLATE 14. Betty's daughters, Anne and Joan Heskett. Private collection.

PLATE 15. Firland Sanatorium. Seattle Municipal Archives, Item No. 2655.

PLATE 16. Vashon Island house. Puget Sound Regional Branch, Washington State Archives.

PLATE 17. Bernice Baumgarten. Bernice Baumgarten, Family Pictures, Single Portraits of Female Relations, undated; James Gould Cozzens Papers, 1878–1978, Box 50, Folder 6, Manuscripts Division, Department of Rare Books and Special Collections, Princeton University Library.

PLATE 18. *The Egg and I* original cover. Author's collection.

PLATE 19. *The Egg and I* reprinted cover with Betty MacDonald photo. Author's collection.

PLATE 20. Joan, Betty, and Anne MacDonald. Museum of History and Industry, *Seattle Post-Intelligencer* Collection (Neg. # 200.107_print_MacDonaldBetty).

PLATE 21. Betty MacDonald riding the Vashon Island ferry. Private collection.

PLATE 22. Betty MacDonald signs *Mrs. Piggle-Wiggle*. Museum of History and Industry, *Seattle Post-Intelligencer* Collection (Neg. # 1986.5.33860.1).

PLATE 23. Howe Street house. Puget Sound Regional Branch, Washington State Archives.

PLATE 24. Betty and Don MacDonald. Museum of History and Industry, *Seattle Post-Intelligencer* Collection (Neg. # 1986.5.33860.2).

PLATE 25. Press agent Jim Moran. Author's collection.

PLATE 26. Betty MacDonald and Claudette Colbert. Copyright 1946, Universal-International Pictures. Author's collection.

PLATE 27. Fred MacMurray and Claudette Colbert. Copyright Universal-International Pictures, 1947. Private collection.

PLATE 28. Betty's family in Hollywood. Private collection.

PLATE 29. Don and Betty MacDonald, Alison Bard Sugia, and Frank Sugia. Private collection.

PLATE 30. Betty MacDonald promoting National Tuberculosis Association's Christmas Seals. Private collection.

PLATE 31. Betty MacDonald signing *The Plague and I*. University Book Store.

PLATE 32. Betty MacDonald, Mary Bard Jensen, and Sydney Bard. Private collection.

PLATE 33. Susannah and Albert Bishop. Aldena Bishop.

PLATE 34. Marjorie Main and Percy Kilbride. Private collection.

PLATE 35. Betty and Don MacDonald in King County Courthouse. Museum of History and Industry, *Seattle Post-Intelligencer* Collection (Neg. # 1986.5.33864.3).

PLATE 36. Betty MacDonald publicizing *Anybody Can Do Anything*. Private collection.

PLATE 37. Betty MacDonald, Anne MacDonald Evans, and Joan MacDonald Keil. Private collection.

PLATE 38. Betty MacDonald with grandchildren. Private collection.

PLATE 39. Betty MacDonald autographing *Onions in the Stew*. Private collection.

PLATE 40. Don and Betty MacDonald in Carmel Valley. Private collection.

TEXT PERMISSIONS

Permission to quote from Betty MacDonald's unpublished letters and from *The Plague and I, Anybody Can Do Anything,* and *Onions in the Stew* courtesy Brandt & Hochman Literary Agency, representatives for the literary estate of Betty Mac-Donald (Anne MacDonald Canham, Heidi Keil Richards, Toby Keil, Kallyn Keil, and Jerrica Keil).

Permission to quote from the unpublished letters of Mary Bard Jensen courtesy Mari Jensen Clack and the Lilly Library.

Permission to quote from Blanche Hamilton Hutchings Caffiere's unpublished letters and from *Much Laughter, a Few Tears* courtesy Jill Andrews.

Permission to quote from *Margaret Callahan: Mother of Northwest Art,* compiled and edited by Brian Toby Callahan, courtesy Mikell K. Callahan.

ACKNOWLEDGMENTS

This book would not exist without the support and encouragement of members of Betty MacDonald's family, especially Betty's daughter Anne MacDonald Canham, Betty's granddaughter Heidi Keil Richards, and her late grandson Tim Keil. My deepest thanks to them all.

Many thanks also to Mary Jo Keil, Kim Richards, Steve and Carol Goldsmith, Chris Goldsmith, Mari Jensen Clack, Salli Jensen Rogers, Heidi Jensen Rabel, and Darsie Beck.

Deepest thanks to the late Blanche Hamilton Caffiere, Betty's longtime pal and a treasured friend of mine for not nearly long enough, and to her daughter Jill Andrews for her ongoing support and counsel.

My sincere thanks to the longtime Betty MacDonald researcher Cathy Bredlau, whose knowledge of all aspects of Betty's life is voluminous and whose generosity in sharing her research with me, answering my questions, and serving as a sounding board greatly influenced and enhanced this project.

This book could have been subtitled A *Love Story about the Research Process*. Thanks to these archives, archivists, libraries, librarians, and volunteers who helped with this delightful treasure hunt: Philippa Stairs, Midori Okazaki, and Michael Saunders at the Puget Sound branch of the Washington State Archives; Greg Lange at King County Archives; Victoria Stiles at the Shoreline Historical Museum; Rayna Holtz, formerly librarian at the Vashon branch of the King County Library System, who was for many years the keeper of that library's burgeoning Betty MacDonald collection; Laurie Tucker at the Vashon branch of the King County Library System and at the Vashon-

Maury Island Heritage Museum; Jefferson County Historical Society archivist Marsha Moratti and volunteers Jesse Stewerd, Mary Stolaas, Charlie Petersen, and Pam Wilson; Aaren Purcell and Maria Elena of the Seattle Public Schools Archives; Alison Costanza at the Northwest Branch of the Washington State Archives; all past and present staff of the University of Washington Special Collections, especially Anne Jenner, Gary Lundell, Jim Stack, and Jennifer MacDowell; Zoe Ann Stoltz at the Montana Historical Society; Caroline Marr and Kristen Hallunen at the Museum of History and Industry in Seattle; Jodee Fenton, John LaMont, Chuck Kwong, Bo Kenney, Ann Ferguson, and all past and present staff of the Seattle Public Library's Seattle Room; Betty Lewis and Margaret Buechel at the Vashon-Maury Island Heritage Museum; Gayle Richardson, longtime children's librarian at the Northeast Branch of the Seattle Public Library, now retired; Lakeside School archivist Leslie Schuyler, who gave me access to Lakeside's archival holdings from St. Nicholas School; University of Southern California Cinematic Arts Library archivists Edward Comstock and Sandra Garcia-Meyers; Princeton University Library reference librarian Gabriel Swift; University of South Carolina Libraries Special Collections archivist Jeffrey Makala; Janet Irwin of the Multnomah County Library; Carmel Valley Historical Society volunteers Elizabeth Barratt and Jeff Ohlson; Monterey Public Library California History Room archivist Dennis Copeland; Sean Lanksbury at the Washington State Archives; Kim Murphy Kohn, Nikole Evankovich, and Ellen Crain, Butte–Silver Bow Public Archives; Conor Cote and Connie Dougherty, Montana Tech of the University of Montana Library Archives and Special Collections; Margaret Hrabe, University of Virginia Library Special Collections; Heather Cole, Harvard University's Houghton Library; Joy Werlink, Washington State Historical Society Archives; George Meek, Placerville Historic Preservation Commission; Wendy Hall and Marti Anderson at Boulder Public Library's Carnegie Branch for Local History; and Eileen McHugh, Cayuga Museum of History and Art in Auburn, New York.

Thanks always to HistoryLink.org, the free online encyclopedia of Washington State history—and especially to its cofounder, the late, great Walt Crowley. Thanks also to my wonderful HistoryLink colleagues, especially John Caldbick, Priscilla Long, Alan Stein, Jennifer Ott, Kit Oldham, Pete Blecha, and Marie McCaffrey.

Thanks to all those who agreed to be interviewed or grant house access and those who facilitated those interviews, including Tanya Roesijadi; Katy McCoy and Phil Vogelzang; Abigail Carter; Diana Hoguet; Dave Larson, the late Ilah Larson Moody, and the late Aldena Bishop, with further thanks to Aldena's children Jim, Loren, Linda, and Carol; Denise Frisino and the late Harriette Frisino; Paul Guimarin; Jill Meyers; Nancy Wilson; David Martin; Mikell Callahan and the late Brian Tobey Callahan; Marjorie Boyd; Gail McNealy; George Huntingford Sr.; David Buerge; Ann Combs, who spoke with me about her aunt, the late Sylvia Gowen, one of Betty's lifelong friends; Sylvia Gowen's son, the late Rodney Wells-Henderson; and Randy Bannecker and Joe Bannecker.

Thanks to the University of Washington Press, especially Regan Huff, Tom Eykemans, Nancy Cortelyou, Rachael Levay, Casey LaVela, Puja Boyd, and Whitney Johnson. Thanks to Tom DesLongchamp for his perfect cover art and to Erika Büky for her thoughtful edit. Thanks (again!) to Panda Photographic Lab, especially to miracle worker Mary Fleenor.

Thanks to those who read this material in draft: Barry Brown, Priscilla Long, Jennifer Ott, Cathy Bredlau, Peter Andersen, Patrick Shanahan, Karen Maeda Allman, Mark Reavis, Nicole von Gaza-Reavis, Meaghan Dowling, and Heidi Keil Richards. Thanks especially to my anonymous peer reviewers, whose insight and suggestions I greatly appreciate.

Many friends have been deeply supportive of this project over the long haul. These include Sally James, Patrick Shanahan, Karen Maeda Allman, Lisa Rivera, Peter Andersen, Harriet Baskas, Amy Caldwell, and Greg Lange.

I thank the legendary Seattle bookseller LeRoy Soper; literary agents Charles Schlessiger and Marianne Merola of Brandt & Hochman; Vaun Raymond; Casey McNerthney; Sara Jane Hall at BBC Radio 4; Paul Dorpat; Diana James; the Seattle Genealogical Society; Seattle public radio station KUOW and host Amanda Wilde for broadcasting all those hits from Betty's era on their wonderful weekly program *The Swing Years*; the band Solas for their album *Shamrock City*, an inspiring tribute to the singular city of Butte; Jeff and Stephanie Hritsco, the Loft at Metals Bank, Butte; Richard Gibson, Butte Historical Adventures; Mark A. Reavis and Nicole von Gaza-Reavis of Butte Urban Safari Tours; the staff at the Mount Moriah Cemetery, Butte; Jill Saleri, St. John's Episcopal Church, Butte; the World Museum of Mining, Butte; the Copper King Mansion, Butte; Lori Hunter of Boulder Walking Tours; the Rev. Susan W. Springer, St. John's Episcopal Church, Boulder; the Jefferson County Title Company; Vashon Print and Design; Jeannie Hale of the Laurelhurst Community Club; Lauren Baldwin; Debbie Covey; Rene Kirkpatrick; David Williams; W. D. King; Heather Henderson; Carlyn Craig; Gary K. Marshall; Scott Hennessy; Christine Barrett; Alexandra Boiger; Ron Edge; Junius Rochester; Katy von Brandenfels and Emily Brandenfels; John Longenbaugh; the Book Club of Washington. And to everyone I am inadvertently neglecting to name—thank you.

Thanks to my mother, Shirleen Becker, and my sister, Susan Becker, on whom I pressed all Betty's books as I discovered them and whom I soon forced to listen to my ponderings, reflections, questions, and conclusions about all things Betty and Mary. Thanks to my father, David Becker, for his ever-ready explanations of obscure technology, and to my brother, Matthew Becker and brother-in-law Kevin Hamilton for their unflagging enthusiasm. Thanks to my father-in-law, Stuart L. Brown, for all his help in Carmel Valley.

Finally, and most heartily, thanks to my husband, Barry Brown, and our children, Hunter, Sawyer, and Lillie, who grew up with Betty and Mary as almost tangible presences in our house. I would (as Betty would say) crawl over broken glass to tell you how much your support means to me.

INDEX

Note: plates 1–16 are found after page 66 and plates 17–40 after page 126.

archives of Betty's letters, 170–73, 204n1

Arctic Club, Seattle, 21

Arnold, Lesley (character), 146

"Around Town" column (*Town Crier*), 53–54

art and artists, 50, 52, 54, 59, 65, 77, 136, 139

Arthur, Jean, 54

Atlantic Monthly: *The Egg and I* serialized in, 71–72, 113

Atlantic Monthly Press, 106

Atlantic Prize submission, 64

attorneys, 45, 46, 49, 90, 91, 115, 120, 188n31. *See also* Guttormsen, George; lawsuits and court cases

Auburn, NY, 12, 77, 183n25

"authing," 74, 108, 129

autobiographical books. See *Anybody Can Do Anything*; *The Egg and I*; *Onions in the Stew*; *The Plague and I*

autographing and autograph parties, 78, 95, 124, 135, 147–48, *plate 39*

B

Baird, Dorothy, 121

baptisms: Betty, 10; Cleve, 14, 183n30; Mary, 8, 182n14

Bard, Alison Cleveland (later Sugia; Beck; Burnett) (sister): 15th Ave. house in name of, 52; in 1930 census, 187n24; about, xvii, 176; as aunt, 41; Betty babysitting for, 141–42; birth of, 27; feuding with, 128; gypsum mine income and, 41; mentioned, 82, 107; photographs of, *plate 29*; at Roosevelt District house, Seattle, 49; schooling, 60;

187n24; Seattle, return to, 44–45; stillborn daughter of, 183n28; as witness at Betty and Don's wedding, 65

Bard, Betty. *See* MacDonald, Betty

Bard, Cleve (Sidney Cleveland) (brother): in 1930 census, 187n24; in 1933, 60; about, 175; archery and, 24; baptism of, 14, 183n30; birth of, 11; Bob Heskett and, 38; childhood, 15; in Chimacum, 38; dairy farm and, 34–35, 37; Don MacDonald and, 65; in family of women, 27; feuding with, 128; gypsum mine income and, 41; Jens and Mary's beach house and, 152; mentioned, xvii, 39, 42, 107; photographs of, *plate 1*, *plate 3*; schooling, 14, 17, 34–35; Seattle, return to, 44–45; spelling of name, 183n24; Vashon bridge effort, 190n1; Vashon road construction, 99

Bard, Darsie Cleveland (father): about, 3, 175; background, 5, 18; in Betty's books, xvii, 24; in Butte, 6, 11–12, 14–15, 16, 25; career, 9, 17–18, 25, 182n10; death of, 25–29, 33, 185n15; Dede, relationship with, 16; engagement and elopement, 6; funeral for, 26; at Harvard, 4–5, 6; mineralogy pamphlets later found in Laurelhurst house, 169; photographs of, *plate 3*; in Seattle, 20–25; Sylvia, loss of, 14; travels of, 7–8, 9, 10, 13

Bard, Dede (Dorothea Darsie) (later Goldsmith) (sister): 15th Ave. house in name of, 52; in 1930 census, 187n24; about, xvii, 176; as aunt, 41; Betty's tuberculosis and, 61; birth of, 16; chicken farm and, 44; childhood, 16–17, 29; Darsie's relationship with, 16; family at Vashon Island, 141–42; fifth birthday, 25; gypsum mine income and, 41; income from, 59–60; mentioned, 39, 82, 107; photographs of, *plate 13*; playing piano at family gatherings, 173; at Roosevelt District house, Seattle, 49; schooling, 37–38, 187n24; Seattle, return to, 44–45; at WPA, 60

Bard, "Gammy" (Anne Elizabeth) (grandmother): in 1930 census, 187n24; about, 175; Alison and, 27; arrival in Butte, 8; in Betty's books, xvii; in Butte, 15, 16–17; on childhood as hazardous, 102; death and interment of, 187n25; descriptions of, 5; divorce of, 5–6; *The Egg and I* and, 69; homemade jam of, 185n25; at Laurelhurst house, 31; Laurelhurst property, 22, 184n10; on lax discipline, 30; matriarchy and, 9; mentioned, 40; move to Boulder, 45; renting in Jefferson County, 41

Bard, James (or "Barde") (grandfather), 5–6, 175, 182n6, 182n8

Bard, Mary Ten Eyck (later Jensen) (sister): about, 175; advertising career, 53; Alison and, 27; *Anybody Can Do Anything* and, 132, 133–34; *Best Friends*, xvi, 138; Betty's cancer and, 158, 159; Betty's death and, 162; Betty's divorce from Bob Haskett and, 45, 48; Betty's frustrations vented to, 153; Betty's tuberculosis and, 61;

birth and baptism of, 8, 182n14; Bob Heskett and, 39, 186n5; Butte environment and, 17; carefully presented in Betty's books, 128; character inspired by, 58; charitable work, 21–22; childhood, 14–15; Chimacum farm and, 38, 44, 186n43; courtship and marriage to Jens Clyde Jensen, 58–59; death of, 163; doctors and, 182n11; as doctor's wife, 59, 137–38; *The Doctor Wears Three Faces*, 108, 137–38, 183n27; Don and, 100; as driver, 31; *The Egg and I* and, 68, 69; family of, 60; finances taken over by, 52–53; *Forty Odd*, 138; German baron and, 55; gypsum mine income and, 41; in Hollywood, 88; homes of, xvi; *Just Be Yourself*, 138–39; at Laurelhurst home, 23–24; on literary stage, 138; Madrona house and Vashon Island beach house, 152, 162; matriarchy and, 9–10; mentioned, 50; mortgages and, 52; *Mrs. Piggle-Wiggle* and, 83; personality of, xvii, 3, 15, 30; photographs of, *plate 1, plate 6, plate 28, plate 31, plate 32*; role of, in Betty's life, 10, 15, 57, 58, 108; at Roosevelt District house, Seattle, 49; schooling, 14, 17, 21–22, 23, 28; in Seattle, 20; Seattle and, 22; snobbery and, 54; sued by Pacific Coast Coal Company, 55; as support for family, 48, 49; Sydney, attempted book on, 162–63; Sydney moving in with Jens and, 66; Vida Pixley and, 52; working at Mandarin tea shop, 32; as writer, 107–8

Brandt & Brandt, 163, 192n23, 204n34; collaboration forbade by, 110; *The Egg and I* and, 69–71, 73; letters, archived, 170; Manhattan offices, 170; sequel to *Egg* wanted by, 100. *See also* Baumgarten, Bernice

breadwinner role, 129

Bredlau, Cathy, 183n20

Breen, Joseph, 90

Bridger Canyon, Utah, 13

Brownies, 138–39

Bruccuoli, Matthew, 203n34

Brute Force (film), 96

Bundy, Edward, 45

Bunyan, Paul, 148, 201n32

burials. *See* funerals and burials

Butte, Anaconda & Pacific railroad, 12, 25

Butte, MT: air pollution in, 18; author's visit to, 168–69; children playing in mines of, 15–16; copper mining and, 12; Darsie's death in, 25; diversity of, 4; eccentricity in, 19; explosion and fire, Granite Mountain Mine, 184n36; as home base for travels, 7; houses in, xix, 8–9, 12, 25, 169; labor violence and stoppages in, 16; McKinley School, 14, 17, 183n32; mines and mining in, 3–4, 12–13, 16, 17; Montana School of Mines, 11–12, 13, 17–18, 169, *plate 4*; move to, 6–7; plans to move from, 17; as "richest hill on earth," 4; Sydney and Darsie's married life in, 3–4; weather in, 14–15; Westside neighborhood, 11–12, *plate 4*

Butte Electric Railway, 12

Butte & Ely Company, 9

Butte Masonic Lodge, 25

Butte Miners' Union, 4, 16

Butte Miners' Union Hall, 16

Butte Mine Workers' Union, 16

Butte–Silver Bow Public Archives, 168

C

Cahoon, Grace, 8

Calkins, Raymond, 27–28, 41, 52

Callahan, Margaret Bundy: "Around Town" column (*Town Crier*), 53–54; Betty's death and, 161; Chimacum farm and, 37, 187n14; as family friend, 29; on Laurelhurst home, 23; on Lincoln High, 28; on Mary, 30, 31, 53; memoir of, 174; mentioned, 45, 157; photographs of, *plate 8*, *plate 10*; on snobbery, 54, 74; on Vida Pixley, 52

Callahan, Tobey, 129

Canada, 182n10

cancer, 154–55, 157–60

Canham, Anne. *See* MacDonald, Anne

Capitol Hill, Seattle, 20–21

Carmel Valley, CA: Corral de Tierra Ranch, 140–42, 148, 149–52, 156, *plate 40*; home in, xix, 148; Los Laureles Grade, 140, 149, 170; move to, xv; roundups, 152; in Steinbeck's *The Pastures of Heaven*, 151; Vashon Island contrasted with, 150

Carmel Valley Horsemen's Association, 152

Carnation Co., 26–27

Carthage, MO, 182n8

cascara, 17

Cedar Falls, IA, 38–39

cemeteries: Golden Gate National

insurance for chicken farming,
42; divorce proceedings against,
45–49, 188n41; in *The Egg and I*,
70, 93–94; film release deal, 91,
93, 186n5, 194n9, 194n19; libel
lawsuit and, 120; marriage to Betty
and chicken farm, 40–45; move to
Olympic Peninsula, xiv; murder
of, 131; public confusion between
Don and, 130
Heskett, Florence, 39
Heskett, Joan (daughter). *See* Mac-
Donald, Joan
Heskett, Katherine, 39
Heskett, Otis, 39
Hicks, Mr. and Mrs. (characters), 112,
114, 125
Hildebrand, John and Bridget, 184n9
Hohoff, Tay, 134, 159, 161–62, 163
A Hole Is to Dig (Krauss), 85
Holland, Barbara, 164
Hollywood, 87–89
Hollywood Ostrich Farm, 87
Holm, Celeste, 96
Holmes, Madeline Bishop, 198n13,
198n21
Hoover, Lou Henry, 7
The Horn Book magazine, 84
hospitals: fan visits in, 159; Firland
Sanatorium, 60–64, 101, 102, 103–4,
189n21, *plate 15*; Harborview,
Seattle, 58; King County Hospital,
62; Maynard, Seattle, 158, 159; St.
John's, Port Townsend, 43
houses and homes: addresses, listing
of, 177–78; *Anybody* house (15th
Ave. NE, Seattle), xi–xii, xvi–xix,
51–52, 66, 99, 165–67, 195n2, *plate
12, plate 14*; Betty's presence in,
174; Capitol Hill, Seattle (former

Danish consulate), 20–21, 169; at
Corral de Tierra Ranch, Carmel
Valley, CA, 150–51, 156, 170, *plate
40*; Dolphin Point Trail, Vashon
Island, 66, 99, 140–41, 142, 167–68,
172–73, *plate 16, plate 20, plate 36*;
duplex near University of Wash-
ington (22nd Ave NE), Seattle,
66; Egg and I Road, Chimacum,
WA, xix, 42–43, 169, *plate 11*; E
Howe St., North Capitol Hill,
Seattle, 99–100, 127, 140, 141, *plate
23, plate 24*; Laurelhurst, Seattle
(The Palisades), 22–24, 34, 36,
41, 169, 184n8, *plate 5*; looking
for, xvi, xix; Madrona, Seattle
(Jensens), 152; Roosevelt District, Seattle, 49–50; Spruce St.,
Boulder, CO (Betty's birthplace),
9, 170, 182n16, *plate 2*; Star Ranch
Road, Placerville, 11, 183n24;
Vashon Island beach house (Jen-
sens), 152, 162; West Copper St.
cottage, Butte, 8–9; West Granite
St., Butte, xix, 8, 12, 25, 169. *See
also* mortgages
Humane Society, 91
Huntington, D. Whitney, 54

I

Illahee ferry, *plate 21*
illnesses (Betty): cancer, 154–55,
157–60; itching (skin condition),
150, 152, 154, 156, 157; pulmonary
tuberculosis and treatment, 60–64;
scarlet fever, 17. *See also* tuberculosis
illustrators for *Mrs. Piggle-Wiggle*
books, 84–86, 194n11

Indians, 75, 192n20
intrapleural pneumolysis, 64
itching (skin condition), 150, 152, 154, 156, 157
Itoi, Kazuko Monica ("Kazi") (later Sone), 63, 106–7
IWW (Industrial Workers of the World; "Wobblies"), 16, 184n36

J

Jackson, Shirley, 143, 204n36
Japanese internment, 106, 107
Japantown/Nihonmachi, Seattle, 63
Jefferson, Maxwell Ford (character), 112
Jefferson County, WA: about, 36–37; Bard women renting in, 41; chicken ranch, Center, 42–46; dairy farm, Chimacum, 34–35, 36–37, 40; egg ranches in, 42; film location scouting trip in, 115; tourists in, 118. *See also* Chimacum, WA
Jefferson County Fair, 75
Jefferson County Historical Society, 44, 169
Jensen, Dr. Clyde Reynolds ("Jens") (brother-in-law): background, 58–59; Betty and, 59; Betty's cancer and, 159; Betty's tuberculosis and, 61; Guttormsen and, 114; Madrona house and Vashon Island beach house, 152, 162; Mary's marriage to, 137–38; wedding, 58
Jensen, Heidi Elizabeth (later Rabel) (niece), 66, 139, *plate 22*
Jensen, Mari Hildegarde (later Clack) (niece), 60, 66, 139, *plate 22*

Jensen, Mary (sister). *See* Bard, Mary Ten Eyck
Jensen, Salli Dorothea (later Rogers) (niece), 60, 66, 139, *plate 22*
"Joanie" (daughter). *See* MacDonald, Joan
jobs (Betty), 53, 60, 64–65, 145–46, 191n5
Johnson, J. C., 20
Johnson, Raymond, 115, 119, 120
Just Be Yourself (Mary Bard), 138–39
"The Just-One-More-TV-Programmers" (Mac Donald), 202n13

K

Kaufman, George S., 55
Keil, Girard "Jerry" (son-in-law), 127, 151, 161
Keil, Heidi (granddaughter), 128, 171–74, *plate 38*
Keil, Joan. *See* MacDonald, Joan
Keil, Rebecca "Becky" (granddaughter), 128, 142, *plate 38*
Keil, Tim (grandson), 172–74, *plate 38*
Kerr, Jean, 143, 164
Kettle, Ma, Pa, and family (characters): Basket as original name, 112, 113; descriptions in *Egg and I*, 117; film roles, 89–90, 96; focus on, 45; as iconic figures, xv; introduction of characters, xiv; Ma and Pa Kettle film series, 116; readers and, 74–75; significance of characters, 115–17; TV series (unrealized), 163. *See also* Bishop/Kettle et al. libel suits
Kettle, Tits, 90
Kilbride, Percy, 89–90, 96, 116–17, *plate 34*

Kimi (character), 102
King County Courthouse, *plate 35*
King County Hospital, 62
Knight, Hilary, 85–86
KOL radio, 58
Korean War, 136
Krauss, Ruth, 85

L

labor adjustor, NRA, 60
Lake Union, 99
Lake Washington, xix, 22, 23
Lake Washington Ship Canal, 20
Lantz, Walter, 95
Larson, Alfred, 118, 198n20
Larson, Anita, 118, 122–23, 198n20
Larson, Dave, 198n20
Larson, Ilah Moody, 198n20
Las Cruces, NM, 78
Laurelhurst District, Seattle, 22–23, 34, 184n11
Laurelhurst house (The Palisades), Seattle, 22–24, 34, 36, 41, 169, 184n8, *plate 5*
lawsuits and court cases: Calkins and gypsum mine proceeds, 41; Edward and Ilah Bishop libel case, 112–15, 122–23; over Mandarin tea house debts, 33; Pacific Coast Coal Company, 55. *See also* Bishop/Kettle et al. libel suits
Lee, Harper, 106, 161
Lesh, Daniel, 184n10
letters. *See* fan mail
Lewis, Sinclair, 134
Lewiston, MT, mineral property, 27
libel suits. *See* Bishop/Kettle et al. libel suits; lawsuits and court cases

Liberty magazine, 191n12
Lieberson, Goddard, 59, 155, 157
Life among the Savages (Jackson), 143
"Life Goes Calling On the Author of 'The Egg and I'" (*Life* magazine), 77
Life magazine, 77, 168
Lilly Library, Bloomington, IN, 163, 203n34
Lincoln High School, Seattle, 28, 30
Lippincott, Bertram, 79, 134, 162
Lippincott, Joseph, 108
J. B. Lippincott Co.: advances from, 100, 154; *Anybody Can Do Anything* and, 134–36; Betty's cancer and, 157; Betty's death and, 161; bio prepared for, 46; correspondence with, 187n21; Don and, 163; on *The Egg and I*, xiii; *The Egg and I* and, 71–73, 76–79, 96; lawsuits and, 112, 113, 115, 146; Lee's *To Kill a Mockingbird*, 106; Manhattan offices, 170; *Mrs. Piggle-Wiggle* and, 81–82, 85, 155; *Nancy and Plum* and, 139; *Onions in the Stew* and, 143–44, 146–47; *The Plague and I* and, 103, 105; publishing process with Betty, 196n26; search for other Bard family writers, 107; sequel to *Egg* wanted by, 100
literary agent. *See* Baumgarten, Bernice; Brandt & Brandt
literary estate (Betty), 163
Loft Candy, 92
Long, William, 131
Los Angeles, 127
Lowell Elementary, Seattle, 21, 184n4
Lumber Research, Inc., 53
Lyon, Marge, 147

M

MacDonald, Anne Elizabeth Campbell (born Heskett; later Strunk, Evans, Canham) (daughter): about, 176; adopted by Don, 131; in *Anybody Can Do Anything*, 133; author's visit with, 172; on Betty's and Don's marriage, 66; Betty's death and, 161; birth of, 40; birth of Johnny and Betsy, 127–28; children in *Mrs. Piggle-Wiggle* compared to, xvii; custody of, 49; Dede's help with, 44; domestic crises, 130; *The Egg and I* and, 77, 192n20; *Egg and I* film role considered, 88; father not seen again after divorce, 49, 188n42; as flower girl for Mary, 58; in Hollywood, 88; home improvements and, 99; Jensen family and, 190n34; "The Just-One-More-TV-Programmers" updated by, 202n13; leaving the chicken farm, 45; MacDonald name and, 99; marriage to Donald Strunk, 127, 141; marriage to Robert Evans, 141; mentioned, 50, 78; middle name, change of, 131; move to Vashon Island, 66; *Mrs. Piggle-Wiggle* and, 82; *Nancy and the Plum* and, 139; in *Onions in the Stew*, 145; photographs of, *plate 14*, *plate 20*, *plate 28*, *plate 37*; pregnancy, 141; at ranch, 157; schooling, 56, 60; in Sydney's care, 56–57, 66

MacDonald, Betty (born Anne Elizabeth Campbell Bard; later Heskett) (also "Betsy"): about, 175; baptism of, 10; biography, need for, xiii, xvi; birth of, 9; books of (overview), xi–xvi; breadwinner role and, 129; called "Betty," not "Mother" or "Grandmother," 152; career overview, xv; childhood in Boulder and Placerville, 9–11; childhood in Butte, 9–10, 11–18; complaints about lack of writing time, 197n30; death of, 161; description of, in *Cosmopolitan*, 98; fame and, 3; family background, 3–10; as grandmother, 127–28, 141–42, 154; her version of her story, xiv; Heskett name dropped by, 50; marriage to Bob Heskett, 38–45; marriage to Don MacDonald, 65–66; as matron of honor for Mary, 58; name change from Betsy to Betty, 31; National Industrial Recovery Administration personal history record, 189n5; no funeral for, 203n29; schooling, 14, 17, 21–22, 23, 28, 31; on Seattle, 20; skill as correspondent, 109; as storyteller, 3, 57, 74–75; suitors, 59; testifying in own defense, 121–22; working at Mandarin tea shop, 32; writing time, finding, 128–30. *See also specific places, topics, book titles, and family members by name*

MacDonald, Betty, photographs of: *Anybody Can Do Anything* publicity photo, *plate 36*; booksignings, *plate 31*, *plate 39*; Carmel Valley, *plate 40*; with Claudette Colbert, *plate 26*; *Egg and I* book cover, *plate 19*; with family members, *plate 1*, *plate 20*, *plate 22*, *plate 24*, *plate 28*, *plate 29*, *plate 32*, *plate 37*, *plate 38*; with friends, *plate 9*; *Illahee* ferry, *plate 21*; King

"Patsy, Who Would Not Take a Bath" (MacDonald), 68–69
Pavlova, Anna, 22, 184n7
pertussis (whooping cough), 13–14
Peshastin, WA, 59
physicians. *See* doctors
Pioneer House, Chimacum, WA, 43
Pixley, Vida, 52
placer mining, 11, 183n23
Placerville, ID, xix, 10–11, 169, *plate 1*
plague. *See* tuberculosis
The Plague and I (MacDonald): about, xiv; *Anybody Can Do Anything* compared to, 135; Betty's presence in, 174; Betty's view of, 101; book signing, *plate 31*; copies of, xviii–xix; cover, 103; as educational, 102; fan mail from, 104–5; female characters in, 102, 106, 136; *Good Housekeeping* condensation of, 103; home described in, xii; idea for, 100–101; *Onions in the Stew* compared to, 143; promotional and publicity for, 104, 105–6; racial issues in, 75; reactions and reviews, 103–4; serialized version of, 190n30; structure of, 102
Please Don't Eat the Daisies (Kerr), 143
pneumothorax treatments, 62–63, 64
Pocket Books, 115, 119, 124
Portland, OR, 5, 77, 116, 121
Portland Academy, 5
Portland High School, 5
Port Ludlow, WA, 122, 186n1
Port Townsend, WA, 36, 37, 38, 43, 116, 122, 186n1, 197n8
poverty, 54, 55, 104, 134
pregnancies: Anne, 141, 154; Betty, 40, 43; Sydney, 8, 11, 25, 26

the press, dealing with, 88, 125, 138
press releases, 65, 72, 95–96
product endorsements, 92–93
Pt. Townsend Leader, 118, 198n21
publicity: *Anybody Can Do Anything*, 134–35, *plate 36*; *The Egg and I* (film), 87–88, 94–95; eggs and, 79, 87, 95–96, *plate 25*; *The Plague and I*, 104, 105–6; tours, 77–79, 88–89, 92–94
Publisher's Weekly, 76, 79
Puget Sound, 18, 19, 20, 67
Pyle, Ernie, 72

R

radio: Betty on, 87–88; interviews on, xv, 69, 78, 88, 112, 138; KOL, 58; listening to, xviii; *Schuyler Square* (Sydney Bard), 58, 166
Raising Demons (Jackson), 143
ranch. *See* Corral de Tierra Ranch, Carmel Valley, CA
rationing, 72
Ravenna Elementary School, Seattle, 56, 187n24
Reader's Digest, 191n12
red hair, 17, 58, 67
red-light district, Butte, 4, 17
"The Red Satin Raincoat" (unfinished) (MacDonald), 201n23
release deal for film (Bob Heskett), 91, 93, 186n5, 194n9, 194n19
reminder books, 128
Repertory Theater, Seattle, 59
reporters, 77, 88, 92, 94, 99, 130, 133
research, xix, 122, 168, 171
Rhodes Department Store, Seattle, 58, 104
Rich, Louise Dickinson, 73

trial. *See* Bishop/Kettle et al. libel suits; lawsuits and court cases

Trocadero nightclub, Hollywood, *plate 28*

Trudeau, Dr. Edward L., 61, 103

Trudeau, Dr. F. B., 103

Trunk, Frank, 119

Tsuyuki, Geary, 106

tuberculosis: antibiotics for, 101; Anti-Tuberculosis League of King County, 190n32; in *Anybody Can Do Anything*, 133; Betty's pulmonary tuberculosis and treatment, 60–64; bovine, 40; children's sanatorium visits, 62, 190n26; fan mail from patients, 104–5; Firland Sanatorium, 60–64, 101, 102, 103–4, 189n21, *plate 15*; gender and racial segregation of patients, 102; law limiting marriage of patients with, 65–66; *Mycobacterium tuberculosis*, 60; National Tuberculosis Assn. Christmas Seals campaign, 104, *plate 30*; pneumothorax treatments, 62–63, 64; rates of, 190n24; relapse, threat of, 64; as sequel topic, 100–101; Tuberculous meningitis, 60; vaccine for, 13; as "white plague," 60; writing about, xiv. *See also The Plague and I*

Twain, Mark, 134

U

Uncle Remus (Harris), 83, 193n5

Universal-International Pictures, 87–90, 95–96, 170, 194n11, *plate 25*

University Book Store, Seattle, 104, *plate 31*

University Club, Seattle, 21

University Congregational Church, Seattle, 185n33

University District, Seattle, 32–33, 188n44

University of Colorado, 9

University of Southern California Film and Television Library, 170

University of Washington, 30, 31, 59, 63, 191n4

University Provision Co., 33

University Village, Seattle, 184n11

University Way Club, 33

V

vaccine for tuberculosis, 13

Vashon Heritage Museum, 204n11

Vashon Island, WA: attempted sale of house, 140–41, 142; bridge efforts, 190n1; chicken project, 99; description of, 67; Dolphin Point Trail house, 66, 99, 167–68, 172–73, *plate 16*, *plate 20*, *plate 36*; *The Egg and I* and, 67; ferry between Seattle and, 99, *plate 21*; as home base for Betty and Sydney after selling Howe St. house, 141–42; home in, xix; house rented out, 150; Jens and Mary's beach house, 152, 162; move to Calif. from, xv, 149; in *Onions in the Stew*, xiv–xv, 145

Verstappen, Henry, 68–69

Viorst, Judith, 164

W

waffles, 28, 29, 32

Wallgren, Monrad, 79

Walsteed, George, 188n31